THE ART OF TELLING

THE ART
OF TELLING
Essays on Fiction

FRANK KERMODE

HARVARD UNIVERSITY PRESS
Cambridge, Massachusetts
1983

Library of Congress Cataloging in Publication Data

Kermode, Frank, 1919–
  The art of telling.

  Includes index.
  1. English fiction—History and criticism.
  2. American fiction—History and criticism.
  I. Title.
PR821.K37   1983   823'.009'23   83–163
ISBN 0-674-04828-8

CONTENTS

THE ART OF TELLING

PROLOGUE

The essays here collected were originally lectures or papers given to audiences of many different sorts, some highly professional and some general, but I have tried to avoid technical terms on all occasions, except when they seemed indispensable and could be explained as one went along. There are certainly variations of tone, some to be accounted for by the different audiences, and some by the author's own development, or, less honorifically, changes of mind. All but the last two of these pieces were written between the publication of a book called *The Sense of an Ending* in 1967, and that of *The Genesis of Secrecy* in 1979. Both of these books are studies in the theory of fiction, and so, to some considerable extent, is *The Classic* (1975). So although I wrote about many other matters in those twelve years, it would be true to say that these essays are the by-products of a more or less continuous effort to understand and contribute to a topic which, as it happens, developed quite suddenly during the same period a central importance it had not possessed since Aristotle.

For in the latter half of the 1960s there occurred a remarkable efflorescence of speculation about the way narratives work. Structuralism, in its origin a method for linguistics, had achieved very novel results in the field of social anthropology, and it appeared to many that it could be used in the analysis of narrative. It was principally a matter of elevating the methods of linguists above the

1

level of the sentence, which was their ceiling. The issue was complicated by the contemporaneous revolution in linguistics, which was almost entirely the work of Noam Chomsky; I remember noticing during a visit to the United States in 1969, many attempts to fit a transformational-generative component into a narrative model. But in the early days this complication attracted little notice in Paris, the centre of structuralism; there it was the linguistics of Saussure (and Hjemslev) that ruled. The basis of French structuralism was a Saussurian semiology (for Saussure associated linguistics with a more general science of signs). It was also strongly affected by a revival, or it might be better to say a discovery, of Russian Formalism, a highly original body of literary theory that flourished in the years immediately following the Revolution. One of its most distinguished exponents, Roman Jakobson, who had influenced the anthropological method of Claude Lévi-Strauss, had survived as a source of inspiration in linguistics and indeed in the larger field which some were now calling 'poetics'.

If there is a single publication that best represents the coming-of-age of this new poetics it is the eighth issue of the Paris journal *Communications* in 1966. This 'little magazine' contained several important essays on narrative analysis (by A. J. Greimas, Claude Bremond, Umberto Eco, Christian Metz, Tzvetan Todorov and Gérard Genette, but it led with Roland Barthes's 'Introduction à l'analyse structurale des récits'. Barthes was already well known outside France for his short book *Le Degré zéro de l'écriture* (1953), his collection *Mythologies* (1957) and his advocacy of the *nouveau roman*. Lately he had published also his *Eléments de Sémiologie* (1964) and engaged Raymond Picard of the Sorbonne in a fierce controversy about the validity of Barthes's little book on *Racine* (1963). The most important outcome of this row was Barthes's drastic and brilliant pamphlet called *Critique et Vérité* (1966), a manifesto that for some reason has never been translated into English. Barthes's adherence to the method of analysis advocated in *Communications 8* was, as it turned out, transient, but it firmly associated structuralist analysis with a critical *avant-garde* more widely conceived, and also ensured that Barthes should at this time be regarded as the most distinguished exponent of the new method. In 1971 he produced an even more influential book, *S/Z*, a highly original semiological analysis of Balzac's short story *Sarrasine*.

I have given what many will recognise as an extremely simplified account of a state of affairs which was historically much more complicated, but my purpose is to recall the importance in those days of Barthes, the invigorating effect of his fertile and surprising mind. As the years went by he became not less exciting but less didactic, and I am certainly not alone in my conviction that much of his finest work came after *S/Z*; but his major impact on students of narrative was felt between, say, 1967 and 1974. My own way of thinking about narrative (as in *The Sense of an Ending*) had nothing, or very little, in common with what was going on in *Communications* or *Tel Quel*, and I remember feeling rather dismally that quite a lot of work had gone into a book which became antediluvian almost on publication. But it seemed necessary to examine specimens washed in by the flood, and it was during those years that I chaired, at University College London, a seminar dedicated to that and to similar enterprises. No other phase of my academic life has given me so much pleasure and instruction. We were quite informal, but did a lot of work, some of which was eventually published; but that was not our primary aim. The constitution of the group changed over the years, and we had many visitors, including some novelists – I remember the late B. S. Johnson as particularly co-operative. Among the participants who were in one way or another exponents of *la nouvelle critique* were Christine Brooke-Rose, Jonathan Culler, the late Veronica Forrest-Thompson, Stephen Heath, Jay Kaiser, Annette Lavers, Christopher Norris, Shlomith Rimmon, Anita Van Vactor, and, on one notable occasion the late Roland Barthes himself; the opposition was in the hands of various no less formidable discussants, Barbara Hardy for one. Not the least of the qualifications of these and many other friends of the group was a willingness to express lively disagreement without rancour; another was to examine one's own prejudices as well as others' and to preserve a tone of good humour in the midst of the most serious, even the most fierce, exchanges. In those days I suppose I imagined that there was nothing unusual in this combination of opposition and civility, but I have seen very little of the kind since 1974, and can only hope that the lack is local and not general.

One important effect of our cultivating these new interests was this: the horizons of our enquiry were constantly extended beyond what would formerly have been thought usual for students of literature. We found ourselves reading many books we might hitherto have left to others: Foucault, Lacan, Lévi-Strauss, to name only three authors. I think everybody felt a little strange but certainly liberated; the training offered by most English universities does little to encourage such 'interdisciplinary' enquiries. But there were limits to our ambition, and I doubt if more than one or two of us shared the view, then earnestly proposed by some, that a new paideia was in the making, perhaps with *Critique et Vérité* as its founding text. As the books and papers multiplied it became clear that there was much less common ground among structuralists than might at first have been supposed; and already in 1967 the books were published that signalled the end of this early version of it. They were the work of Jacques Derrida, and among much else they used a novel and de(con)structive method of analysis to question, in the most radical manner, the tacit assumptions on which structuralism, Saussurian semiology, Lévi-Straussian anthropology, and pretty well every other mode of enquiry, including its own, might be shown to depend. The 'post-structuralism' which ensued was a protean and eclectic affair. The idea of deconstructionism gathered momentum only slowly, but with the powerful advocacy of Paul de Man it made its way in the United States, first at Johns Hopkins and then at Yale and Cornell. The strange 'ludic' (spontaneously playful) anti-philosophy is now well established in the United States, together with the kind of interpretation that follows from it; in the UK it has never really taken root, and is still regarded with suspicion and derision by serious persons, many of whom seem to have very little idea of what it is. The career of Jonathan Culler is instructive. As late as 1975, when he was still working at Cambridge and Oxford, he was opposing Derrida in his *Structuralist Poetics*, generally thought to be the most authoritative guide to the subject; but he returned thereafter to the US and joined the Derrida party. His earlier book may well seem to him now as academically conservative as it does to such commentators as Frank Lentricchia, whose excellent book *After the New Criticism*[1] includes the observation that when the Modern Language Association awarded *Structuralist Poetics* the James Russell Lowell Prize for 1975, this on the whole conservative organisation was not so much engaged in disinterestedly applauding merit as in recognising that Culler had made structuralism safe, partly by his judicious dismissal of Derrida. The Association was not merely applauding, but bestowing 'an ideological nod of recognition'. Culler's conversion to deconstructionism is quite an important moment in the history of the American movement, but the distance, in this respect, between the two nations is great, for the British academic establishment offered no prizes or nods even to the conservative-structuralist Culler, and I should expect its response to his later work (if it could be bothered to have one) would be that it was well rid of him.

The seminar came to an end in 1974, without ever (so far as I remember) taking on Derrida or deconstructionism. Although, as I have suggested, I gained much by it, I was never tempted to declare myself a structuralist, or a post-structuralist, or even a narratologist or poetician. There are doubtless many reasons for this resistance, not all of them creditable. One was, simply, inertia; I was too old, and by formation too much of an historian, to be comfortable with all the implications of structuralism; I was a diachronic sort of person, who indeed once published a book called *Continuities*. A good part of the pleasure I derived from my profession had come from finding out what texts seemed to be saying as it were voluntarily, and in conveying this information to others; and I should have felt uneasy to join a party whose sole business it was to elicit what they were saying in spite of themselves. Since I have put the matter so crudely I should add that I do not share the comfortable opinion of the English academic (and, it seems, journalistic) establishment that the critics of the new persuasion are self-evidently absurd; or, more seriously, that they are unprincipled; or, when their arguments seem persuasive, that they are, like the forces of Monostatos and the Queen of the Night, wickedly threatening the citadels of Imagination or indeed Humanity, as alarmed academics sometimes claim.

Concerning deconstructionism, the most frightening manifestation of the newer criticism, I myself have reservations. First, when deployed with a fervour no less evangelical than ludic, it can be extremely dull, and since dullness is a contravention of what I take to be the purpose of criticism – briefly, illumination – I could not join a party which did not mind about *that*. Derrida himself, ranging eccentrically over great tracts of literature and philosophy, is full of surprises and hardly ever dull; but his followers do tend to say the same thing about everything they choose to discuss – that those texts are 'always already' self-subverted, that they contain, in some occulted form, that which violates their ostensible meaning. I take this to be an hyperbolical expression of a partial truth, like the confident assertion that the history of criticism is necessarily a history of error. 'Their life a general mist of error' – Webster's words might therefore serve as a motto for the tribe of literary critics. There is something, but not everything, in it, and of course it applies as much to the deconstructors as to everybody else, as Derrida has always engagingly allowed. 'Deconstruction,' says Hillis Miller, an eminent disciple of Derrida, 'is not a dismantling of a text, but a demonstration that it has already been deconstructed.'[2] As Suresh Raval quite fairly remarks, 'Deconstructionist practice does not merely remain bound to its governing theoretical premises; it rather ceaselessly seeks to confirm those premises. . . . The reason deconstructionists cannot help endlessly repeating the same synchronous tale in all their interpretations is that the limits of what they can say are defined by the concepts they hold . . . the concepts . . . determine the limits of their experience.'[3] The method is not only monolithic, it is entirely absorbed in demonstrating its own validity. It may be argued that there is nothing very wrong in that, but the kind of criticism one does is, in the end, an ethical choice, and I myself do not believe that this kind of thing is what criticism *ought* to do.

A second, and to a teacher a more compelling argument against some advocates of deconstructionism is paedagogical. The success of the new critical philosophy has come at the very moment when, as almost every competent reporter would agree, students arrive at the universities knowing much less, having read much less, than ever before. This may be less true of the great institutions in which the new style has been most successful – Yale, Cornell, Hopkins – though I doubt it, and in any case such exceptions would make no difference to the general argument. It is natural for a man who has found the truth to wish for the most effective means of communicating it widely, and Professor Miller, with others, would make deconstruction an undergraduate subject. Yet it depends for its operation on the existence of more or less canonical texts, which have already an accepted range of constructive meanings. The leading deconstructionists are all very learned men, indeed learning is an obvious prerequisite of their practical programme; and students will always have to be conducted into some initiatory mist of error before they can hope to emerge on the sunlit, ludic uplands of deconstruction. *O welch ein Glück!*

My purpose in sketching an attitude to deconstruction is to emphasise that the essays in this book reflect what is called in the argot a 'recuperative' temperament. The best exponents of the new approach are at least as aware as their opponents that it cannot last for ever; indeed the people who think they possess methods and assumptions of perpetual validity are precisely these opponents; their veneration for what they take to be the directly accessible structures of past cultures, and for the historical record unsullied by intrusive modern perceptions, has never enabled them to observe that change is just as obvious as continuity in the history of interpretation. I am interested in the record of both. The history of modernism could be written as an account of the conflict between excited catastrophe theorists on one side and panic-stricken reactionaries on the other. Deconstructionism is, in part, a catastrophe theory, for behind it there is the assumption that the whole Western metaphysical tradition can be put into reverse. It is at this point that the orthodox, who dislike having to consider such unsettling propositions, man the walls with their dusty banners: principle, imagination, the human world, though the most vocal of them are manifestly unacquainted with the first, lack the second and seem to know the third only by hearsay. They are therefore unable to see that just as some of the innovations of Empson and the New Critics (who were also in their day derided by a conservative establishment) have been absorbed into their practice, so will the methods of the deconstructionists, who could perfectly well claim Empson as an ancestor. We cannot foretell the history of interpretation in detail, but we can say with some confidence that it will continue, that it will not be deconstructionist, and that contemporary polemic against the new criticism will, if anybody bothers to consider it, look foolish.

We lack a great man who might, like Eliot, hold together the new and the traditional, catastrophe and continuity; unfortunately we do not lack doctrinaire and unconsidering people on both sides of the argument. My own inadequacy as a mediator has already been adequately demonstrated. There is a war on, and he who ventures into no-man's-land brandishing cigarettes and singing carols must expect to be shot at. Christopher Norris took this point in a perceptive (by which I do not mean wholly favourable) review of

The Genesis of Secrecy,[4] when he said that the two positions are 'in theoretical terms . . . beyond all reach of moderating judgment,' so I expect no medals for going on trying; but it seems that I can do no other, there is no possibility of retreat. It is not easy to act aggressively from a position of moderation, and I shan't try – not here, at any rate. But I will try to explain, as I look back over the essays here included, all records of various attempts to understand the new without abandoning the old, where I now stand. Sixteen years ago Christopher Ricks offered a description of 'the true reader and critic': he is 'open-minded but not vacuous; he does not surrender his own opinions, experiences, beliefs and knowledge, but neither does he clutch them desperately. He is both independent and accessible.'[5] In pre-war 1966 these words must have seemed almost too obvious or even banal to be worth the trouble of writing down, but they are worth recalling at a time of embattled vacuity and inaccessibility; I shall try to bear them in mind, and hope against hope that they are frequently recited in the 'traditionalist' trenches, if only in the spirit of bishops blessing cannons.

UNCLE WILLIE AND THE WEDDING CAKE

I begin with what I take to be a useful historical instance of a problem in interpretation of the sort that cannot honestly be avoided by any party to the current dispute. There are, in fact, two instances, but only one problem. Let us first look at what E. M. Forster described as his 'nicest' novel, *A Room with a View*, which was published in 1908 though in large part written some years earlier. It is the story of an English girl at her moment of social and spiritual crisis, for she is in danger of permanent absorption into the darkness of middle-class manners and prejudices. Chaperoned by an older woman who has, it seems, already gone into that night, she encounters in a Florentine *pensione* two unusual souls, the Emersons, *père et fils*. Old Emerson is a rather uncouth, truth-telling, agnostic life-worshipper. Young Emerson has his own dark, and may disappear into it, but it is not the dungeon of public school refinement. They are a rather garden-city pair, but are clearly 'saved', or will be. Hearing the ladies lament the absence of a view from their rooms, they offer to exchange; bad form, but the offer is accepted. Lucy, the young woman, happens to be standing nearby when a man is stabbed to death in the Piazza

Signoria, and she faints in young George Emerson's arms. Later, encountering her in a glade full of violets, he kisses her. This outrage is observed by Charlotte, the chaperone, and Lucy's response is modelled on Charlotte's. They leave for Rome. But the Emersons turn up again in the English village where Lucy lives; she gets kissed again, is again outraged. However, she breaks off her engagement to a truly awful man called Cecil, who, though an aesthete, was not going to save her from the dark. She does spend a little time there, but eventually elopes with George to Florence.

A year before *A Room with a View* Forster had published a much more complicated novel, *The Longest Journey.* In it Agnes, the darkling wife of the hero Rickie, complains at one point about the kind of stories he writes, and asks, 'Couldn't you make your stories more obvious? I don't see any harm in that. Uncle Willie floundered helplessly. . . .' When Edward Garnett reviewed *A Room with a View* he quoted this passage, and commented, 'In truth it is not easy to explain the subtle quality of Mr. Forster's brilliant novel to Uncle Willie and his kinsfolk. . . . How can the art of telling, this network woven of a succession of tiny touches, be brought home to Uncle Willie?' Garnett, a most enlightened publisher's reader, was at the time the principal mediator between writers who thought of the novel as art, and a public which as a whole cared nothing about that but wanted a good read. Among the writers he tried to bring home to Uncle Willie were Conrad and Lawrence. Forster, not surprisingly, was much gratified by the review; he wrote that it 'gave me tremendous pleasure for the Uncle Willies are encompassing me sorely.'[6]

For a number of reasons the position of writers who wanted to practise the art of the novel was, at this time, both difficult and promising. The sudden death of the three-decker in the 1890s had changed the pattern of fiction and fiction publishing. Novels could be shorter and cheaper, and with luck they commanded very large sales. Freed of the constraints lamented by Gissing, they enjoyed new formal freedoms, though Uncle Willie still held the purse-strings. The artists were under two powerful influences: Meredith's, but it was fading; and James's. The Prefaces to the New York edition were appearing in these years. What followed was new – an intense concern for the potentialities of the instrument itself, for the latent and neglected capacities of narrative fiction. The 'art of telling' underwent the sort of critique that was being applied, in these same years, to music and painting, but also to philosophy and physics, and to technology in general.

This passion for technique, for a new novel that might escape the constraints of conventional narrative, was by no means confined to Britain. In France, where the revered ancestor was Flaubert, it already seemed by the turn of the century that the Novel was more interesting than novels; that fiction could be less *récit* than *recherche*. By 1913, the year of *Les Caves du Vatican* and *Du Côté de chez Swann*, it was commonplace to decry mere story. The Symbolist horror of the accidental and the quotidian passed over into fiction, and Valéry deplored the 'absence of necessity' in novels. About this time there also developed a sense that many of the old tasks of novels could be left to the cinema; but the first appearance of symptoms of 'une crise de l'affabulation' were evident at the end of the nineteenth century.[7] The rest of this history is more familiar: Sartre, Camus, Queneau, Butor, and above all Robbe-Grillet with his fully fledged manifesto of a *nouveau roman*; and then, before long, the *nouveau nouveau roman*.

What happened in England was, as usual, less bold and less a matter of manifestos and proclamations; and even Ford frequently insisted that the novel of technique should not reject the more popular tradition. And it would certainly be possible to maintain that the technicians were not so much inventing a new novel as developing features already in the tradition; for example (but the development of the theme must await another occasion) the deeply excogitated time-shifts of Conrad and Ford are merely a conscious extension of quite ordinary expository devices to be found in most novels. (Hardy presumably did not think of himself as using new techniques in the opening paragraphs of *Jude the Obscure*, though they can be shown to use a quite elaborate set of time-shifts.) Nevertheless, Conrad and Ford were among the writers who failed to please Uncle Willie any more than James did. Forster's correspondent Garnett understood their art, but belonged to the world of commercial publishing and wanted for them the huge rewards achieved by the popular yet still 'serious' novelists like Galsworthy, Wells and Bennett. It may not seem credible, but I calculate that Bennett's income in 1913, expressed in terms of our money in 1982, amounted to something over £800,000.

Doubtless such riches were somewhat beyond the hope, perhaps beyond the desire, of Forster; unlike Conrad, Ford and Bennett he had a decent private income. But it was his character Cecil Vyse and not Forster himself who sweepingly condemned success: 'all modern books are bad . . . Everyone writes for money these days.' And Garnett usually found the younger, unestablished writers quite willing to let him help them find a compromise between art and Uncle Willie. He would have argued that in doing so he was not only attending to their material needs but maintaining contact between their work and the history of the novel, which was created for a bourgeois audience not ordinarily very interested in art, and quite ready to judge fiction by standards that might seem, to those engaged in technical research, tediously or even lethally conventional. The response to *A Room with a View*, so far as it may be judged from the reviews collected in the *Critical Heritage* volume,[8] gives one some idea of how a rather unorthodox new novel might be received. The word that recurs in almost all of them is 'clever', which probably enticed some readers but scared off Uncle Willie. The *Times Literary Supplement* added to 'cleverness' both 'sheer fun' and 'occasional beauty'. The *Morning Post* headed its review 'A Clever Novel' and affirmed that Forster had 'one aim only: he sets out to make clear the limitations of the cultured middle-class.' Elsewhere he is commended for 'sighting the comedy of ordinary social intercourse'. A Chicago paper complained of Forster's 'irritating desire to be clever' and called the book 'a would-be difficult and would-be novel trick in the gymnastics of psychology'. On the whole it seems that everything in the least unusual or disquieting about Forster's procedures could be dismissed with the one word 'clever', while the remainder was assigned to standard categories, whether eulogistically or dismissively. There is no reason to suppose that modern reviewers would do the job any better.

It is true that some contemporaries alluded to the 'symbolism' of the book – to the not wholly naturalistic use of rooms, views, various Italian painters and so forth – as giving the work a penumbra of inexplicit senses. Later commentators, unhampered by deadlines and also benefiting by changes in critical fashion, have deepened these perceptions. More is going on than meets, or is intended to meet, Uncle Willie's eye. Twenty years later Forster, in his *Aspects of the Novel*, gave some attention to this conflict between the art of the novel and 'the grossness of its material'; this was after he had written his most complex and, as it turned out, his last novel, *A Passage to India*. Meditating the quarrel between

11

James and Wells, which turned on this very issue, he says that he is on Wells's side in that he 'gives the preference to life' over art. But he also meditates upon the device he calls 'rhythm'. 'Rhythm' is not obvious symbolism of the Meredithian kind, as when, in *The Egoist*, a cherry tree follows Clara Middleton around; it is more like the 'phrase de Vinteuil' in Proust, itself a musical phrase, deriving its meaning not from reference but from repetition in different contexts. These 'rhythms' are not as simple as the *Leitmotive* of Wagner, as Forster conceived them – that is, as referring quite straightforwardly each time they occur to ring, sword, Valhalla, and so forth. A rhythm is something that recurs less obviously, yet gives the work its wholeness, its 'expansion', its closing on a conviction that something rather mysterious, probably unnameable, has been added, so that the novel 'has a larger existence than was possible at the time', and when it is over may seem not to have been 'completed', not rounded off but rather opened out.[9]

This is an important idea, and Forster was not alone in his day when he shunned the thumping dominant-tonic endings expected by Uncle Willie. They had been derided by Henry James, deplored by Conrad. That 'relations stop nowhere' but must appear to do so is a point made by James in his Preface to *Roderick Hudson*; and he would have maintained that what enables them to continue in 'a larger existence' after the apparent completion of the story is composition, the discovery, by the delighted novelist, of the occult elements in his theme, elements which resound together and are in their nature not consumable by Uncle Willie as simple story. For, as the Preface to *The Ambassadors* puts it, 'There is the story of one's hero, and then, thanks to the intimate connexion of things, the story of one's story itself.' It was by means of such 'intimate connexions' that Forster, albeit more timidly than James, sought to prolong his novels beyond the time of their ending. In 1906, lecturing to a Working Men's College Old Students' Club, he said that the modern author 'wants to end his book on a note of permanence, but where shall he find it? . . . Where shall such a man find rest with honour? Scarcely in a happy ending.'[10] Scarcely, indeed, in any conventional ending at all. To 'find rest with honour' entails providing a plausible stopping place but allowing the story, or some compositional essence of it, to live on; giving its quietus to the gross material while conferring liberty on its rhythms, its Ariel, which must survive in a different order of time. Thus the problem of ending and the problem of rhythm, of occult, non-referential patterns, coincide, and both must be solved without insult to Uncle Willie.

In *A Room with a View* the most striking episode – for all its other instances of violence are merely verbal – is the murder in the Piazza Signoria. We know from the surviving early versions how Forster reworked the passage, and indeed radically altered the conception, for in its original form it described the victim as an almost naked and beautiful youth, and Lucy was not even present at the murder. In the book as it was published the scene has no part in the story except as a decisive moment in the relationship of Lucy and George Emerson; he catches her when she faints, picks up the postcards she has dropped, now covered in blood, and takes her back to the *pensione*, throwing the postcards into the river *en route*. Postcards, their sellers, and the river all assume an obscure importance in the texture of the book, but more remarkable is a certain trick of language, a rhythm, in the sentence describing what happened the second after the stabbing: 'Mr. George Emerson happened to be a few paces away, looking at her across the spot where the man had been. How very odd! Across something?'

This is a palpable disturbance of the narrative flow; it draws attention to itself as peculiar. We may reasonably expect in what follows to find some explanation of 'across . . . across something.' But none is forthcoming. Forster remarks of his 'rhythms' that 'there are times when the little phrase . . . means everything. There are times when it means nothing and is forgotten.' And he adds that such is, in his view, 'the function of rhythm in fiction: not to be there all the time like a pattern, but by its lovely waxing and waning to fill us with surprise. . . .' In fact 'across' has waxed earlier, in the opening chapter of the novel, where George Emerson 'seemed to be smiling across something.' Odd, certainly; but not every eye will pause or stumble at it, and Uncle Willie, together with a great many other people, will probably have forgotten the small surprise by the time they come to the murder scene. In any case, 'across' thereafter wanes, almost as if there has been a deliberate effort to suppress it. Over a hundred pages later, on the climactic day of the story, we are told that 'gray clouds were charging across tissues of white'; but so far as I know the word occurs again only there, though there are many other places where it would seem quite natural.

What are we to do with 'across'? Manifestly the second occurrence recalls the first. But what are they *for*? One might say they touch upon the theme of views, often seen across sills; mountains are seen across valleys; and so forth. It is seeing Lucy across the dead man that changes George, and seeing him seeing her so that commences the salvation of Lucy. Yet all this merely rationalises something that essentially lacks such references; it is, as Forster might have said, like fitting programmes to symphonies. What we have here is not so much a secret as secrecy, an inexplicable consonance. We know it is there because the disturbance in the prose signals its presence. It is so arranged that we, or Uncle Willie, may ignore it if we choose; but it is there, and has to do with expansion, with the reconciliation of art with honourable rest.

Forster lacked the temperament of Conrad, in whom the self-lacerating determination to be an artist was never truly to be reconciled with the need to make money from a public he despised. Forster wanted to deploy his rhythms in novels that need not alienate Uncle Willie: 'the effect can be exquisite, it can be obtained without mutilating the characters, and it lessens our need of an external form.' (By this he meant, I think, the perfection of formal patterning he deplored in *The Ambassadors*.) The great triumph of 'rhythm' is *A Passage to India*, in which the extraordinarily complex rhythms are so successfully concealed that for a long time everybody behaved like Uncle Willie and left them unheard; probably the last word has still not be said of them. At the end of his career as a novelist Forster was equal to the challenge Garnett had so long been posing: he wrote a book that was very successful with a public uninterested in secrets, willing to read it as a study of the British in India and approve or condemn it for its accuracy or its partiality; and at the same time wrote the novel he wanted for himself. Conrad was quite incapable of such a compromise, and the public success of *Chance* is a still mysterious fluke. As I have tried to show in Chapter 6 below, *Under Western Eyes*, a novel which cost him a serious breakdown, is a secret diatribe against the public notion of novels, which required story to be as obvious as beer in a glittering Swiss glass. There is a sort of hysterical alien nobility about the performance; perhaps it is related to Conrad's refusal of a knighthood, probably on the ground that he was already noble and scorned to accept an honour tainted by bourgeois ambition.

The technical innovations of Conrad and Ford, unlike those of Forster, were not to be finessed; they stood fiercely between the ordinary consumer and the story. It cannot have been easy to see why *The Good Soldier* was worth the bewilderment induced by a first reading, or why one should comply with its tacit but inevitable claim that it should be read at least twice. The problem of the ordinary reader is amusingly illustrated by Theodore Dreiser's review of Ford's book. Dreiser was by formation and conviction unable to feel the technician's doubt as to the continuing validity of the methods of normal realism, his conviction that the more usual way of doing things deserved to be labelled mendacious or in bad faith. He likes Ford's story, but finds that he has not 'made it splendid in the telling.' A wonderful idea, but clumsily executed. 'I would have suggested to Mr. Ford ... that he begin at the beginning ... go forward in a more or less direct line. ... In the hands of a better writer this jointure of events might well have been articulated into one of the finest pictures in any language. ... The whole book is indeed fairly representative of that encrusting formalism which, barnacle-wise, is apparently overtaking and destroying all that is best in English life.'[11] In short, Dreiser so exactly misread *The Good Soldier* that he almost suggests, by contraries, how it ought to be read. And although he had a special dislike for British Uncle Willies, he shared their view about the right way to tell a story. He wanted to find in a novel an easily recognisable version of the world as he saw it (in his case, though not in Willie's, a Social Darwinist world). Curiously enough, he and Ford would have agreed about some of the symptoms of Anglo-Saxon malaise in the opening years of the century, for example, the cult of gentility that smothered passion; but the aetiology was different in each case, and in each case a wholly different myth of the past informed the prescribed treatment. Dreiser could never have understood Ford's explanation of the evils of modern sexuality in terms of the European disaster of the Reformation, and Ford can have had no notion of how the lives of the Chicago poor appeared to a writer trained in science in a midwestern college; the quality of feeling about sex was different in each of them, but, much more decisively, the pressure of the past demanded of each a completely different method. Ford's whole view of the truth called for obliquity, for the conduct of microcosmic 'affairs' which reflected, in the eye of a good reader, not the mere sequence of

15

history as represented by theories of conflict and survival, but the great historical crises which transcend the temporal sequence, like the signing of the Protest at Speyer. Later, a little surprisingly, Ford and Dreiser became good friends, and Ford spoke generously of the American's achievement; but they represent well enough the opposition between naturalism and formalism, or pseudo-reference and auto-reference, and Dreiser must always have been irritated by writing which directs attention from one part of the text to another, rather than to some intelligible world without: though Ford believed that his opacities, his centripetal allusions, were the right way, in the end, to represent in art a world and its history.

Forster's 'across', then, represents a compromise of a kind not really available to Ford or Conrad or indeed James, whom he expressly rejects as a model; for he gave much thought to these matters, and knew what he was rejecting. His response to James and Joyce, Gide and Conrad, is not philistine, but the gentle rhythmical arrangements of *A Room with a View* are nevertheless consistent with a respect for the requirements of generations of Uncle Willies, though at the same time they enable him to do some of the work he conceived it possible for novelists as artists to do. There are certain regularities, certain conventions of completeness and representation, that do not rule out those rhythmic arrangements which allow the book its 'larger existence'.

For another view of the relations between art and Uncle Willie we may turn to Arnold Bennett. As a young aspirant he had taken the modernist (which is often in practice also the patrician) view of his craft. He thought that the English must somehow acquire a French passion for 'the artistic shapely presentation of the truth', and learn to care less for 'subject' than for 'presentment'.[12] Yet by 1914 Henry James could single out Bennett, by now very famous, as an example of the sort of writer who put down every fact required for verisimilitude 'in dense unconfused array'[13] without ever answering a reader's desire to give these facts a formal centre. In other words, Bennett had given up 'presentment', abandoned his interest in the Jamesian 'doing'. And indeed he confessed that he gave up *The Ambassadors* after 150 pages, finding it 'not *quite* worth the trouble of reading it'.[14] Of course these comments put the matter in a misleading light; Bennett was a refined and careful technician, as the excogitated shape of *The Old Wives' Tale* testifies. But he was not interested in 'experiment'. In 1914 (the year of James's critique) he noted that 'as the years pass, I attach less and less importance to good technique in fiction'; he admired it, but except for Turgenev he thought that 'the greatest novelists of the world' ignored it.[15] Here as elsewhere he seems to reserve the term 'technique' (as he might have done in his prentice years) for the innovations of the modernists; he admired Conrad greatly, and understood him. But he chose a different way, and made a fortune.

When Bennett came, in 1923, to write *Riceyman Steps*, his reputation had waned a little from its fullness at the time of *Clayhanger* (1910), the book that had been James's principal target in the assault of 1914. But for this novel admiration was general; it pleased the technicians as well as the public. Conrad, Wells, Moore and Hardy applauded; Sir Herbert Grierson awarded the book the James Tait Black Memorial Prize, the only literary prize Bennett ever won. Bennett himself ventured to describe *Riceyman Steps* as a 'jolly well constructed and *done* book.'[16] Meanwhile the people who judge novels by buying them or not, took Elsie, the perfect, submissive young charwoman, to their bosoms. Bennett was exasperated with them for doing so, but nevertheless wrote them a sequel, all about the later life of Elsie. Garnett had long before said of Bennett that 'the most interesting thing about him is the strange amalgam he presents of *commercial* man pure and simple, and author',[17] and Bennett behaved accordingly by satisfying the demand for more Elsie, while at the same time asserting that 'the quality of the book' had nothing to do with 'the sympathetic quality of Elsie'. Its quality was in the skill of the 'doing', in its capacity to suggest elements of secrecy, to emit signals indicating, to the higher sort of reader, a larger existence than the simple narrative, read in ignorance of these signals, could propose or sustain.

Bennett's registration of reality in *Riceyman Steps* is as complete, as dense in array, as James would have predicted. The book is set in Clerkenwell, a London district Bennett did not know as he knew the Five Towns. So he walked around it, read a history of it; he gave it a genuine past but specified it exactly as it was at his chosen moment. His principal character is a miserly bookseller, and he bought, in a second-hand bookshop in Southampton, a book about misers. How much he looked into the life of the Clerkenwell poor after the first World War I do not know, but he knew enough about them to represent them convincingly as rough people who despite undoubted privations retained genuine decency and good nature. Elsie herself is a war widow; her 'follower' still suffers from shellshock and malaria, contracted in France after troops from the Middle East had brought it there (this is the sort of unusual information Bennett always loved for its authenticating power). The miser, Mr Earlforward, thinks his hoard threatened by Communism, raising its head in Clerkenwell working men's clubs in the time of postwar disillusion. Elsie has a waitress cousin who gets mentioned in the newspapers for bravely intervening in an affray in such a club; and Mr Earlforward, who takes all the services performed by the lower classes as his natural right, fears that Elsie's remote and innocent connection with these goings-on 'brings communism right into the house'.

The calm and righteous oppression of servants by the lower middle classes, here represented by Earlforward and the woman he marries, is very accurately represented; this is the most crucial battlefront in the class war, and it is interesting that Bennett's readers admired Elsie for her pacific acceptance of her conditions of employment. In these and in other respects, *Riceyman Steps* is worthy of the author of the Five Towns books, and instantly readable by the readers of *Clayhanger*. If it is a mark of the modern, as Auden implied, to 'prohibit sharply the rehearsed response', then *Riceyman Steps* may not, on this view of it, seem very modern; it may be said to have encouraged a more complex response to Elsie, but it didn't prohibit the rehearsed one. Yet there is much in the novel to remind one of another 'simple tale' of London streets, the admittedly more apocalyptic *Secret Agent* of Conrad. Bennett had clearly not forgotten Conrad, but his tale is more acceptably simple. There must be a certain irony in Conrad's subtitle and even in the dedication of the book to Wells; he wanted the simplicity that brings success, but the complex imposed its presence on Uncle Willie's attention all the same. Bennett, both commercial man and author, ordered these things better.

Earlforward's bookshop is in a small square at the top of a flight of steps, near the King's Cross Road. A healthy middle-aged man with a limp, he conceives an admiration for a widow who keeps a confectioner's shop nearby. When they marry, Elsie, who has served them separately, becomes their 'general'. Though ill-paid and overworked, Elsie is ardently loyal. When her lover shows signs of unseemly behaviour she dismisses him; he insults a World

War general in Piccadilly and goes to prison; he is forced to sell his 'papers' – his identity – for a meal. Meanwhile indications accumulate that Earlforward is a pathological miser. At first these signs are trivial: malefunct light bulbs are not replaced, books purchased are wrapped in crumpled brown paper, there is a marked lack of heat. But these economies are condoned by a considerate narrator; electricity, he notes, is expensive. Mrs Arb, who marries the bookseller, begins by admiring his respect for money, but it soon proves incompatible with any notion of a decent married life. Their honeymoon is a trip to Madame Tussaud's (no catalogue). When they return home (no taxi) they receive three presents from Elsie: rice, which she throws at them; a slipper; a wedding cake. With an anomalous burst of gluttony the Earlforwards instantly consume the whole cake. The bridegroom's present to his bride is a safe, to be kept in the bathroom. Hers to him is more remarkable: while they were out enjoying themselves she had hired a professional vacuum-cleaning company to clean the filthy bookshop.

Shocked and amazed by this intrusion, Earlforward laments the loss of the dirt, and asks the workmen if they will sell it. He is right to fear so great an upheaval in his way of life; the wedding is decisive. After it, Earlforward maintains a starvation diet, while Elsie, full of guilt, eats whatever she can lay her hands on – bread, cheese, even a steak offered to her husband by Mrs Earlforward as a marital treat and perhaps a sexual invitation, but spurned by him, as she is. The miserliness of the husband grows more and more crazy; the house and shop become dirty again. The premises are sealed off from the world, like a safe. Only Elsie comes and goes, sometimes leaving the door open. Both the Earlforwards are sick, she with a fibroid growth in the uterus, expressly related to her sterility, and he with a cancer of the upper stomach. Mrs Earlforward dies during an operation, not because it was dangerous in itself, but because she is so undernourished. The immediate cause of Earlforward's death is his discovery that Elsie, needing sixpence to send a message to the hospital, has got into his safe and borrowed one. At the climax of the book plump, loving Elsie is nursing both her employer and her lover, whom she has smuggled into the house prostrate with malaria. Both take service with the good doctor, who has saved the young man but failed to do the same for the emaciated and finally insane bookseller.

Most novelists would admire the fertility and control of detail in this book – the progression of Earlforward's mania, the assurance with which the tricks of the bookseller's trade are noted, much in the manner of earlier records of the manufacture of pots in the Five Towns, the pacing of the narrative, the colour and lighting of the piece. Yet these skills do not seem to belong to the same tradition as, say, Ford's; we are not talking about what he meant by *progression d'effet*, or *charpente*; there is nothing he would recognise as the 'exhaustion of aspects', and very little he would recognise as the 'baffled relation between the subject matter and its emergence'. Yet there is nevertheless available to the reader a pleasing sense of being in expert hands; and in fact the good stern Dr Raste is, in this story, a kind of surrogate for the novelist. There is a sort of plenitude, a world is there as it is, rich and mean, poor and loving, with Dr Raste and the novelist on hand to offer diagnosis without foolish confidence in any power to heal. Just as it is, *Riceyman Steps* might be thought to earn the condition of rest with honour.

And yet there is in the novel – even in the very simple condensed account of it I have given – a surplus of sense on which any good reader will find himself working; an indication of larger existence, of something seen as it were 'across' the story. I will take only one set of signals, Elsie's wedding presents. They come in, almost looking like a jolly little decoration, at the crisis of the tale (though we learn that it is so only later). The story of miserly employers growing thin while a generous servant grows fat would have taken a very different form in James, and it might not be amiss to say that the high technology of *The Sacred Fount* looks a little barren by comparison with Bennett's novel. Elsie, careless of business when life is opposed to it, careless of money when it is needed to serve an important ritual, buys the cake out of her meagre wages. From the moment of their guzzling it the Earlforwards are doomed. Is this a matter of mere sequence, or of cause? By eating the cake they are saving money, the cost of a meal, on their wedding day. But their response to the cake is wilder than even this lucky economy can explain.

> They lost control of themselves, and gloried in so doing. The cake was a danger to existence. It had the consistency of marble, the richness of molasses, the mysteriousness of the enigma of the universe. It seemed more fatal than daggers or

20

gelignite. But they attacked it. Fortunately, neither of them knew the inner meaning of indigestion.

The note of facetiousness here is traditional in the English novel; all the hyperbole can be ascribed to it, and so readers can use it to screen out the signals of another less explicit plot. How is the cake 'a danger to existence'? Eighty pages on, Earlforward, in a passage that is actually free indirect discourse but may be taken as a direct report, admits parenthetically that 'he had first begun to feel ill either just before or soon after the eating of the wedding-cake on his bridal night.' 'Just before' might allow him to attribute his illness to the wedding itself rather than the cake; but after another sixty pages he reflects that 'he had never suffered from indigestion until the day after his wedding-night, when he had eaten so immoderately of Elsie's bride-cake. The bride-cake seemed to have been the determining cause, or perhaps it was merely the occasion, of some change in his system.' After his death, Elsie holds herself responsible for it:

> She had noticed that he had never been the same since the orgy of the wedding-cake, and she had a terrible suspicion that immoderate wedding-cake caused cancer. Thus she added one more to the uncounted theories of the origin of cancer, and nobody yet knows enough of the subject to be able to disprove Elsie's theory.

The suspicion that there is some magical link between the cake and the cancer is dismissed with a jocose remark at Elsie's expense; 'her notions of the value of evidence were somewhat crude,' we are told; and as one might expect of Bennett, there is a sufficiency of medical detail in Dr Raste's diagnosis to allow us to suppose the connection no more than a fantasy, just as we may dismiss all the talk about its mysterious, enigmatic fatality as a passing jest. Yet the cake does make an emblem of the married state, and Earlforward's invincible objection to spending money implies an unwillingness to perform his marital part; his wife expressly complains about this. When she herself fears financial ruin her dread is described as 'a cancer – not a physical one', and indeed her illness is not cancer, though it is said to be a consequence of sexual privation. They are sealed from each other, again like safes, harbouring within them growths which accumulate like money. (Mrs

21

Earlforward bitterly compares her husband to a 'locked-up, cast-iron safe'.) As we have seen, it is Elsie's act in breaking into his safe that kills the husband. When Elsie finds the slipper in her mistress's wardrobe she weeps: 'All the enigma of the universe was in that shoe . . . Elsie had never heard of the enigma of the universe but it was present to her in many hours of her existence.'

Obviously the wedding-cake, and the slipper, and the inappropriate rice, belong, like Forster's 'across', to a quasi-magical, non-sequential plot that is at odds with the prevailing idiom of the story; though the author takes care to make them assimilable, or dismissible, on terms acceptable to readers who do not want to bother about such matters. We may take, or leave, 'the enigma of the universe'; it is a banality or a fact. The cake brings, or does not bring, illness; we can take it either way, we can provide the Freudian explanations that are ready at hand (the dirt, the money, the cake, the slipper). More important, we can take all these things as they come, one at a time, and not seek to see them as a chain of half-occulted senses in the text. But they exist, the signals are there, quite strongly marked if one looks for them, deep shadows in the story, though easily dismissible; indeed we are told how to dismiss them by responding to their pomposity, their naivety, their suitability to the notions of a charwoman.

In this way the novelist may practise his art, have his own wedding-cake and at the same time let Uncle Willie eat it. Others may, if they choose, contemplate it, put in under their pillows like Elsie; they may practise slow reading, of the sort Nietzsche called 'philological' reading; they may process that unidiomatic surplus, recombine the fragmented hints of the story's larger existence.

A natural language may have a quantity of formal machinery that doesn't generate meaning, that remains inert or merely phatic, simply maintaining communication or attention. At a higher level of discourse, novels also have such elements. But it comes to the attention of the inquisitive technician that such elements may be put to use; that all the language that is simply discarded as insignificant by a casual reader may be given the power to bear less obvious meanings. No designer likes to include weight that contributes nothing to the effective functioning of the instrument; the designer of Dreadnought did not, and neither did his contemporaries, the Edwardian novelists, though some of them also knew that it was necessary to allow Uncle Willie his extravagant and old-fashioned requirements.

Story for story's sake got an increasingly bad press from the technicians; Ford thought 'story' a wicked word, and Forster (with some of that protective facetiousness we have noted as part of the novelist's inheritance) defined it as simply the highest factor common to all novels, an atavism. Some came to think of novels as instruments of research; some, as we have seen, tried to have it both ways, and succeeded. But in the two novels of the 1920s I have just been considering, we observe that as in Conrad there are little disturbances in the surface that indicate the existence of activity below, little breaches of the idiom of simple narration: symptoms to be interpreted. In his case history of 'the Wolf Man', Freud remarks that his patient, 'like so many other people ... used his difficulties with a foreign language as a screen for symptomatic acts.'[18] The application of this perception to Conrad is, I think, obvious; but we need adapt it only a little to make it apply also to Forster and Bennett.

SIGNALS, AUTHORS, INTERPRETERS

It may not have escaped notice that in talking about 'signals' I have allowed the inference that they are emitted from an identifiable source, namely the author; and the further inference that their emission is under conscious control. And indeed it seems clear that all concerned knew what they were up to, so that there was no other way to talk. My argument was that there were deliberate attempts to transform an older way of writing, or without offence to make the old accommodate the new, in the interest of Forster's 'larger existence'.

But the question arises, whether what seems merely consumable, formal and inert, in older fiction, cannot also have a potentiality of meaning. We should find it difficult, indeed impossible, to argue that in all cases there was a conscious intention to make it available to readers. There are amongst us two – at least two – sorts of dogmatist in these matters: the first rules out of account any interpretation that cannot be shown to be consistent with an author's intention, or with what is known to be the sort of intention he might have had; the second seeks to put a stop to the discussion by claiming that whatever the author wrote must be what he intended – so that anything said about the sense of what he wrote is said, correctly or incorrectly, about his intention. Neither of these positions seems to me right and neither is in the least useful.

The modern critical tradition, for all its variety, has one continuous element, the search for occulted sense in texts of whatever period. It has learnt from modern poets and novelists how to think about unmodern poems and stories. It may allow, as I do, a certain element of conscious self-surveillance, a certain technical self-consciousness, in modern practitioners, and this will in some measure distinguish them from their predecessors. But neither the New Criticism nor the *nouvelle critique* in its many forms has been willing (in practice, and usually not in theory either) to accept the dogmatic positions mentioned above. It may be said that in this refusal they have many precedents, for the pedantry they resist is an ossified form of a philological method developed only in the eighteenth century.

I think we can see how things are by a simple exercise. The author of a story is its first interpreter. In modern times it is extremely unusual for another hand to rework that story, but it was not always so in the past, as the example of the Hebrew Midrash shows. When Leah is substituted for Rachel in Jacob's bed, he is, in Genesis, the victim of what may reasonably be called a 'gratuitous swindle'. The Midrash motivates this bed-trick; Jacob, suspecting foul play, arranges that Rachel should carry certain identifying symbols. But she gives them to Leah, who all night answers to the name 'Rachel', and from being merely a silent woman in the dark becomes a character playing a part. Next morning Jacob accuses her, and her father Laban, of cheating, and she retorts that Jacob had after all cheated Esau, as indeed he had. Zwi Jagendorf, of the Hebrew University, in an interesting unpublished paper on this subject, correctly observes that the Midrash does two things: it provides more motivation than the older text contains (for instance, it doesn't simply assume that Leah went to Jacob in the dark; it says that for modesty's sake the lights are put out); and secondly, which is more to our purpose, it links two disparate passages, bringing into the text a common feature that had not been stressed before. Not only was there trickery in both instances; the reason for it is also similar in both instances, for Esau surrendered his birthright for a meal, and in both cases it is the trickster who gets the blessing. One might add that a bit later

24

Laban himself is tricked by Jacob when he sets up the wands before the animals; this is a revenge, since Laban has tricked Jacob out of his wages. And Rachel, when she flees with Jacob, tricks Laban again when she hides his household gods in the camel's saddle and sits on it, claiming that she can't get off because she is menstruating. In other words, the second writer got strong signals from the text of the first, and wrote the unstated plot into the story. I have heard this process, which is of course repeated over and over again, described as the provision of 'hermeneutical increment', which is an expression applicable to all interpretation of narrative. Of course the authors of Midrashim would be clear that they must not interfere with the original sense in adding others, and also that in doing so they were not really adding at all, but merely working towards the restoration of the full original meaning, a plenum that human endeavour cannot ever hope to achieve.

There are, of course, other ways of interpreting such texts, and Jagendorf illustrates them by means of the allegorical readings given to the Rachel story in the Zohar. But allegory of that kind, though it has a very long history, is another thing. What we may keep in mind is the antiquity of the practice of rewriting a story to help it attain its full possibility of meaning, its larger existence; and this, I think, may be said to be what Forster and Bennett, in their different ways, were doing. Reading their fables by writing and rewriting them, novelists are the first of their interpreters; the process continues as long as they are creatively read.

The history of such reading might, in some cultural circumstances, be represented as a prolonged attempt to recover a plenitude that was originally present; this, as I have said, is the case of the Midrash, which, with all its accommodations, updatings and euphemisms, still aspires to the condition of the impossible presence of the Word. I suppose it might be said that the conservative or 'recognitive' theorists mentioned above hold a rationalised form of this doctrine. Thus it is maintained that interpretations are false if they cannot be said to belong to 'the type of meaning willed by the author'. In its more moderate form this position is expressed as a matter of professional ethics: we ought to behave as if it were correct; but as I have suggested there are more extreme versions. To avoid prolonging these introductory remarks I have discussed one of these in an Appendix. The question of what can properly be said of a text inherited from the past is one of the most troubling issues of modern criticism. If it is acknowledged that the history of interpretation must in part be a history of error, and of transient fashions wrongly assumed to be permanent and obviously right, then it is a sort of arrogance for anybody to suppose that he can stand aside from that history and securely judge, for example, what does and doesn't conform to the author's type of meaning.[19] It is a matter of fact that some interpretations, and some modes of interpretation, die, while others survive; the decision may be made by professional consensus, and after due consideration, but it may simply be a consequence of neglect or accident. The one thing certain is that new interpretations are affected by the interpreter's historical position; that readers of twentieth-century novels, for instance, will read earlier fiction in ways affected by that experience. It is equally clear that in a later generation there will be interpretations of the same text that differ from ours. It would be absurd to think of this 'perpetual *aggiornamento* of sense', as I've called it elsewhere, as a systematic progress towards a plenitude identifiable with an author's intention; plenitude would have to be less personally, more mystically, conceived. An understanding of this fact lay behind the old structuralist attempts to find ways of defining *how* rather than *what* texts meant; this solves the problem of criticism by making it a secondary activity of importance only to the history of taste. A later criticism cuts the text off entirely from an author, and by speaking of its meanings as endlessly deferred, endlessly subject to the play of signs within it, tries to subvert the myth of presence and offer inexhaustibility as a replacement for plenitude, no rest, honourable or otherwise, for the people of God.

But we are not obliged to choose between courses so extreme, and if we are to give an acceptable answer to the question with which I began this section – whether, in the absence of the special information we have about modern writers, we may still act upon 'signals', indications of the 'larger existence', in older texts – we need to find another way. What is most necessary is a view of history which is neither simply historicist nor simply *anti-passéiste*; which accepts that there exists such continuities as the culture elects or anyway receives; and ours is still a culture of texts and monuments. There is a variety of hermeneutics, much misrepresented in Britain and possibly also in the United States, which allows this to be the case. It is principally associated with the name

26

of Hans-Georg Gadamer, who seems to be thought of by literary people, if they think of him at all, as merely the unworthy opponent of E. D. Hirsch (whose rival 'recognitive' hermeneutics is also subject to misrepresentation by the dogmatists). One hears it said that on Gadamer's view the past is inaccessible or even worthless, an opinion deplored, as one might expect, by rigorous antiquarians; but it is not Gadamer's. It would be more accurate to say that he wishes to ask what it is to take into account the historical response to texts, including that of the original audience so far as it can be determined, when we formulate our own. The process involves what Gadamer calls 'the fusing of horizons'. (The term 'horizon' in this sense has been characterised as a bizarre innovation; as Gadamer explains, it has been in philosophical use since Nietzsche and Husserl.) What he means can be understood, in part at any rate, by a single quotation:[20]

> It is a hermeneutical necessity always to go beyond mere reconstruction. We cannot avoid thinking about that which was unquestionably accepted, and hence not thought about, by an author, and bringing it into the openness of the question. This is not to open the door to arbitrariness in interpretation, but to reveal what always takes place. The understanding of the word of the tradition always requires that the reconstructed question be set within the openness of its questionableness, i.e. that it merge with the question that tradition is for us. If the 'historical' question emerges by itself, this means that it no longer raises itself as a question. It results from the coming to an end of understanding – a wrong turning at which we get stuck. It is part of real understanding, however, that we regain the concepts of an historical past in such a way that they also include our own comprehension of them. I [call] this 'the fusion of horizons'.

Setting aside the unfamiliarity of some of this language, and the special sense in which Gadamer uses the word 'question', we have still, I think, a view of the matter that is attractive to common sense. Nor is it essentially new, even if one thinks only of Gadamer's predecessors in hermeneutics; he himself quotes an interesting passage from a work by Chladenius (1742) to the effect that understanding an author is not the same thing as understanding speech: 'since men cannot be aware of everything, their words, speech and writing can mean something that they themselves did not intend to say or write.' The interpreter, Chladenius concludes, must therefore understand more fully than the author. Gadamer finds this statement ingenuous, but himself expresses the same idea with more force: 'Not occasionally only, but always, the meaning of a text goes beyond its author.'[21]

Doctrines of this kind are far from asserting that we cannot achieve understanding of old texts. The point is neatly put by D. C. Hoy: 'a certain incommensurability exists between the theoretical and aesthetic outlooks of different periods,' but 'this incommensurability only means that such outlooks are not reducible to the present outlook. Irreducibility, however, certainly does not entail incomprehensibility. It will, of course, allow for some variation in judgments about aesthetic characteristics, since such judgments will involve, without distortion of the artwork, different readings of the work because of different weighings of a complex set of factors. Historical considerations will be part of this set, and will themselves include questions about the extent to which the actual effects a work did have even in its own "time" (and one now sees that even this is only an interpretive variable that cannot be rigidly specified) alter that time's own aesthetic self-understanding.'[22]

The attempt to reconstruct a past response (though it must be governed by its own historical conditions: it projects a fusion of horizons) is, for most of us, an important element in all acceptable interpretation. Even the deconstructionists are of the consensus, for in order to exhibit the *aporia* caused by the collision of uncontrollable signification and fixed consensual meaning they must have some notion of the latter. It is, I suppose, possible to imagine a cultural revolution of the Chinese sort that might alter this state of affairs. If it succeeded all texts might be read as what Barthes used to call *scriptible*. But as things are it appears that *lisibilité*, which depends on the fixing of signification by an informed consensus (aided by many reassuring signals from conforming authors) is, in our tradition, a necessary preservative; the dependence of the modern on the past continues, and not only in the more authoritarian kinds of modernism where this dependence is gloried in, but in the more anarchical varieties also. The claim of Dada that it was a 'beginning at zero' could never be made good, and even its adherents were divided as to whether, for all its nihilism, it was not rather a new art than the instrument that would end art. In the 1960s Neo-Dada hit the streets, or the campuses, and soon it had some effect on criticism, not only in the third-rate apocalyptic ramblings of *soi-disant* Postmodernists, but also, more curiously, in Deconstruction which, in its radical questioning of the highly academic school of structuralism, developed its famous 'ludic' quality. That mixture of destructiveness and playfulness descends from earlier avant-garde activity in the arts; Apollinaire and Dada are among its ancestors. So with Lacan; the attack on orthodoxy, conducted with a certain playfulness, notably in the use of wire-drawn puns, was, avowedly, a *retour*, a fundamentalist return to the true Freud. The purely synchronic method of Saussurian structuralism, which is highly academic, is in fact the only *anti-passéiste* element in the apparatus of modern criticism, and it is, for reasons suggested above, more or less obsolete.

It seems, then, to be a fact of life that all our interpretations depend in some measure upon historical interpretations; of these some survive and some do not, a point made very simply in Chapter 9; and communities maintain, with indefinite but quite powerful criteria, some and not others, as I suggest in Chapter 8. The question, whether to argue thus is to betray an adherence to a covert conservative ideology (as Jürgen Habermas believed to be the case with Gadamer), is not to be considered here; one might be willing to accept the charge and yet remain clearly distinguishable from the reactionaries who profess a belief in the Single Correct Interpretation. We can say that it is the very *alien-ness* of texts that makes interpretation possible; that this estrangement is caused by the action of history; and that the action of history also maintains our lines of communication with whatever texts we still want to, and can, interpret.

We may now return to the question of 'signals' in texts other than those in which we have reason to believe 'signals' were deliberately planted by authors interested in giving them a 'larger existence'. Such signals are detected because we have discovered a method, suitable to our historical situation, of looking for them. It is a method that is unlikely to resemble any that happened to be current at the time when the text was written; it assumes the possibility of 'fusion'. All theorising apart, there is a tacit assumption among all practitioners that their interpretations ought to contain something new, and that this will continue to be true if

29

ever the antiquarians contrive to add the last cumulative word to their historicist analyses. Interpretation, says Paul Ricoeur, 'is the work of thought which consists in deciphering the hidden meaning in the apparent meaning, in unfolding the levels of meaning implied in the literal meaning'; such meanings he calls symbolic, giving as a definition of symbol 'any structure of signification in which a direct, primary meaning designates, in addition, another meaning which is indirect, secondary and figurative, and which can be apprehended only through the first.'[23] It is not, I think, part of the premise that these indirect meanings are fixed and constant, only that they can be apprehended only through the literal sense. And here is one means of distinguishing between the value of interpretations, and between true and false secrets. We shall have to agree that the signals are there in the text before we can use them to speak of the work's larger existence.

This is clearly what we do with texts new and old, without regard to the issue of the consciousness of the signalling system. Our era of interpretation might be said, without too great an oversimplification, to have begun when Freud published *The Interpretation of Dreams*; it is therefore as old as the century. (Of course he had his acknowledged precursors, and so had the novelists I have been talking about; they did not invent 'signals' but merely saw how to use them.) We know what, for Freud, constituted signals of a buried discourse; and we could perfectly well use such terms as condensation and displacement to speak of the examples I gave from Forster and Bennett. Forster's *across* means that a primary sense is confused, overdetermined or displaced; Bennett's carcinogenetic wedding-cake is a sort of secondary elaboration; all these things can be provided with a façade acceptable to Uncle Willie. The kind of writing here exemplified is what Allon White, after Althusser, calls 'symptomatic',[24] a term which reminds us of the Freudian connection. 'Symptomatic reading', which depends on a sort of literary third ear, took some time to develop; it arrived unmistakeably with early Empson, and had to be ushered in by a new sort of poetry. But the symptoms and signals were always there; it became possible to produce them as it were under laboratory conditions. Our awareness of what is happening in Forster's strained use of the word *across*, or in some of Conrad's strategic desertions of English idiom, derives from modern writing, but what we are aware *of* is something that is by no means new, and is indeed an inherent property of written texts. Writing and reading can be, and in the novel for most of its history, were, conducted on the assumption that the simpler forms of communication were to be primary, that signification ought to be controlled. The reasons for making this assumption are extremely complicated; they are social, economic, paedogogical and so forth. We need not suppose that we have reduced its power without silently substituting some other assumption.

My conclusion, then, is that the twentieth-century interest in the Novel, in its technical potentialities, made some writers especially conscious of what might be made of certain hitherto unregarded aspects of narrative texts; of what might be suggested as apprehensible beyond or *across* those texts. There are difficult questions I cannot raise here and one of them is the nature of the rules we apply to discourse when we know it to be fictive. In the ordinary business of life we give great emphasis to the pragmatic aspect of language, screening out hesitations, parapraxes, fumbled performances. If by a slip of the tongue a woman, say a princess, promises to marry not her bridegroom but his father, the ceremony is not invalidated, and any speculation about the cause of the slip is secondary and probably facetious. But in the 'depragmatised' language of a novel such a mistake (whether in accordance with the author's intention or not) might be of great importance, as a sign of that larger existence beyond the confines of the text as read by Uncle Willie. It is not surprising that we have grown more aware of these unpragmatic possibilities, these secrets lurking in the tale-bearing text. These are the modern modes of interpretation, continuous with older ones and yet proper to their epoch. They need to be taken into account when we try to delineate the horizon of our understanding, and the measure of its fusion with those historical horizons. That the fusion is necessary we know from the modernity of our perception of the signals; that it is possible we know from the continuity of the whole interpretative tradition; that it is transient we know from the transience of every phase of that history. As I mentioned at the beginning of this Prologue, there are those who argue that the history of criticism is a history of error; but if we stay within the tradition, rather than seek to overthrow it, we shall have to say rather that it is a history of accommodations, of attempts to earn the privilege of access to that kingdom of the larger existence which is in our time the secular surrogate of another Kingdom whose horizon is no longer within our range.

NOTES

1 Frank Lentricchia, *After the New Criticism*, Chicago: University of Chicago Press, 1980, pp. 103–4.
2 *Georgia Review*, 30 (1976), p. 22.
3 Suresh Raval, *Metacriticism*, 1981, pp. 227, 234.
4 *Essays in Criticism*, xxx (1980), pp. 84–93.
5 *Poems and Critics*, 1966, p. 23.
6 George Jefferson, *Edward Garnett*, 1982, pp. 102–3.
7 See P. Raimond, *La Crise du Roman*, 1966, from which I derive much of this paragraph; the quotation is from p. 55.
8 *E. M. Forster: The Critical Heritage*, ed. Philip Gardner, 1973, pp. 101–21.
9 *Aspects of the Novel*, end of Chapter 8.
10 *A Room with a View*, Abinger edition, ed. O. Stallybrass, 1977, Introduction, p. xvii.
11 *Ford Madox Ford: The Critical Heritage*, ed. F. MacShane, 1972, pp. 47ff.
12 *Journals*, 1 January 1898 (Penguin ed., 1971, p. 45).
13 'The New Novel' 1914, in *Selected Literary Criticism*, ed. M. Shapira, 1968, p. 366.
14 *Journals*, 11 January 1905, p. 118.
15 *The Author's Craft*, 1915, p. 47.
16 *Journals*, 16 February 1924, op. cit., p. 473.
17 From a report on Bennett: *The Truth about an Author*, quoted in George Jefferson, *Edward Garnett*, 1981, p. 84.
18 'From the History of an Infantile Neurosis' ['The Wolf Man'], *Standard Edition*, ed. J. Strachey, xvii, 1917–19, p. 94.
19 As Gadamer observes, 'It is the tyranny of hidden prejudices that makes us deaf to the language that speaks to us in tradition. . . . Historicism . . . is based on the modern enlightenment and unknowingly shares its prejudices.' (*Truth and Method* [*Wahrheit und Methode*, 1960], trans. G. Barden and J. Cumming, 1975, p. 239.
20 *Truth and Method*, p. 337.
21 *Truth and Method*, pp. 161–2, 264.
22 'Hermeneutic Circularity, Indeterminacy, and Incommensurability', *New Literary History*, x, 1978, p. 168.
23 Paul Ricoeur, 'Existence and Hermeneutics', in Josef Bleicher, *Contemporary Hermeneutics*, 1980, p. 245.
24 Allon White, *The Uses of Obscurity*, 1981.

CHAPTER 1

THE ENGLISH NOVEL, *CIRCA* 1907

Around 1907 great changes, we may confidently announce, were either occurring or pending, both in English society and in the English novel. Joyce and Lawrence were already at work; so was Gertrude Stein. James was publishing his Prefaces, and Ford, who had worked with Conrad, was excogitating a new theory of the novel. Arnold Bennett was writing *The Old Wives' Tale* on what seemed to him sound French principles. 1907 wasn't a bad year for novels, for it saw the publication of both *The Secret Agent* and *The Longest Journey*. Who would read them? Three years earlier a public had been found for both *Nostromo* and *The Golden Bowl*; the next year they would accept, though at first without enthusiasm, Bennett's novel, as well as *The Man Who Was Thursday*, *The War in the Air*, and *A Room with a View*. There were Wagnerites and Ibsenites in the audience: William Archer's translations started to appear in 1907 and so, as I've suggested, did the New York edition of James. Many people had read some Flaubert and Tolstoy, Nietzsche and Whitman; a few had encountered *The Interpretation of Dreams*. Husserl was little known, but Russell was famous. The climate, at first glance, seems one in which there might have been an audience for fictions aspiring to art and seriousness.

Of the society more generally, it is necessary to say only that there were signs of a more critical attitude to the past, a developing habit of national self-examination. The fragility of the Empire had become more evident after the Boer War. The educated conscience had discovered the poor, whose plight, like that of women, troubled the liberal mind as much as the low standard of national health disturbed those whose property might, before long, be dependent on the country's ability to find fit men for the army. There was a powerful sense of transition, accompanied as always by mixed reactions to all the new evidence of decadence or of renovation, according to how one interpreted such signs of relaxation as the criticism of capitalism, the questioning of conventional sexual morality, and the treatment in literature of previously forbidden subjects. The early years of Edward's reign showed a real loss of nerve, which was in some measure recovered before its end. There was a feeling of crisis, that there was no telling how things might go; and this is caught in James's tragic retrospect at the outbreak of war in 1914: 'the plunge of civilisation into this abyss of blood and darkness . . . is a thing that so gives away the whole long age in which we have supposed the world to be, with whatever abatement, gradually bettering, that to have to take it all now for what the treacherous years were all the while really making for and *meaning* is too tragic for any words.'[1]

How do such concerns affect the works of the time? There ought to be a relation between the Condition of England and the condition of the English novel. Such a relation would be not merely a matter of what novelists say about the state of the nation, and specific aspects of it – but how they go about doing so. Is there, so to say, a period lexicon? If so it should be easier to describe than a period syntax. Successful novels normally use language understood by many people. Let us glance first at a little group of novels that did well with the readers of 1907. In one way or another they might tell us something about the lexicon, and the grammar, of mid-Edwardian fiction. Of course we should remember that many of these readers were not fully extended by the works here discussed, since they could also read *The Secret Agent*, a work – to continue the figure – that made much severer linguistic demands.

Elinor Glyn's *Three Weeks* is, if not read, remembered still as a sexual fantasy, and in a way this is just; though the American preface defends the book against the charge that it is merely 'a sensual record of passion,' and, in its fashion, it *is* more than that. The lovers are a young Englishman of great beauty and stupidity and the Imperatorskoye, a royal adventuress whose sensuality, at once mystical and practical, uplifts and exalts the young man, so that after the three weeks he spends with her – ending at the full of the moon – he finds himself transformed into a man of intellect and embarks on a career of distinguished public service. The Imperatorskoye separates love from all else, including domestic convenience and learning and art and 'feverish cravings for the impossible new,' blaming such mixtures for the 'ceaseless unrest' now generally felt. (' "Yes," said Paul, and thought of his mother.') The consequence of all this is that the Empress bears Paul a son, but is murdered by her husband. He in turn falls to the hand of an avenging Kalmuck loyal to the Empress, and the child becomes, apparently, Czar or Czarevitch. Paul is able to attend his fifth birthday celebrations in the cathedral of the capital and sees his son, 'a fair, rosy-cheeked, golden-haired English child, future ruler by right.'

This curious and successful dream appealed to an increasingly felt need to abandon not only official morality but also cultural isolation. English virtue could reasonably be exchanged for alien virtuosity. The bedroom scenes, like the foreignness of the lady's manners, catch the exotic in an unserious way, or anyway in dreamlike fashion. The lady is 'beyond the ordinary laws of morality,' and the novel offers the satisfaction of a solution in which this Nietzschean wickedness is paid for by death, yet contributes to the advancement of the real, that is the British, Empire. Paul is saved from his hearty English fiancée but nevertheless produces an heir, and a pure English heir for an empire previously the domain of foreigners; while he, purged by an admittedly unrepeatable sexual experience, returns to the true imperial centre, London. He is able to give it the benefit of all the knowledge and experience it had lost sight of during its protracted estrangement from Europe, for this is what he had acquired during his three weeks in an exotic but undeniably imperial bed.

Miss Glyn's rejection of middle-class English women may be seen as a measure of the desire of her female contemporaries to liberate themselves from the old roles, much as her rejection of the provincialism of the British Empire reflects a growing mood of the time. But she does not consider the possibility of asking the very considerable audience which was somehow ready for this kind of thing to abandon social and national assumptions inconsistent with the changes currently proposed. Her new man is a boring English-man transformed and liberated by coming into the knowledge, conveniently represented as sexual experience, which his own society denied him. He remains an upper-middle-class Englishman whose powers had been concealed, not destroyed, by the barren-ness of his life, and he continues to behave in conformity with class conventions. The new Emperor is wholly English, apparently with-out genetic inheritance or early training from his foreign mother, who simply educated the husband, produced the son, and died. Thus the growing uneasiness lest imperialisms clash, a new aware-ness that British arrangements would have to be changed, defended, and perhaps even overthrown, that stupidities of education and rank urgently required correction, and that extreme sexual repres-sion might be dangerous, are eased and calmed in a dream, in a best-seller. Taking it seriously is likely to seem odd or offensive because the text is not of a kind that advertises its connexions with reality. They exist, perhaps inevitably; only sometimes the discrep-ancies are so huge as to conceal them.

The sense that one was entering a new age, in which some transformation of the British might be necessary if they were to maintain their hitherto effortless supremacy, inspired a whole range of invasion novels; and as the period wore on the outcome of these novels tended to change, first from easy victory to hard struggle, then to disaster. Erskine Childers, in the best of them, still showed some confidence in British racial superiority;[2] Wells, in a book serialised in 1907,[3] showed the coming world conflict through the eyes of an undereducated English mechanic, but transferred the capital of the world to New York. But conscious enquiry into contemporary problems – as in Wells, or in *Major Barbara* (1905), or even in Galsworthy – isn't perhaps as good a guide to the capacities and needs of the audience as fiction which has no such explicit purpose. Florence Barclay's *The Rosary*, of 1908, will serve as an example of such fiction. This extraordinarily bad book was still being reprinted in my youth, and I read it somewhere around 1933 in a cheap edition; apparently it went on satisfying a public, albeit an unsophisticated one, for a quarter of a century.

The American publishers claimed that it was a modern book; ('modern' was already a hard-sell word); it is in fact a dream of the new woman, in this case represented as having been a nurse in the Boer War, a golfer, and very strong and healthy. She gives up an affair with an exquisite painter because she is too old and plain for him. The setting is a ducal home, and the upper-class dialogue works because the author has learned how to do it from, among others, Oscar Wilde. The poor are represented by a railway porter who when heavily tipped by the heroine imagines her an angel sent from heaven to provide delicacies for his sick wife. This fantasy about the poor is contemporary, it should be remembered, with the conscience-stricken sociological enquiries into their lot that were well under way with Fabianism and with the fear of rioting mentioned by Shaw in *Major Barbara*. Galsworthy surrounded his rich with a frieze of poor in attitudes of misery and sickness. Chesterton professed to regard them as the champions of a gay Christendom. Conrad knew they were exactly what the police existed to control. But Miss Barclay's new woman still treats them as beneficiaries of upper-class generosity, and this social imperceptiveness fairly represents the general level of her imagination.

Her artist goes blind and, incognito, she nurses him, pulls him through his worst time, and not only marries him but assists his completely effortless translation from painter into composer. Problems of art become, in this imaginative light, as simple as those of poverty. The impassioned dénouement, incidentally, is visible a mile off, and is an emblem of the easy gratifications expected of popular fiction.

Yet the success of the book transcended that of the ordinary cheap romance; it was taken more seriously. What is of some interest is the coexistence of decent, even accomplished, upper-class dialogue and an immense vulgarity of imagination and technique. It was possible to learn to do certain things, which probably sounded quite modern, without the slightest notion that there was a crisis in the relations between fiction and society which had already elicited much more radical modernisation. And to have them taken seriously; one American reviewer, gratefully quoted by the publisher, called *The Rosary* a book that 'strengthens faith in the outcome of the great experiment of putting humanity on earth' and held that it was one of those unusual stories that appealed to 'all classes of readers of fiction.' This credits it with powers which were at the time much sought after, for example by Conrad. There existed a real desire to maintain the popularity of fiction while modernising it.

But the urgency of technical innovation as a means to modern truth is felt by novelists rather than their readers. In general people probably wanted then, as in a measure they still do, old techniques applied to genial, or anyway familiar, materials. 1907 produced one novel worth examining in this light, William de Morgan's *Alice-for-Short*. De Morgan had been an associate of Morris in the pottery business and was himself a distinguished artist; only when at sixty-five he lost his studio did he turn to writing long novels, the first and most successful being *Joseph Vance* (1906).

De Morgan's manner was deliberately archaic. In a message to his readers at the end of *It Can Never Happen Again* (1909) he says, excusing himself for a particularly cosy, omniscient chat: 'I know that gossiping with one's readers is a disreputably Early Victorian practice, and far from Modern, which everything ought to be. . . .' In *Alice-for-Short* he does much the same thing: 'We are dwelling (to your disgust, we doubt not) on these points because we really want to take you into our confidence about Charles and Alice, and what they thought and felt. Never you mind how we come to know these things! We answer for their accuracy. Be content with that!' (p. 464). The jocose unease of these interpolations suggests that the Modern was a trouble to de Morgan, and its presence in his thoughts produces some odd twists in his novels. *Alice* is about a waif brought up as an adopted daughter by a good family; eventually, despite their long adherence to the notion that their feelings are purely fraternal, she and the son of the house marry. The facetious chapter heads and the waggishly archaic tone don't quite gloss over the fact that much of the story is about death, broken marriage, drink, and slums, 'the great hells of civilisation,' the stunted, abandoned children of the very poor. The time of the action is the early Victorian period, and there are obvious sources in Dickens; but to anybody interested, de Morgan is talking about Edwardian slums – his date and his tone exempt whoever does not want them from disagreeably topical reactions.

That he was conscious of doing more than producing a pastiche is indicated by the subtitle of his book, 'a dichronism.' Not content with a complicated Victorian plot, he makes unusual play with a character called Mrs Verrinder, whose basic narrative function is to bring the lovers together. But Mrs Verrinder is also the agent of further festoons of plotting. Having been knocked on the head at the age of twenty, sixty years before, she has only now come to; there is a good scene when she first sees herself in a looking glass, but the interest really lies in her being a sort of human time machine. Also we are told of her views on the art of fiction. She is surprised to learn that the poet Scott has turned to novel writing and, since the lovers cannot persuade her of the merits of Dickens and Thackeray, she reverts, in her search for entertainment, to *The Vicar of Wakefield*.

Since de Morgan was a man of intellect and imagination, this book poses some odd questions. Nowhere else, so far as I know, can one point to novels that please by a deliberate thematic and technical archaism, yet at the same time carry within them an awareness of technical change and the complex action of time on the authenticity of narrative.[4] De Morgan doesn't of course propose this as the main interest of his book; but his object is to give to readers who feel about the Victorian novel what Mrs Verrinder felt about *The Vicar of Wakefield* more of what they wanted, with as little change as time and conscience permitted. *Alice-for-Short* is therefore an example of a number of complex relationships – of changes in the life of forms in art, changes in the relations of writer to reader – all of which, given practised intelligence and practised conscience, continue to occur even in situations where they are for other reasons not wanted. A book caught like this, reluctantly but consciously, in an inevitable change of period, may well be something of a monster, and probably a short-lived one; but it has its interest.

The three books I've mentioned so far all illustrate, in different ways, the pressure of the times – of the Condition of England – on popular fiction. None of them was written on the assumption that serious changes in technique might be required to accommodate the dimly perceived new shape of the world; de Morgan's awareness that this might be so was deliberately dulled by his archaism. Yet this was also a time in which the technique of fiction was a matter of intense concern, not only because men wanted, as artists, to refine the instruments they had inherited, but because they felt with much urgency that the condition of the world required kinds of understanding which could not be provided otherwise than by technical innovation. There was even a characteristically patriotic motive, since it was not thought right to allow the English novel to remain technically inferior to the foreign. This was the age of the dreadnought; one needed to overgo Flaubert and Maupassant as one needed to keep ahead of the German navy.

Much of the history of the novel in the present century is dominated by the notion that technical changes of a radical kind are necessary to preserve a living relation between the book and the world. Here I am concerned only with the earlier stages of this technical research. Serious writers lived not only with the knowledge of the problems of naturalism but also with the example of James. The marvellous Prefaces were appearing. James had failed to interest a large popular audience, but had written, and commented upon, novels of great importance to technicians, who certainly did not believe that the interest of these works was limited to the area of professional know-how. *What Maisie Knew* was especially venerated and not only for its 'technique.' It was a model of how technique is necessary to imaginative apprehension of the times. And James's audience was not confined to practitioners; he could not, in the early years of the century, have repeated his complaint of 1884 that 'the "serious" idea of the novel appeals apparently to no one.' In 1897 the *Academy* reviewer greeted *Maisie* with 'amazement and delight.' In the opinion of the *Edinburgh Review*, James so far succeeded in his determination to achieve 'an immense correspondence with life' as to have 'added a new conception of reality to the art of fiction.' The *Saturday Review* said that this novel was 'very easily followed'; and many echoed the views of Oliver Elton in his fine essay of 1903 associating James with a specifically *modern* beauty and significance. Elton was a professor of English, and we would not ordinarily associate him with desperately adventurous opinions.[5]

These and similar observations imply a newly developed interest, confined no doubt to a smallish circle of readers, in the technical and theoretical aspects of fiction. Brownell, in a remarkable long essay published in the *Atlantic Monthly* in 1905, observed acutely that 'the present time may fairly be called the reign of theory in fiction . . . and Mr James's art is in nothing more modern than in being theoretic.' Admittedly he goes on to complain that James is obsessed with theory to a damaging degree, 'palpably withholding from us the expected, the needful exposition and explanation.'[6] But this is the normal reaction against technical developments which proceed from an understanding that the routine product often has features which, on rigorous inspection, turn out to be archaic, redundant, and falsifying. Those features served no purpose relevant to the nature of the novel as it was coming to be understood, but they did give assurances to the normally inactive reader that whatever was going on matched his own comfortable and quite arbitrary expectations, so that he, unlike the new novelist, mistook them for the main business of the art. In short, the more reflexive, the more technique- and theory-obsessed the fiction, the more it asked its readers to give up and the more it asked them to supply;[7] so the 'new' novel demanded a large increase in that art of collaboration which was of course always needed but by convention mitigated and understated. Hence the assertion that the reader of *What Maisie Knew* or *The Golden Bowl* was called on to develop a sharper and more subtle feeling for *relevance*. This was identified as modern and attributed to a modern increase of 'general consciousness.' The point was taken, even by opponents of James – by Wells, for example. So the new techniques were firmly associated with the new changed times; both were abandoning some certainties, looking into attitudes and devices that had come to seem false, and facing a new situation in which more things had to be thought about and in different contexts of relevance.

And here we have to consider Conrad, who was responsible for much of this radical enquiry. By 1907 he had abandoned hope of popular success, supposing that the public was incapable of the sacrifices he required, for example, in the matter of endings – a most important matter, for the 'full close,' the 'nail hit on the head,' was among the most falsifying of the time-honoured conventions, as well as the one that seemed especially dear to ordinary readers 'in their inconceivable stupidity.'[8] By a freak which astonished and possibly annoyed Henry James, but which is of a kind we have later grown more familiar with, Conrad did in 1913 slip into the best-seller list with *Chance*, a book obsessed with method, theory, technique to the point where even hardened Conradians begin to protest. This is testimony either to a rather rapid evolution of public taste or to the truth of Conrad's own view that the public will swallow anything, even occasionally and fortuitously something that is properly 'done.' Earlier, Conrad shared the view of his collaborator Ford that there was a genuine though obscure relation between techniques and the times, the condition of fiction and the Condition of England. Ford regarded James not only as a great technician but also as a great historian of the culture. He may already have been contemplating *The Good Soldier*, which is not only a profoundly researched novel as to its techniques but precisely intended as a history of the culture. Ford's friend Masterman, as Wiley reminds us, had written in his book *The Condition of England* of the need to diagnose 'the hidden life of England' and suggested that fiction might be the instrument employed.[9] The development of that instrument, Ford was sure, would require study of alien examples rather than of the indigenous novel – a cosmopolitanism acquired for reasons of national health and security in a manner analogous, though remotely, to that dreamed of by Elinor Glyn.

Techniques developed in order to study so great a subject without looseness and bagginess are likely to be of the sort that can propose without explicitness the symptomatic quality of a fictive event. The circumscribed 'affair' used by Ford in *The Good Soldier*, and so much admired by him in *What Maisie Knew*, should reverberate within the chambers of the reader's attention in such a way as to induce him to select, from an indeterminate range of possible inferences, those that have significance. Their number is not to be limited by the conventional coding of the old novel, by, for example, the formal close or by steadiness of tone, or by what James called Bennett's 'hugging the shore of the real' or by the vouched-for authenticity of narrator, because these are no longer relevant except in so far as the disappointment of illegitimate expectations on the part of the reader may be a legitimately suggestive device.

It is easy enough to see why other writers who were capable of understanding the new thing – Bennett and Wells, for example – nevertheless rejected it. Finally the difference of opinion comes down to incompatible estimates of the rights and duties of the reading public, and to the question of whether the dismantling of all expectation-satisfying devices isn't in the last analysis the dismantling of the novel. The true heirs of Conrad are the modern French, with their demand for full collaboration from the reader in an act – all *lexis*, no *logos* – that can scarcely any longer be called fiction, so that the *roman* slips undifferentiated into *écriture*. But that was a long way off, and both Ford and Conrad cherished some hope of winning the attention of *la cour et la ville*, of a general reading public that might be induced to collaborate in the techniques required by the times. To some extent it was so induced. The outcry over the ending of *Jude* was evidence, as Alan Friedman says,[10] of the fact that tampering with the closed ending was tampering with public morality. But in the years that followed there was a change, and the famous hung ending of *Women in Love* seems not in itself to have upset people. There was a change, a recognition that totality, solidity, *rondure* may falsify the truth, especially when not achieved with the laborious sophistication displayed in *Nostromo* and *The Good Soldier*. Bennett, though perhaps he had more natural endowment than Ford or Conrad, was wrong about what was needed. Whether one thinks of such changes in terms of technology or in terms of grammar, they did make possible a modern and in some sense a more truthful fiction.

As an instance of how a writer, one who may be said to be of serious intent but of less natural ability than Bennett and less intelligence than Conrad or Ford, can fail significantly at such a moment, consider Galsworthy's novel *The Country House*. It appeared in 1907, a year after *The Man of Property*, which is rightly, for all its faults, the more celebrated. The easiest way to say what's wrong with *The Country House* is to declare, perhaps unreasonably, that it ought to be a Fordian novel. It is about a single 'affair' – the prevention of a divorce suit – but is much concerned with the Condition of England. Galsworthy is writing about an upper-class family and the troubles that come upon it when the son and heir gets involved with a New Woman whose husband threatens to cite him in divorce proceedings. The author knew the divorce law from personal experience and was writing at a moment when campaigns to change it had made it a prominent issue in the understanding of the new England.[11] But Galsworthy's hero escapes all the humiliation and obloquy, and does so by a quite deplorable bit of novelism.

His affair is conducted in a London which certainly contains poor people – they stand outside his club in Piccadilly; sick and weary, they wait on him in the discreet restaurant where he takes his wicked lady; at Newmarket they are jockeys in the pay of unscrupulous masters. But the affair of the book is essentially an affair of the rich, for since divorce was for the rich alone it could hurt only them. They are never focused in relation to the sufferers who crowd around; that there is no sorrow like that of the rich is written into the book's texture. This inability to focus may have disturbed the tender-hearted author – and it certainly makes a hash of his story, which, though rumpled and torn by ineffective ironies, arrives at a conclusion in which almost everything of interest in it is ignored or betrayed. What is certainly true is that there is a relation between this social falsity and failures of tone in the writing.

The boy's father, Mr Pendyce, is a collector.

His collection of rare, almost extinct birds' eggs was one of the finest in the 'three kingdoms.' One egg especially he would point to with pride as the last obtainable of that particular breed. 'This was procured,' he would say, 'by my dear old gillie Angus out of the bird's very nest. There was just the single egg. The species,' he added, tenderly handling the delicate porcelain-like oval in his brown hand covered with very fine blackish hairs, 'is now extinct.' He was, in fact, a true bird-lover, condemning cockneys, or rough, ignorant persons who, with no collections of their own, wantonly destroyed kingfishers or other scarce birds of any sort, out of pure stupidity. 'I would have them flogged,' he would say. . . . Whenever a rare, winged stranger appeared on his own estate, it was talked of as an event, and preserved alive with the very greatest care, in the hope that it might breed and be handed down with the property; but if it were personally known to belong to Mr Fuller or Lord Quarryman, whose estates abutted on Worsted Skeynes, and there was grave and imminent danger of its going back, it was promptly shot and stuffed, that it might not be lost to posterity.

(All quotations from *The Country House* are from the 1907 edition.)

This is firm enough, a little too sarcastic perhaps, but well made, down to the 'very fine blackish hairs.' There is no posterity save one's own; if Pendyce cannot possess the egg or the bird the species might as well die. The delicacy with which his animal hand touches the egg, his privileged knowledge of it, do not in the end distinguish his barbarity from that of the vandals. In itself it is not inconsistent with a desire to flog such people. This, though not subtle, is quite clear and sharp. Later we see him as a Justice of the Peace:

There were occasions . . . when they brought him tramps to deal with, to whom his one remark would be: 'Hold out your hands, my man,' which, being found unwarped by honest toil, were promptly sent to gaol. When found so warped, Mr Pendyce was at a loss, and would walk up and down, earnestly trying to discover what his duty was to them. There were days too . . . when many classes of offender came before him, to whom he meted justice according to the heinousness of the offence, from poaching at the top down to wife-beating at the bottom; for though a humane man, tradition did not suffer him to look on this form of sport as really criminal – at any rate not in the country.

It was true that all these matters could have been settled in a fraction of the time by a young and trained intelligence, but this would have wronged tradition, disturbed the Squire's settled conviction that he was doing his duty, and given cause for slanderous tongues to hint at idleness. And though, further, it was true that all this daily labour was devoted directly or indirectly to interests of his own, what was that but doing his duty to the country and asserting the prerogative of every Englishman at all costs to be provincial?

Here the sarcasm produces tired locutions, even very clumsy sentences; but the focus is again sharp enough, both as to the way the poor are judged and as to the assumption that the preservation of his own property is the sole important task the world sets a man. And the only reason for our hearing so much about the Squire is that his son's behaviour is a threat to his interests and pleasures, but also to the perpetuation of his property; so there is some expectation that this heavy 'placing' of him will tell when the plot begins to question him. There are matters within his upper-class competence, as when, with the Parson, he charges like an officer at the head of his troops to put out a fire in a tenant's barn. But the New Amoral Woman and Divorce should confront him with more difficult problems. Galsworthy, however, has a novelist's trick to play. Mrs Pendyce is a dull lady and no New Woman, but she is as highly bred as her husband; and by acting with ladylike decision she settles everything satisfactorily. She leaves her husband, thereby shaking momentarily his notions of property and propriety, goes to London, interviews her son and his mistress (who has by this time given the boy up), and then visits the lady's husband, who is still threatening proceedings. He is persuaded to drop them on the sole ground that Mrs Pendyce *is* a lady. So she sorts out the entire imbroglio at no cost save the speaking of a few sentences she would rather not have uttered.

When this has been done we hear no more of the poor or of bullied jockeys, for Mrs Pendyce returns home, where all is restored to its prelapsarian calm. The cloud has lifted (even the actual weather is fine) and in the garden are the Squire and the Parson looking at a tree; 'symbol of the subservient underworld – the spaniel John was seated on his tail, and he, too, was looking at the tree.' She notices weeds, but a word to the gardener will put that right. She picks one of her own white roses and kisses it. So the book ends. Later, no doubt, they will sit down to the modest seven-course dinner, served without champagne, which is all the family allows itself when alone.

This conclusion certainly proves that the rich can be lucky. Galsworthy wrote in a preface to *The Country House* that he had got the name of a revolutionary for speaking as he sometimes did about the upper classes, but argued that he was 'the least political of men. The constant endeavour of his pen has been to show Society that it has had luck; and if those who have had luck behaved as if they knew it, the chances of revolution would sink to zero.' Nothing else is done, and all the promises that something else will be done are frustrated, ignored. The ironies of the concluding tableau, insofar as they are effective at all, belong to a different book; it could have started from the same *données* and contained the passages on Mr Pendyce's collecting, but its middle would have been less lucky. It may be worth adding that Galsworthy himself owned a spaniel called John and treated him as the lucky should treat the poor; for when his conscience prevented him any longer taking part in bloodsports, he sent John every summer to Scotland for the shooting, that his instincts should not go unsatisfied.[12]

It is curious that in the much more inclusive and more finely imagined *Man of Property* Galsworthy should have made Soames a 'great novel reader'; this prompted him to write a somewhat satirical passage on the ways in which novels 'coloured his [Soames's] view of life,' giving him the false expectation that Irene would eventually come round to him again. Galsworthy, in *The Country House*, takes refuge in Soames's kind of expectation, having created expectations of another kind. His irony creates an amusing problem for interpreters, for its undoubted existence in some places creates a presumption that it may be found in others, whether he wanted it or not; as when Mrs Pendyce, seeking knowledge of her son, writes a solicitous letter ostensibly concerning the misfortunes of a poor girl in whom she is interested. We hear no more about the girl, whether she got into the home or not, any more than we hear of the worn-out waiters who so adored the adulterous rich young couple. She uses this pitiful case as a cover for the really serious business of her letter, and this is clear to her correspondent. Our hearing no more of the girl is part of the way things are, the way the lucky behave. What we hear about is how upper-class virtues saved the heir of a great estate from the consequences of his own conduct; and we hear it in no such way as to persuade us that the serving poor, the underworld, are still there in the text. The spaniel John does pastoral duty for them.

One sees in Galsworthy how it may be possible for a writer to command to admiration some traditional technical devices without knowing that the sort of honest dealing with the world he wanted to achieve might require him to control much more machinery, some of it very new. It was nine years later that Ford showed the way in another story of adultery; his narration hardly glances at the poor at all – only describing, as he says, the death of a mouse by cancer, but in such a way as to make it imply the sack of Rome.

Most would agree that the best novel of 1907 was *The Secret Agent*, a story with an enormous hole in the plot; so this particular kind of invitation to exceptionally strenuous hermeneutic activity on the part of the reader must be attributed to Conrad and not to Alain Robbe-Grillet, who has an admittedly more difficult hole in *Le Voyeur*. This is not the place to compare these holes, nor to expatiate on *The Secret Agent*. Conrad in his sub-title called it 'a simple tale,' but its simplicity is precisely of the kind that makes for interpretative difficulty, like the notion of angels as simple in substance. I shall say something instead of a book published in the following year: Chesterton's *The Man Who Was Thursday*, which may have been a response to Conrad's novel and surely, it must be said, a weak one. It is another tale of 'those old fears,' of anarchist plots and terrorism. In *The Napoleon of Notting Hill* Chesterton sets his action in a London of the future identical with that of the present, a protest against social change which would presumably extend to those technical changes advocated by writers of less conservative and optimistic outlook. Chesterton would dislike 'cold mechanic happenings' as much in fiction as in life. 'The old trade of story-telling is a much older thing than the modern art of fiction,' he believed.[13] He did, however, call *Thursday* a 'nightmare' – that is his sub-title, and it may be a comment on Conrad's – and thought it worth reminding people of this fact many years later. He was trying, he said, 'to describe the world of wild doubt and despair which the pessimists were generally describing at that date.'[14] Most of their fears are dissolved in the dream. Saffron (Bedford) Park was the centre for aesthetes of the Godwin kind, but also housed the anarchist Stepniak, who was killed there on a railway line;[15] Chesterton makes it a sort of Cockaigne where the anarchist Gregory and the policeman Syme, disguised as a poet, can meet. A believer in order, poetry, and life, Syme ousts Gregory and gets himself elected to the Central Anarchist Council, having first explained – it is Conrad's point but differently put – the similarities between anarchists and policemen, which make the war between them a holy one. Chesterton gets some strikingly stagy effects: the seven top anarchists meet on the glassed-in balcony of a Leicester Square restaurant and observe on the street below them not only a policeman, 'pillar of common sense and order,' but also the poor, entertained by a barrel organ and full of the vivacity, vulgarity, and irrational valour of those 'who in all those unclean streets were . . . clinging to the decencies and charities of Christendom.' The sight fills Syme himself with 'supernatural valour.' Compare the extraordinary moment in *The Secret Agent* when the *agent provocateur* Verloc calls the policeman in the park; it is like the difference between fancy and imagination; it expresses a contrast between the modes of paradox and poetry. And it helps to distinguish the kind of inventiveness proper to a new form of novel from the kind of fantasy permitted in the old.

Conrad's London is the raw, dark, dirty middle of the world, where there is no structure in space or in time that enables men to know one another, or even to familiarise themselves with inanimate objects. In a Soho cafe his policeman knows nobody and nothing; human contact is arbitrary and fugitive. But Chesterton finds order and charity in the dirty city and uses a Soho cafe to bless its alien inhabitants. Conrad's anarchistic aristocrats are sleazy politicians,

Chesterton's are heroes. He is answering Conrad with counterassertions that are belied even by his own text with its fake ending; and his truth is of nightmare, which the paradoxes whitewash. Thus in Chesterton it is a joke that anarchists and policemen turn out to be 'just the Syme.' And the primary process of his book *is* nightmare. We remember not what the comically educated policeman says on the Embankment, but the essentially horrible pursuit of Syme through London by an immobile but nightmarishly speedy ancient in a snowstorm, or the duel with the bloodless Marquis.

The difference between *The Secret Agent* and *The Man Who Was Thursday* is instructive in the context of the present discussion. Chesterton was convinced of the existence of evil as a permanent feature of life; it was a sort of world-conspiracy represented by Jewish adventurers who, as he believed, began the Boer War 'and set two simpler and braver peoples to kill each other for their profit.' But the answers were old and paradoxical, unlike those of the 'pack of dirty modern thinkers' he declared incompatible with 'the mass of ordinary men.'[16] Conrad's novel contains specimens of the dirty modern thinker, but he handles them so originally, with such disregard for the mass of ordinary men, that he is in his way a dirty modern thinker himself. Chesterton takes Conrad's mixture of anarchist and policeman, rich and poor coexisting uneasily at the heart of the world; but Chesterton wants it to be ultimately a benign mixture and a good place, and in the pageant with which he ends, time itself takes on a ritual character as the seven policemen anarchists become days of the week and a mimesis of a good and ordered creation. For Conrad the attempt on the Observatory where time and space are zero and the imperial city is the devourer of the world's light is all the more nihilistic in that it is carried out by an idiot at the instigation of an informer whose master is a corrupt and foolish politician. The frescoes in the pub, the journey of the decrepit cab horse, are nightmares that no paradox will tame; the term 'mystery' in this novel belongs in the newspapers that further soil the filthy streets and corrupt the mind, not to a traditional theodicy. Empire, the English poor, the impact on Englishness of alien and often horrible thoughts are as much Conrad's concern as Chesterton's, but his way of seeing them belongs to another world.

Thus it was the alien who saw that the Condition of England was but a shadow of a deeper condition, which could only be diagnosed with transformed instruments. So radical is the change that in order to understand it we should have to look back at least to Nietzsche to discover how a text might have to stand in a new relation to reality to be truthful; and forward, half a century or more, to see more fully its technical implications for fiction. All we can say on this evidence is that it is one thing to know about or sense the issues – in a way, Elinor Glyn did that for those who shared her language and her expectations – and another to research the means by which a text might be caused to illuminate them. The need was felt by de Morgan, but the new novel was still a little too hard for Englishmen of 1907; it was for them too modern a way of rephrasing a proposition they might, at heart, accept: that the critical condition of England was the critical condition of life, if one had the means to know it.

NOTES

1 *Letters of Henry James*, ed. Percy Lubbock, 1920, ii, 384; quoted by Samuel Hynes, *The Edwardian Turn of Mind*, 1969, p. 358. Hynes's book not only characterises the general mood of the period but provides much helpful detail on the whole 'Condition of England'.

2 Erskine Childers, *The Riddle of the Sands*, 1903.

3 H. G. Wells, *The War in the Air*, 1908.

4 But one should mention John Fowles, *The French Lieutenant's Woman*, 1969, and William Golding, *Rites of Passage*, 1980.

5 These quotations are all from Roger Gard, *Henry James: The Critical Heritage*, 1968, pp. 149, 269, 347, 382, 349ff.

6 Gard, *Henry James*, pp. 401–7.

7 With the consequence, as Brownell hinted, that the reader gave up James instead: 'I know of nothing that attests so plainly the preponderance of virtuosity in Mr James's art as the indisposition of his readers to re-read his books' (Gard, *Henry James*, p. 404).

8 Quoted in John D. Gordan, *Joseph Conrad: The Making of a Novelist*, 1940, pp. 306–8.

9 Paul L. Wiley, *Novelist of Three Worlds: Ford Madox Ford*, 1962, p. 40.

10 Alan Friedman, *The Turn of the Novel*, 1966, p. 74.

11 See Hynes, *The Edwardian Turn of Mind*, pp. 185ff.

12 Dudley Barker, *The Man of Principle: A Biography of John Galsworthy*, 1969, pp. 22–3.

13 Reported in Anonymous [Cecil Chesterton], *G. K. Chesterton: A Criticism*, 1909, p. 202.

14 From a late article reprinted in the Penguin edition.

15 Ian Fletcher, 'Bedford Park: Aesthete's Asylum?' in Fletcher, ed., *Romantic Mythologies*, 1967.
16 Cecil Chesterton, *G. K. Chesterton*, p. 142.

CHAPTER 2

LOCAL AND PROVINCIAL RESTRICTIONS

We could save ourselves much trouble by agreeing that a novel is a fictional prose narrative of a certain length, which allows for a great deal of variation between novels. But it is obvious that people want to expand it; they plump it out in various ways, and this enables them to make such observations as 'This is not really a novel,' or 'Where have all the novelists gone?' They can specify a novel with much more accuracy than my simple formula allows; the trouble is that in doing so they represent accident as essence. This is one reason why the death of the novel is so often announced. Provisional and local characteristics are mistaken for universal requirements. The difficulty is made worse by the desire of those who understand this to dissociate themselves vigorously from the old novels that exhibit such restrictions. Not only do they wish, understandably, to write novels which are free of those local and provincial restrictions so long mistaken for essential elements of the kind; not only do they sensibly want to enquire into what sort of a thing a novel really is, what goes on in the mind that reads it; they also, and less happily, assert that the newness of what they are doing distinguishes it decisively from anything that has been done before. So both sides may agree that the old novel is dead, one rejoicing and the other lamenting. The New Novel is parricide and usurper, and the Oedipal parallel is strengthened, some might say, by the self-inflicted blindness of the son.

If we have the patience to look at the difficulty more closely, we may find that a family resemblance persists, as between Laius and Oedipus, who were both lame, both deceived by oracles, and both married to the same woman. Novels new and old may have congenital defects, may take oracles too literally, and have an intimate relationship with the reader. Differences of course exist, though commentary and advertisement exaggerate them. Certain old habits have been discontinued; for example the old assumption that a novel must be concerned with the authentic representation of character and milieu, and with social and ethical systems that transcend it – what may be called the kerygmatic assumption – is strongly questioned. The consequence is a recognisable estrangement from what used to be known as reality; and a further consequence, which can equally be defended as having beneficent possibilities, is that the use of fiction as an instrument of research into the nature of fiction, though certainly not new, is much more widely recognised. But if we admit novelty to this extent, we must at once add that none of these new things was outside the scope of the long narrative of the past; what we are *learning* about narrative may be, in a sense, new, but narrative was always potentially what we have now learned to think it, in so far as our thinking is right; though perhaps for good reasons the aspects that interest us seemed less important, and were the subject of fewer or even no enquiries.

It seems doubtful, then, whether we need to speak of some great divide – a strict historical *coupure* – between the old and new. There are differences of emphasis, certainly, as to what it is to read; and there are, within the narratives themselves, rearrangements of emphasis and interest. Perhaps, as metacritics often allege, these are to be attributed to a major shift in our structures of thought; but although this may be an efficient cause of the mutation of interests it does not appear that the object of those interests – narrative – imitates the shift.

Compare an older historical problem. W. P. Ker tells us in his *Epic and Romance* that the yielding of the first of these kinds to the second was an epochal event: 'the change of temper and fashion represented by the appearance and vogue of the medieval French romances is a change involving the whole world, and going far beyond the compass of literature and literary history.'[1] He is talking about what later came to be called the Renaissance of the Twelfth Century, of which the change from a 'stronger kind of poetry'[2] to another, more eclectic, less heroic, more ambiguous, was but a part. Within the larger changes in society he detects not only changes in poetry and rhetoric, but also new kinds of story-telling, which 'imply the failure of the older manner of thought, the older fashion of imagination.'[3] 'Failure' here is too strong, surely: 'change' would serve. It must be said that the re-examination of the nature and design of an instrument, in this case fiction, might well be related to other kinds of cultural change, as Ker suggests. But within the history of narrative this is interesting mainly as an example of how, from time to time, it becomes possible and desirable to think about the nature of narrative not as if it were given and self-evident, but as if it were susceptible of widely different developments. 'No later change in the forms of fiction,' says Ker, 'is more important than the twelfth century revolution. ... It ... finally put an end to the old local and provincial restrictions upon narrative.'[4]

This is perhaps extravagant; 'finally' is also too strong. But we can add to Ker's authority that of Eugène Vinaver, who speaks of related matters in his remarkable book, *The Rise of Romance*. Look first at the kinds of difficulty encountered in the *Chanson de Roland*: its discrete, discontinuous scenes, its lack of 'temporal and rational links and transitions.'[5] It seems impossible to speak of its possessing an overall structure, or a narrative syntax, for that would imply sequence, connection, subordination – not this par-ataxis. The same event may dominate successive strophes: Roland dies three times, always with a difference, almost as if in a novel by M. Robbe-Grillet. Vinaver insists that if we try to lay out these strophes as temporally successive we shall distort the work, which appears not to be as interested as we have come to be in the registration of an even flow of time and causality. Romance, on the other hand, does have continuous narrative of a sort, but the problems it sets us are equally difficult. So much is not explained. The writers seem consciously to require their readers to work on their texts (*gloser la lettre*) and supply meanings to them (*de lor sen le sorplus mettre*).[6] The reader's job is like the writer's own, the progressive discovery of non-linear significances, the reading, in narrative, of clues to what is not narrative. Creative inferences of this kind are necessary in all competent reading; here the fact is recognised with and exploited in what seems a peculiar way. The coherence of a narrative may be of such a kind as to frustrate certain cultural expectations.

The complexities of Chrétien de Troyes are such that he may still, in up-to-date books, be accused of 'lapses of coherence'.[7] His Grail story is particularly vexatious, and scholars have solved it by inventing a Quest sequence: Miraculous Weapon, Dolorous Stroke, Waste Land, Healing. But this sequence, and a fortiori its mythic archetype as we discover it in the work of Jessie L. Weston, occurs neither in Chrétien nor in any early text. (Such is our rage for order that when Eliot dissolved this myth in The Waste Land his critics crystallised it out again.) Chrétien was not aiming at this kind of coherence, and to provide it is to violate his text – to import irrelevant constraints into the interpretation of the narrative. What he sought to produce was what Vinaver – adapting a famous formula of Cleanth Brooks's – calls 'a pattern of unresolved stresses.'[8] He did not assume that all good fiction must be of the kind of which it can be predicated that everything 'fits in.'[9] This position may be hard to hold; in the thirteenth century what Vinaver calls 'the restraints of design'[10] – the requirements of sequence and closure – grew strong again.

Certain qualities which we may, on a narrow view, associate with well-formed narratives, are absent from that of Chrétien: closure, character, authenticated reference to settled notions of reality. The modern rejection of these qualities is, in part, a rediscovery of properties of narrative known in the twelfth century: the qualities Vinaver calls entrelacement, and polyphony, of resistance to closure, and to certain other expectations bred by narratives of a different emphasis.

What we discover, then, from listening to Ker and Vinaver on the Chanson and Chrétien is that discoveries about the nature and possibilities of narrative may, perhaps must, take place at times when there are in progress revaluations of much larger cultural scope, but that the discoveries themselves are about narrative, and are not necessarily of a character that connects them in an obvious way with the changes that accompany them. Nor do they constitute an irreversible evolution; that is why in both works there are what we think of as anticipations of the fire-new research of our contemporaries. We note also the recurrent desire to reimpose local and provincial restrictions. Narrative is prior to all such, and we need to understand how it works without identifying it with its local and transient manifestations.

I want now, for a moment, to talk about a single novel; for reasons which I shall try to make clear it is a detective story. This kind of narrative began to develop in the nineteenth century and reached a very remarkable degree of specialisation in the twentieth. It is therefore a good example of the overdevelopment of one element of narrative at the expense of others: it is possible to tell a story in such a way that the principal object of the reader is to discover, by an interpretation of clues, the answer to a problem posed at the outset. All other considerations may be subordinated to this interpretative, or, as I shall call it, hermeneutic activity. Clearly this emphasis requires, to a degree much greater than in most stories (though all have hermeneutic aspects) the disposition, in a consecutive narrative, of information which requires us to ask both how it 'fits in', and also how it will all 'come out'; and this information bears up an event, usually a murder, that precedes the narrative which bears the clues. So there is a peculiar distortion of more usual narrative conventions (though readers rapidly acquire the competence to meet the new demands). I have chosen a recognised classic of the genre, E. C. Bentley's *Trent's Last Case*, published in 1912.[11] There is not much detailed study of such books, partly because they are by some thought unworthy of it, but also because there is a tabu on telling what happens in the end. This tabu, which, observed, frustrates comment, is relevant to my enquiry, because one of the most powerful of the local and provincial restrictions is that a novel must *end*, or pretend to; or else score a point, by disappointing the expectation that it will do so. There must be *closure* or at least an allusion to it. The tabu sacralises closure; it suggests that to give away the solution that comes at the end is to give away all, so intense is the hermeneutic specialisation. But in the present context profanity is necessary and also good.

The detective story is much more concerned than narratives normally are with the elucidation of a series of events which closed either before or only shortly after its own starting point. The narrative is ideally required to provide, by variously enigmatic clues, all the evidence concerning the true character of those earlier events that the investigator and the reader require to reconstruct them. Clues are of many kinds. Some information is conveyed simply, other information looks simple but isn't. Still more appears to have a bearing on the problem but does not, or does have a bearing while seeming not to. Of course another kind of information must also be provided and processed, the kind that moves the narrative along, establishes a milieu or characterises the detective – as a priest, a don, an aborigine, or a peculiar old lady – or explains why so many people disliked the deceased, and so on. This information may or may not be irrelevant to the hermeneutic enterprise on which the reader is embarked; also it can conceal clues or introduce false ones. It will certainly, in so far as it takes his attention, distract the reader from his hermeneutic task. And the interplay between narrative and hermeneutic processes is so complex that information which has no bearing on the pre-narrative events may be processed by an attentive reader in senses which alter the whole bearing of the book. Ideally however, we are always sorting out the hermeneutically relevant from all the other information, and doing so much more persistently than we have to in other kinds of novel. For although all have hermeneutic content, only the detective story makes it pre-eminent.

In *Trent's Last Case* the title itself is enigmatic: we don't find out why it's his *last* case until the final paragraph. The first sentence of the book is: 'Between what matters and what seems to matter, how should the world we know judge wisely?' This has the characteristic ambiguity. The narrator explains it thus: very rich financiers, such as Manderson the victim in the book, are extremely important in the international money markets, though they have no effect at all on the world in which wealth is really produced. (Notice also the false complicity of 'the world we know', which suggests that our reading is always going to be the one prescribed by the narrator.) Of course the words refer equally to the difficulty of distinguishing what, hermeneutically, matters and does not matter in the pages that follow. It is worth adding that it does not matter whether this ambiguity was intended or not. An important and neglected rule about reading narratives is that once a certain kind of attention has been aroused we read according to the values appropriate to that kind of attention whether or no there is a series of definite gestures to prompt us; of course we may also decide not to be docile, and evade these local and provincial restrictions.

The millionaire Manderson is found dead in the grounds of his house.[12] He has been shot through the eye. No weapon is found, and there are scratches on his wrists. He is oddly dressed in a mixture of day and evening clothes; his false teeth are missing; his watch is not in the pocket designed for it; his shoelaces are badly tied. Yet he was known to be a neat dresser; he had clearly put on some of his clothes with his usual leisurely care; and he had parted his hair. Trent finds among Manderson's otherwise perfect shoes a pair slightly damaged, as if by the insertion of too large a foot. This enables him, though reluctantly, to suspect Manderson's English secretary Marlowe. He duly finds Marlowe's pistol to have been used in the killing, and he finds the right fingerprints on Manderson's tooth glass and elsewhere. However, Marlowe has a perfect alibi: he had driven through the night to Southampton on business of Manderson's. Trent correctly concludes that death must have occurred much earlier than had been supposed – the ambiguity of evidence on this point has been scrupulously indicated – and that Marlowe, on the previous evening, had dumped the body where it was found, entered the house wearing Manderson's shoes, conducted a daring imitation of his employer – even conversing with the butler and Mrs Manderson – and then, having planted the clues which suggested that his employer died the following morning, departed for Southampton. Trent writes all this out and takes the document to the young widow, whom he likes but suspects of an attachment to Marlowe, and perhaps even of complicity. He leaves her to decide whether the facts ought to be revealed.

This is the famous 'false bottom' of the book. Almost every clue, including some I haven't alluded to, has been caught up into a satisfactory pattern. Nothing happens for some time, until Trent meets Mrs Manderson again, is assured of the mistake he has made concerning her relations with Marlowe, and proposes marriage. He confronts Marlowe, who is able to give a satisfactory explanation of his conduct on the night of the murder; he was the victim of Manderson's fiendish plot (well motivated by much talk of the millionaire's ingenuity and jealousy) to achieve revenge on his wife's supposed lover by sending him on a journey with a large quantity of money and diamonds belonging to his employer. Manderson would shoot himself; Marlowe would be found to have shot his master and absconded with the loot. Luckily Marlowe was a skilled chess player as well as a clever actor; he saw through Manderson's plot in the nick of time, correctly interpreting certain anomalies in his behaviour, and, turning the car round, found Manderson dead near the spot where they had parted. Believing in the impossibility of establishing his innocence otherwise, he behaved then exactly as Trent had deduced, driving the body back, replacing his pistol in his room, and executing the charade in the house before leaving for Southampton.

The position now is that while the police still accept the explanation – good enough for them, it's implied – that Manderson was murdered by the emissaries of an American union he had antagonised, Trent believes that he committed suicide as part of his crazy scheme for revenge. But this is still another false bottom, and gentle old Mr Cupples, scholarly confidant of Trent and uncle of Mrs Manderson, now reveals that he happened to be nearby when Manderson pointed the pistol at himself. Darting forward and seizing the weapon, he accidentally shot the financier. This incident is not, by the way, unclued; it is prepared for by concealed clues in the opening pages. Trent did not notice them, nor did we. He will not inform the police, but he does despair of human reason, which is why he calls this his last case.

If Trent had attended as closely to Cupples as to Marlowe he might not have missed these clues. The reason why he overlooked them is simple: Cupples is honest, English, and upper-middle-class. Trent prides himself on knowing the intrinsic value of people, but they rarely win his esteem unless they conform closely to that description. They must not be policemen, servants or Americans. The characters who, as he senses it, are incapable of evil are Mrs Manderson, Marlowe and Cupples. Manderson, on the other hand, is too rich, too puritanical, too ruthless, and not English. In a way the police are right; the killer is an American, as it happens Manderson himself rather than American Labour desperadoes.

Tricking us about the clues is of course the writer's business here; but it is important that in order to do so he may be obliged to provide information which he cannot stop us from processing in a quite different fashion. Thus it is important that Manderson is jealous, a plotter, an exploiter of the poor, and that this reflects on his nation. Mr Cupples himself remarks that in these unprecedentedly bad times the 'disproportion between the material and the moral constituents of society' is especially marked in the USA. In trying to throw suspicion on American Labour the book willy-nilly invites the reader to make inferences on an entirely new system. We gather that money-lust, godless and narrow morality, social unease, insane plotting, napoleonism, eventually madness, are typical of Americans. Not content with merely nationalist snobbery, Marlowe ventures a racial explanation. He has looked into Manderson's genealogy and found early Mandersons mating with Indian women. 'There is a very great deal of aboriginal blood,' he says, 'in the genealogical make-up of the people of America.' He is, wrongly, under the impression that this discovery of the Indian taint was what set his employer against him. But the charge remains true, even if he wasn't ashamed of his aboriginal blood, since Cupples can speak of his 'apparently hereditary temper of suspicious jealousy'. Mrs Manderson is much better off married to Trent.

Bentley dedicated his book to Chesterton, who was capable of a foolishly naive anti-Semitism, and doubtless shared the ordinary Edwardian Englishman's attitude to colonials; this may help to explain a certain chauvinism in the tale, though Bentley presumably meant it to remain inexplicit. Yet the processing of clues leads us inevitably to the conclusion that this novel has a cultural significance which, if we had to attempt a formal description of the text, we might subsume under some such heading as 'early twentieth-century myth of America'. The processing of hermeneutic material has entailed the provision of other matter from which we may infer an ideological system: American is to English as the first to the second term in each member of this series: rich-not rich, uneducated-educated, cruel-gentle, exploiter-paternalist, insensitive-sensitive, and so on, down to coloured-white. So the hermeneutic spawns the cultural.

It also spawns the symbolic. For example: Trent solves the riddle only in part (the whole solution requires the aid of old Cupples (a goodish name for Tiresias)); he supplants a man who, since he is old enough to be his wife's father, is also old enough to be Trent's. There's a good deal of displacement, of course, but the myth is Oedipal. So we see that Bentley's novel, though primarily a hermeneutic game, inevitably provides information which, if we are not docile, we may process independently of the intention or instruction of the author, who is therefore neither the source of a message nor an authority on reading. All narratives are like this, whether they belong to the nursery, the analyst's casebook, or the library shelf. Bentley's genre is evidently one in which hermeneutic information predominates; but to provide it in a narrative is to activate other systems of reading or interpretation. Trusting the tale can have unforeseen consequences, as all readers of *Studies in Classic American Literature* ought to know. The multiple, perhaps unfathomable possibilities which inhere in a narrative 'of a certain magnitude' declare themselves under this kind of examination, even though the text is generically so limited, so resistant to plurisignificance.

It happens – to continue with this example of highly developed hermeneutic interest – that in rejecting the old novel some self-conscious makers of the new have taken a special interest in detective stories. Their reasons for doing so are that they mistrust 'depth'; they regard orthodox narrative, with its carefully developed illusions of sequentiality and its formal characterisation, as a kind of lie. Thus they admire the detective story, in which the hermeneutic preoccupation is dominant at the expense of 'depth', in which 'character' is unimportant, and in which there are necessarily present in the narrative sequence enigmas which, because they relate to a quite different and earlier series of events, check and make turbulent its temporal flow. The presence of ambiguous clues is also of great interest, especially if you give up the notion – and here is a major change – that they ought to lock together with great exactness, and abandon the attempt at full hermeneutic closure (all loose ends tied up).

As early as 1942, in a comment on his own *Pierrot mon amour*, Raymond Queneau was talking about ' "an ideal detective story" in which not only does the criminal remain unknown but one has no clear idea whether there has even been a crime or who the detective is.' Eleven years later Alain Robbe-Grillet published the first of the new wave of new novels, *Les Gommes*, which is an approach to that ideal. His detective goes much more seriously wrong than Trent, and it turns out, if that is not too strong an expression, that the murder he is investigating has not yet been committed, and that when it is the murderer is the detective Wallas, and the victim his own father, perhaps. Since Wallas appears to be physically attracted by someone who appears to be his stepmother, is repeatedly asked riddles about what animal is thus and thus in the morning, at noon, etc., and searches devotedly for an eraser of which the brand name may be *Oedipe*, he has inherited Trent's

Oedipal qualities; but he lives in a very different kind of narrative, in which events and characters are doubled; in which objects – including a famous tomato – are described in hallucinated detail but have at best very obscure hermeneutic relevance; and which is in itself as it were false, not just false-bottomed. Trent lives without trouble in a book which has a double flow of time, but Wallas gets hopelessly swamped in it. Trent masters most of the clues; the clues master Wallas. And the erasers are always at work, rubbing out the novel. The closure is, in Barthes' expression, *à la fois posé et déçu*. Novels, it seems, may erase themselves instead of establishing a permanent fixed reality. There are many internal relations and echoes which have no significance outside the text, point to no external meaning. The book seems to be trying to seal itself off from everything outside it.

The fashion prevailed: Michel Butor's *L'Emploi du temps*, written a few years later, is also, in its curious and complicated and unclosed way, a detective story. A young Frenchman, passing a year in the bleak English northern city of Bleston, finds himself at war with it; after seven months of passivity he rouses himself to defeat the city in the remaining five by recapturing the lost time, writing an account of those lost months. The double flow of time becomes extremely turbulent. In May Revel is recounting, straightforwardly, the events of October; in June the events of June mingle with those of November; and so on, with increasing complexity, until in September the events of September, July, March, August and February are all boiling up together, as he not only recalls the past but frantically re-reads his manuscript. The young writer concerns himself incessantly with maps of the city – they have a magical relation to its labyrinths. Among these the most interesting is a detective story called *Le Meurtre de Bleston (The Bleston Murder*, but also *The Murder of Bleston*), a work of great topographical accuracy. Revel meets its author, and reveals his identity, an indiscretion which perhaps causes an attempt on the author's life.

The Bleston Murder is, by all accounts, an elaborately clued story. And in *L'Emploi du temps* there are hundreds of clues of many kinds; but they do not work traditionally. We can see how Revel forms them into hermeneutic sequences and we even try to do it ourselves; but they do not work out. They lie in the past of the manuscript: the Cain window in the Old Cathedral, suggesting not only fratricide but the first city and also Bleston, is incomplete, like the novel itself and other works of art in it; it is related – but how? – to all the other cities that are mentioned – Petra, Baalbek, Rome in flames, and the labyrinth at Cnossos. In the same way the mythical Ariadne underlies, but not with a perfect fit, the girl Rose; and Theseus (a mythical twin of Oedipus) underlies, with imperfect fit, the author. The book becomes arbitrarily encyclopaedic: the Old Cathedral offers one systematic world-view, the New Cathedral, with its careful carvings of plants and animals in proper modern botanical and zoological orders, a world-view appropriate to the nineteenth century; the detective-story murder took place there, and was finally avenged in the red light from the Cain window in the Old Cathedral. But all these and many other hints about the hermeneutic fit are false; all remains unclosed, incomplete, and we watch Revel fail in his attempt to hammer it all into a unity, to make the clues work like clues in a detective story.

J. C. Hamilton, author of *The Bleston Murder*, lectures intermittently on the genre. It must, he says, have two murders; the murderer is the victim of the second, which is committed by the detective, his weapon an 'explosion of truth'. The detective is, as so often in the tradition, at odds with the police (for Butor an allegory of the best possible relationship between himself and the reader) because he is concerned, not with the preservation of an old order, but with the institution of a new; so he cheats the police (as Trent did). The climax of his existence is the moment when his accurate vision transforms and purifies reality. Furthermore, he is a true Oedipus, 'not only because he solves a riddle, but also because he kills the man to whom he owes his title and because this murder was foretold him from the day of his birth.'[13] Hamilton argues further that 'in the best of such works the novel acquires, as it were, a new dimension,' giving among his reasons for saying this the view that such novels have narrative which 'is not merely the projection on a flat surface of a series of events' but which, in addition, 'rebuilds these as it were spatially.'[14] Revel adds that in exploring events anterior to its opening, such a novel has a truth missing from other kinds, for we muse on our disasters after they have happened, and live our lives in these cross-currents of past and present. It was for this reason that he felt obliged to abandon the simplicities of May, when he set down what happened in

October, in favour of the detective story writer's complex movements in the labyrinth of time and memory.

But the attempt fails; the clues don't fit, or close; all the receding series of objects, works of art, mythical equivalents, are askew. No blinding explosion of truth will destroy Bleston. And these myriad disymmetries, displacing the symmetries, force us to peer, each from his own angle, into the text, make our own adjustments, institute within the text a new order of reality, our own invention. Butor himself speaks of 'spatial polyphony'. Barthes, examining such phenomena, will speak of 'stereographic space'; in terms of the relations established within it we produce our own reading, so changing our view and, ideally, ourselves, altering our opinion as to what matters and what does not. For ordinarily we go on living in a state of truce with the world, supposing an identity between it and the arbitrary notion we happen to hold of it. The novel can be a criticism of common consciousness. It can show that our normal 'fitting' is bogus; it attacks the way in which we 'legitimate' our beliefs. Without forgetting that it could always do these things – it would not sound strange to say that George Eliot's novels are criticisms of common consciousness – we can allow that we are forced to produce, rather than merely assent to, an order, and that the order must be new.

Thus are the hermeneutic specialisations of the detective story transformed in the interests of *truth*, in the cause of enabling us to live in the world as it is, as it simply *is*, lacking all meaning but that signified in our texts. Every novel, on this view, should be an affront to the simple hermeneutic expectation that it will *work out*, because it can only work out if we accept the false implication that the world itself is simply coded, full of discoverable relations and offering closure. Since, as sociologists assure us, 'conceptual machineries of universe-maintenance are themselves products of social activity, as are all forms of legitimation,'[15] we need not be surprised that in adapting the detective novel to their purposes these French writers change it with revolutionary intent; they are usually willing to see in what they are doing a model of larger changes in politics, or more generally in the institution of a modern *Weltanschauung*. For them the Oedipal detective, no longer concerned with puzzles guaranteed soluble and limited, becomes a herald of the new order. The problem of reading, including re-reading, because it requires us to remake ourselves, to move about in worlds not conventionally

realised, becomes the central problem. The novel is thus deconstructed; mysteries like those of Chrétien once more challenge the
reader. He must forget how he used to read, deluded by local and
provincial restrictions; he must cease to invent structural myths,
and instead develop the creative activity which narrative always
demands in some measure, but which may be deadened by over-
familiarity and by trained expectations too readily satisfied.

This is, I think, to allow the new its full quantum of novelty. It
amounts to a lively awareness of, and a new way of stating, what
has always been at least intuitively known: the 'openness' and the
'intransitivity', and the esential 'literarity' of texts. This new awareness is such that it ought to change conventional attitudes to all,
and not merely new, texts; but there is, of course, a difficulty here,
namely the restrictiveness of the criticism to which the new critics
aggressively oppose themselves.

How are we to give up the kind of reading which reinforces and
complies with 'local and provincial restrictions'? We began to do
so long ago; occasionally one regrets the bad communications with
Paris, for we, who have had Professor Empson and the New Criticism with us for forty years, hardly need to be told that texts can
be polysemous, and will hardly believe that all professors deny
this. But such differences will not excuse our neglect of what is
being said; nor will our mistrust for the politics, philosophy and
polemics of the new French criticism. They may have something to
teach practical critics about method – and not only in their operations on new texts. Roland Barthes, an early champion of
Robbe-Grillet, was carried away by the theoretical possibilities of
the *nouveau roman*; he proclaimed, before its authors were able
to, that the desired '*anéantissement de l'anecdote*'[16] had finally
been achieved. Later, with other structuralist critics, he grew interested in the attempt of the Russian Formalists of forty years
earlier to find methods of describing a story or novel as a linguist
describes a sentence – without regard, that is, to the meaning it
may communicate, only to its structure. This suited his view that
literature must struggle against the temptations of meaning[17] – that
the 'science of literature', as he called this new enterprise, should,
like linguistics, deal with systems not of *pleins* but of *vides*. He
devised the expression *écrivance* to distinguish an older literature
of reference from the true *écriture*. The neo-Formalist or structur-

alist enterprise was in full swing a few years ago, and much machinery was devised for the scientific description of texts.[18] But Barthes grew discontented with it; it was unequal to the really important task of describing a text in its individuality and difference. In *S/Z* (1970) he developed new procedures, and tested them on Balzac's story *Sarrasine*.

A text, he argues, is not to be referred to a structural model, but understood as a series of invitations to the reader to *structurate* it. It is a network of significations, of *signifiants* lacking transcendant *signifiés*, and a reader can enter it anywhere. He must produce, not consume it; he must as it were *write* it; and in so far as it avoids external reference it may be called *scriptible*. Classic texts he calls *lisible*; they lack the plurality of the *scriptible*, possessing meaning which can only be ideological, and in some respects, such as story, possessing also a directionality that must be avoided by the *scriptible*. In other words, the *lisible* has local and provincial restrictions, the *scriptible* (of which no example is available) has not.

Barthes's analysis is conducted in terms of five codes, which are to account for what we do in the process of reading a text, to one or more of which each *lexie*, or unit of discourse, is assigned. These codes, though as yet unsatisfactory, are rather promising. Two have to do with what we think of as narrative, distinguished as the proairetic and hermeneutic codes: that is, the sequence of actions (dependent on choices), and the proposing of enigmas which are eventually, after delay, concealment, deception, and so on, solved. The other codes relate to information not processed sequentially: semantic, cultural and symbolic, they stand as it were on the vertical rather than the horizontal axis of the work, and remain rather vague, especially in view of the prohibition against organising some of them on a thematic basis. To study these codes is not to study meanings, but only to describe the plurality of the work as apprehended by (presumably competent) readings. In *lisible* writing (Balzac's, for instance) this plurality is limited. In a *scriptible* text it would not be so. The *lisible* adheres to an obsolete *episteme*, a kerygmatic civilisation of meaning and truth. But even in the *lisible* there is movement from code to code: the same signifier may operate in both symbolic and hermeneutic codes (the castration of Zambinella in Balzac's story, or the false clues about American violence in *Trent's Last Case*). Despite the constraints of

limited plurality – the commitment to closure – symbolic, hermeneutic and proairetic may, in the *lisible*, stand in an and/or relation.
We now see clearly what the authors of the *lisible* were prevented
from seeing. Above all we understand that there is no *message* that
is passed from writer to reader: *dans le texte, seul parle le lecteur*.[19]

If we ignore his ideological bias – itself a local and provincial
restriction – we may find in the codes of Barthes a way of approaching the task of describing what happens when we read a
narrative. On the question of the hermeneutic operations of the
reader he seems, in *S/Z*, very limited, partly no doubt because of
the character of the text examined. But there seems little doubt
that he has got behind the arbitrary constraints that have been
mistaken for rules; the kind of reading he describes will perhaps
enable us to cleanse our perceptions in the matter of narrative.
One instance might be that we should alter our notions of acceptable closure, so exploited by the specialised hermeneutic of the
detective story. The questioning of this by Queneau and Robbe-
Grillet was a prelude to a new understanding that hermeneutic and
other forms of closure are contingent not necessary aspects of
narrative. This, rather than a purely modern dissociation of narrative from kerygma, is the lesson of the new novel and also of the
codes.

For it seems wrong to argue that all this establishes a sharp
distinction between something called the novel, with all those qualities and conditions that seemed essential but turn out to be period
trappings, and some leaner narrative that has cast them off. We
have seen how even the classic detective novel, with its not always
perfectly fitting clues and its uncontrollable play between hermeneutic and symbolic codes, prefigures 'stereoscopy'. New insights
into the nature of modern fiction are equally insights into the novel
– for all novels verge on the stereographic in so far as they satisfy
the reader (a crude criterion, admittedly, but defensible).

Because *Sarrasine* is interesting in this way, though it was published in 1830, Barthes calls it a *texte-limite*; although it is an
instance of what he calls, sardonically, *pleine littérature*, it stresses,
by its very subject, namely castration, and in many of the ciphers
which reflect it, an interest in want, in emptiness; it exploits the
collision of castration with sex, of emptiness with plenitude, of Z
with S. So that although it is on the wrong side of that firm line
which, for Barthes, cuts off the modern from the classic, *Sarrasine*

happens to be a book that not only illustrates the limited plurality of the classic, but adumbrates the *littérature vide* which, in the present *episteme*, succeeds it, just as sign is held to have succeeded symbol.

The inference appears to be that all the novels of the past in which we find much to admire partake of the modern precisely in so far as they are not patient of interpretation that assumes limited meaning. Barthes, under the influence of a domestic French quarrel, always talks as if establishment critics deny that position. Outside France this is, of course, untrue. In a sense he is saying, in a new way, something we have long known about the plurality of good texts.

Yet many critics do continue to feel some *horreur du vide*. The invention of myths to explain Chrétien's allusions to the Grail stories is a handy example of a continuing critical passion for closure, the more interesting in that there are fictions more or less contemporary with these mythical inventions that are expressly designed to frustrate closure. James provides classic instances, notably in *The Sacred Fount*. It does seem to be taking us a long time to understand the implications of these experiments in enforced plurality and imperfect closure. Yet the success of our interpretative enterprises on the novels of, say, Dickens, is evidence that in our unmethodical way we have made good guesses about it, and noticed that there seems no easily ascertainable limit to the number of *structurations* they will bear: what we reject we reject intuitively. More simply still, the very length of anything we call a novel should warn us that it will contain much information of which the critic, no matter how committed to the single full interpretation, makes no use. He explains it away or ignores it; sometimes behaving as if he thought there are things necessary for novels to do – because they are novels and need to seem 'true' – that are nevertheless hardly his business ('pour faire vrai il faut à la fois être précis et insignifiant,' as Barthes[20] remarks). At best he is dealing with a remarkably small proportion of the information provided in the text, information which may, as we all know, be processed in so many ways that a plurality of readings is ensured.

As I've noted, novelists themselves long ago exploited their knowledge that their medium was inherently pluralistic; to the name of James one need add only that of Conrad, who invented the hermeneutic gap long before Robbe-Grillet expanded it to engulf the whole text. These writers saw ways of using the fact that the senses of a narrative are always, in some measure, *en jeu*; they exploited this discovery and wrote to show how crucial it was despite the obscurity in which it had remained. So Barthes has found a possibly useful way of talking about something which the researches of novelists had already brought to light.

To take a simple example: in *Under Western Eyes* Rasumov leaves Russia to serve as an agent *provocateur*. We are not told until later how he contrived to do so: his cover was provided by an oculist. The novel has a great many allusions to eyes and seeing, few of which could be regarded as important to the narrative, simply considered. Some of these relate to the difference between Russians and others to the difference between Russia and Switzerland; and others are concentrated in the representation of Miss Haldin. All this could be schematised in terms of Barthes's codes as proairetic, hermeneutic (he provides for delay in the solving of an enigma), semantic, cultural and symbolic; and the fluent interplay between the codes is evident. It is indeed very complex, much more so than in Balzac; and it is from writing of this kind that the need to invent formal means to describe the pluralities grows, rather than from a wish to develop an instrument capable of analysing any narrative (though Barthes might deny this). A copious interplay of plural significances was the invention of novelists examining the potential of narrative; our competence to read them is dependent upon the existence of texts requiring such competence.

It is, by the way, perfectly correct to say, as Barthes would, that the question as to whether Conrad intended the visit to the oculist to signify in all these ways is beside the point. It is simply in the nature of the case. This is the sense in which it is true that *dans le texte seul parle le lecteur*. And having learned from certain texts how to speak, the reader will do it in others, including the classic, the *lisible*; that is why we can always find new things to say about a classic text; we can structurate it anew. There has been a change in our reading, not in the texts; we know that a novel does not simply encode a message from the author, and this knowledge became explicit when we had to deal with novels like *Under Western Eyes*, which asserts the fallibility of all that it seems to assert right down to its last page, which offers not closure but a hermeneutic booby-trap.[21] Its views on Russia, whatever they may be said to be, are not Conrad's; his were not western eyes. Here is a difference in points of view that produces an authentic stereography. And that expression 'points of view' will serve to remind us that there have been earlier attempts, in the Anglo-American tradition, to come to terms with the problems that engage Barthes. They are inherent in narrative; he did not discover them, nor has he shown that they came into being with the great cultural changes of the modern era.

The French theorists want a novel without transcendental reference as they want a world without God. They want it to be impossible for anybody to 'recuperate' the local and provincial which is inherent in the *lisible*. And in the course of their research they have made interesting observations. They have noticed, as D. H. Lawrence did, that the novel may be a way of demonstrating that it is possible to live, because it is possible to read, without accepting official versions of reality. Excited by this hope, they formed the belief that there may be a kind of novel in better faith than any before it by virtue of its abandoning the old assumptions and cultivating the text of pure sign, without external reference, without symbolism, without structure, receptive of all structures the reader produces. But this exaggerates – perhaps for ideological purposes – the novelty of some aspects of narrative, which, though now given much attention, are a selection from the set of permanent possibilities. As we saw at the outset, it was as possible for Roland to die three times as it is for a Robbe-Grillet personage; and Chrétien understood something of the now fashionable 'emptiness'. Nor would it be difficult to multiply historical instances; after all, when we speak of a classic what we mean is a text that has evaded local and provincial restrictions.

There has, in short, been a renewal of attention to aspects of narrative which did not cease to exist because they were not attended to. When we remake our great novels – as we must, and as we have, of recent years, remade the nineteenth-century English classics – we shall find that they all have certain qualities of *Sarrasine*, as Barthes defines them, and also certain qualities of twelfth-century romance, as Marie de France defines them. They will always invite us to plural glosses on the letter, to ingenious manipulation of the codes; it is their nature to demand that we produce rather than consume them, and that we liberate them from local and provincial restrictions, including, so far as that is possible, our own. As to Barthes, it may seem odd to suggest that he has outlined a method for the formal description of a classic; but I believe that is what he has done, and the keenness and brilliance of his insights into *Sarrasine* tell us the same story.

NOTES

1 W. P. Ker, *Epic and Romance*, 1896; ed. of 1931, p. 6.
2 Ibid., p. 49.
3 Ibid., p. 322.
4 Ibid., p. 349.
5 E. Vinaver, *The Rise of Romance*, 1971, p. 5.
6 Marie de France, quoted by Vinaver, op. cit., p. 16.
7 R. S. Loomis, *Arthurian Tradition and Chrétien de Troyes*, 1949, p. 6; quoted in Vinaver, op. cit., p. 40.
8 Vinaver, op. cit., p. 47n.
9 Ibid., p. 51.
10 Ibid., p. 52.
11 Bentley said his original intention was to write 'not so much a detective story as an exposure of detective stories' (Julian Symons, *Bloody Murder*, 1972, p. 95) but it was always taken 'straight' as an example of the genre.
12 It is only fair to say that this banal summary does no justice to a very entertaining puzzle.
13 Michel Butor, *Passing Time*, translated by Jean Stewart, ed. of 1965, p. 143.
14 Ibid., p. 158.
15 P. L. Berger and T. Luckmann, *The Social Construction of Reality*, 1966, ed. of 1967, p. 108.
16 Roland Barthes, *Essais critiques*, 1964, p. 65.
17 Ibid., p. 267.
18 See Roland Barthes, *Communications* 8, 1966, and *Théorie de la Littérature*, ed. T. Todorov, 1965.
19 Roland Barthes, *S/Z*, 1970, p. 157. There is a more detailed consideration of these codes in the next chapter.
20 Ibid., p. 75.
21 For a fuller discussion of *Under Western Eyes*, see Chapter 6.

CHAPTER 3

THE USE OF THE CODES

> ... the great problem is to outplay the
> *signifié*, to outplay law, to outplay the
> father, to outplay the repressed.
>
> —Roland Barthes[1]

My chapter title is capable of two interpretations, so I had better
explain what I mean to talk about. The codes are those of Roland
Barthes's *S/Z*, but I do not intend to offer detailed discussion of
what he calls his 'stereographic' method of textual analysis. My
concern is less with the how than with the why. The codes may
come to be recognized as an interesting advance on the Neo-formalist descriptive techniques which preceded their invention; that
they will hardly do so without considerable modification is my
belief, but not my present theme. I am interested in the normative
aspect. Barthes, let us remind ourselves, is dealing with the kind of
text he calls *lisible*, distinguished from the authentically modern
scriptible text by the fact that it is not indefinitely open to 'production' by the reader. *Lisible* texts are said to have a limited degree
of plurality and are subject to various kinds of closure. Barthes
investigates the way we read such texts, and in so doing indicates
their limitations – as to restricted plurality and closure – by comparison with ideal modern texts which have neither.

St Augustine explained, in his book *The City of God* that 'those things which have no significance of their own are interwoven for the sake of things which are significant,' and Barthes is making a not wholly dissimilar point when he observes that 'there is text everywhere . . . but not everything is text.'[2] St Augustine's expression retains some relevance to the way novels are written and read, with this important qualification: unlike us he was quite certain about which things were significant and which not. Lacking that assurance, we have to assume that narratives capable of interesting competent readers are likely to be in some ways inexplicit and indeterminable to the extent that there is no universal agreement as to what kinds of significance, if any, are to be attributed to any particular moment of a text; so there is in effect, in all such cases, an indefinite measure of plurality. If it were not so teachers of literature would soon work themselves out of jobs. Whatever Professor Raymond Picard and others nearer home may think, most of them have long assumed the plurality of the texts they choose to study.

There can obviously be new ways of talking about this interesting situation, but they can hardly succeed if they also pretend to have invented it. That the reading of a novel is a highly individualized performance by the reader, its virtue depending upon his competence, is surely common knowledge, and I doubt if Stendhal thought he was proclaiming a new truth when he compared the novel to the bow and the reader to the violin.[3] This analogy falters, of course, since novels, unlike fiddle-bows, can nudge and prompt. It is also true that readers of restricted competence can allow themselves, as it were, to be played by the novel. The mere existence of a story-line, and the more or less traditional devices by which a text can pretend to establish the authenticity of its account of the world, can ensure the abandonment of strenuous analytic activity. There are banal performances and there are also banal novels; but literary critics (competent readers, we hope) like the works they like precisely because performances are possible which are not banal, and which, moreover, may be indefinitely various, not only as between readers but also as between readings.

It will be observed that I have already begun to 'recuperate' the Barthian codes. Of the five, two are what he calls 'irreversible': the hermeneutic and the proairetic, the voice of truth and the voice of the empirical. It is true that people really do like to see how it all comes out, and like to think it's real. In so far as this is the case, the linear codes do account for a restriction on plurality,[4] an appeal to passive consumption. There is, however, a possibility of a problematical use of these codes. This is a possibility Barthes is unwilling to consider, except as deviation from the norm of the *lisible*; instead he invents his antithetical (but empty) category, the *scriptible* text, which would be a galaxy of signifiers with no signifieds. Such a text, he says, would be rather like an onion, whereas the texts of the *lisible*, which always *close* on something, offer at best an apricot. There is a stone or pit of content.[5]

How does the *lisible* come by the limited measure of plurality it has? Barthes does not allow that there is any hierarchy in the codes, but it is clear from his demonstration of the method that the symbolic code is much the most important, for, aside from the linear codes, the cultural code is what he calls *endoxal* (referring to vulgar knowledge, opinion, ideology) and the semic is largely concerned with the obsolete notion of character. Whatever it is that may redeem the classic – make it somehow anticipate the modern – seems to arise in the symbolic code. In the Balzac story he analyses (*Sarrasine*), it is the means by which a classic narrative may say more than it knows, for instance by elaborating symbolic themes related to castration and money. And only when it both says more than it knows and contrives to bring into question the validity of the assumptions on which it was written can the classic text find its only value: as a prophecy of the modern. As Philippe Sollers remarks, the classic text is 'an economized plural. . . . It does not have to take account of the fact that it is written. . . . The classic text . . . is a fetish, a chimera that half-speaks. It spirals round a barred empty subject.' It is this emptiness, which the classics, except in their moments of prophetic unease, suppose to be plenitude, that the modern would acknowledge and exhibit. The best the *lisible* can do is, more or less by accident, to offer us the chance to let it escape from its habitual representation of 'life' as 'a nauseous compound of general opinions'[6] and provide the reader with something he can, as Barthes says, *write*, that is to say, read creatively, 'produce.'

We must consider what is implied by this doctrine of the ambiguous innocence of the classical text. The *lisible*, it appears, assumes that its relation to the world is one of specularity, or of transparence; the text pretends to be absent – as if, to recall Coleridge's invaluable expression, it is, in the course of reading, defecated to a pure transparency. This is the basis of Barthes's distinction between *écrivance* (classic, transparent) and *écriture* (modern, announcing its difference, a text among texts). People who believe in the simple specularity and transparency of novels are indeed very naive, and they are certainly prevented by their simplicity from reading texts in their textuality, narratives in their narrativity, and so on. (Any acceptable notion of competence would presumably exclude them.) And inasmuch as *lisible* texts pretend to accept these myths, they have to be subjected to a process of deconstruction before their authentic though limited pluralities become available to the modern reader or producer; what is more, they must offer, in spite of themselves, opportunities for the application of these procedures.

We can now approach the central issues. For Barthes, the only hope for *lisible* texts is that they allow themselves, in limited ways, to be treated as modern. He is always quite explicit about his modernism, longing for mutatory texts to make us even more modern than we already are, to take us beyond the point of the last great mutation, associated with Mallarmé. The notion of the great historical mutation, which has dominated so much of Anglo-Saxon criticism in this century, happens in France to take this form: the crucial date is often given as 1870, give or take a year or two; and after that time no text ought to be naively unaware of its own existence as something *written*. Nor should it, considered as a fruit, possess a stone. All closure is in bad faith. The modern 'galaxy of signifiers' would have nothing to signify, or rather it would be in constant circulation and signifying ceaselessly, 'mais sans délégation à un grand ensemble final, à une structure dernière.'[7] To put it crudely, the *lisible* is *about* something, it refers to some validating plot within it. One reason why Barthes gave up the Formalist attempt to establish a narrative *langue* of which every *récit* is a *parole* was precisely his fear that success in that operation would revive the old organicist myth of a structure peculiar to a particular work. Thus the work we wanted to open up would close again, again possess a signified secret. Such closure he would condemn as ideological, the consequence of false assumptions, occidental and endoxal, about the nature of signs. Our business as moderns is to read in order to maximize plurality, not in order to understand secrets. The apricot stone must go. We must not seek to discover structures but to produce structurations.

Neither the Formalist nor the organicist model will serve: 'il faut à la fois dégager le texte de son extérieure et de sa totalité.'[8] Japanese *vides*, not European *pleins* – oriental onions, not occidental apricots – are what we require. And we can protect ourselves against story (which dishonestly claims to reveal truth) and against specularity which is naive and dishonest, and against all the other threats. We have semiological defences; we know that our bourgeois culture habitually transforms history into nature by imposing on us myths of various kinds;[9] and so we should not be so simple as to believe in narrative structures, even when texts pretend to have them, or in bogus closures. Our motto: 'Point de dieu, de vérité, de morale *au fond* de ces signifiants.'[10]

We might once more ask whether Barthes, with rather extravagant (and for that matter, ideological) additions, is not saying something that in a way we know already. But a more urgent question is, what do novels themselves know about all this? Can it be said that the *lisible* novel solemnly refuses (save when its composure is betrayed by some accident in the symbolic code) to consider sceptical enquiries as to whether it has a stone or not?

Let us look at a novel which may help us to answer this question. It may be objected that a better example would be a much older novel than Anthony Burgess's *MF*, and that I am cheating by choosing a book which is modern, and problematical in ways that suit my purpose. It would be quite easy to meet this objection by speaking instead of *The Scarlet Letter*, for example, a work which would give Barthes a lot of trouble. But Burgess's novel happens to raise the whole issue in a simpler way, and it is undoubtedly what Barthes would call *lisible*; it is not even a *nouveau roman*; it has linear codings and closure. And I think it neatly illustrates the point that non-*scriptible* texts are perfectly capable of being the sort of fruit that can ask whether it contains a stone or not.

Miles Faber, a clever lad, quick with polyglot puns, addicted to word-games of all kinds and especially riddles, has a rage for disorder. As a protest against order, the past, the dividedness of the world, and so forth, he copulates, on the steps of his college library, with a girl called Miss Tukang. We meet him in New York, discussing this event with his father's lawyer, a Mr Loewe, the first of a polyglot of lions in the book. Mr Loewe is charged by Miles's father to prevent him from visiting the Caribbean island of Castita, where he wishes to study the works of a neglected but great anti-artist called Sib Legeru. His father's secret motive is a horror of incest. He has arranged for his son to marry a Chinese girl, seeing in miscegenation the greatest obtainable measure of exogamy. And since Miles's sister is in Castita, he must be kept away from there.

Miles is staying at the Algonquin. He enjoys a new soft drink, sold in owl-shaped bottles and called Coca-Coho. He dreams of owls. After many adventures, he evades Loewe and flies to Miami. There another leonine representative of his father (Pardeleos) asks his views on incest. Freedom-loving, rational Miles says he thinks it permissible in principle; but in the absence of absolutely dependable contraceptives he would not, for genetic reasons, practise it. When Pardeleos informs him that he, Miles, is the product of an incestuous union, he understands why he suffers from certain minor ailments.

After sailing through a storm which casts some doubt on the proposition that all disorder is good, he reaches Castita, only to find himself in a situation of apparently irrational complexity. There is a circus, Fonanta's circus, with a female Welsh bird-trainer, who seems to recognize Miles. A lionlike cripple, a sphinx, having moralized on man as 'the great unifier of disparates,' asks him a riddle, to be answered on pain of death. He refuses to answer, and saves himself by blowing a football referee's whistle, which he has found, together with the rulebook of soccer, in his hotel (a notion picked up, I dare say, from *Heart of Darkness*). He discovers that he has a foul-mouthed obscene double, son of the birdwoman Averyn (Welsh for 'birds'); and when, in searching for the works of Sib Legeru, he runs into his sister, he finds himself under the necessity of saving her from rape by this double, at whose death he then presides. To protect himself from her vengeance he must now convince the birdwoman that he is her missing son, and the only way he can do this is by undertaking to marry his sister.

The circus, as it happens, has a riddling priest among its clowns, and he marries the siblings, amidst the din of circus bands and animals and the insults of the performers, who hate the young man they take Miles to be. Dr Fonanta, owner of the circus, arrives to bestow his blessing, regretting only that there is no eclipse that night. Taking his bride to bed under surveillance, Miles just manages not to consummate his union; but there is another trial in store. The birdwoman has talking birds who ask riddles, and hunting birds (all named after living English novelists) who hunt. She puts Miles's identity to a final test by requiring him to answer a riddle set by a talking bird on pain of having his eyes pecked out by the hawks. He survives, by using his whistle, escapes, and marries the Chinese girl. He finally turns out to be a black man, from Cardiff, Wales.

This is a simplified account of a much more agitated jostle of events, puzzles, riddles, jokes, connections, and disconnections. *MF* looks like a difficult book to systematize. Lest we should think it a merely random medley of picaresque detail, it offers a few hints about its structure, many of them vouchsafed by Dr Fonanta himself. Some riddles, it appears, should remain unanswered, however simple; especially if asked by sphinxes, themselves riddles. 'The riddler has to be itself a riddle. But no, the ultimate organic creation's emissary rather, granted a voice. With this voice it says: *Dare to disturb the mystery of the universe.* For order has both to be challenged and not to be challenged, this being the anomalous condition of the sustention of the cosmos. Exogamy means disruption and also stability; incest means stability and also disruption.' The harder you try to avoid incest, by randomness, the more you are likely to commit it. For example, Tukang is Malayan for 'skilled workman' (*faber*). Z. Fonanta – *zoon phonanta*, the speaking animal – is man, product of incest, inventor of the archetypal sign-system, language. Siblegeru, pseudonym of Fonanta, is Old English for incest; and there is, even in his works, a banal order, for the speaking animal cannot avoid it. Fonanta also explains that not all of Miles's explanations, systematizations, were correct; some were insignificant, some were unsystematic, coincidences; there are texts everywhere, but not everything is a text.

Miles finally exhorts us not to answer the riddle of the book. Abandon this impassioned decoding, he says, cease to limit pluralities. And apart from the explanations the book itself offers, and which I've sketched in, it seems to be mostly random inventions and riddling fantasies. It makes ambiguous claims for order without apparently having much of it – it has a touch of Siblegeru.

Yet the book is much more closed than appears on the surface. The secret is that one needs to distinguish 'that which belongs to the order of structure and that which belongs to the order of event';[11] and the author of that formula, Claude Lévi-Strauss, provides more specific aids. He believes that the incest prohibition is universal, and the *sine qua non* of social organization. Its universality entails, given the model he employs, the existence of identifiable transformations of the Oedipus myth. One such is the Algonquin myth of a girl who suffered attempted rape by the double of her brother, who kills the attacker, and is then required to establish to the mother of the victim that he is her son. She happens to be a mistress of owls (called 'Coco-cohu' in Algonquin). The young man tries to mislead her by marrying his sister, but there is another test, as a consequence of which the woman is fooled; the birds aren't, but he escapes. 'The very precautions taken to avoid incest make it unavoidable.'[12]

Oedipus is himself a double (supposed dead but living), and thus far there is correlation between the two myths. But what about the Sphinx's riddle? Riddles are extremely rare in Amerindian cultures. However, it happens that in Algonquin myth owls ask riddles that must be answered under pain of death. Further, the Pueblo Indians have ceremonial clowns, themselves thought to be the products of incestuous unions. The correlation is complete. Puzzles and riddles, like incest, bring together elements that ought to be kept apart. There are many more transformations; for instance, these myths are transformations of the Parsifal myth. When the Indian hero gives the right answer the eternal winter ends; when Parsifal asks the right question the land is renewed. Chastity is related to the answer that lacks a question, incest is related to the question that lacks an answer (and however simple, better unanswered). The Algonquin-Oedipus myths invert Parsifal; incestuous unions engender not spring but storms and fermentation and decay (as in the noisome works of Sib Legeru and in the joint of beef Miles cooks for his fat sugar-loving sister).

Certainly this seems to weld contradictions, reduce dispersity. And it's only a beginning. There is more – enough to create, though perhaps only in the naive or incompetent, the notion that the book is laying down the law about the world. Zoon Fonanta is incestuous because any myth of human origin must be either that, or demonic; but his descendants, the Fabers, are programmed for system-making, and should therefore avoid incest. Their business is with the perception or invention of systematic relations homologous with language – which is to say: their business is to be human. The Jakobsonian triangles[13] which chart our learning to speak also chart our cooking. Culturally, cooking is the avoidance of incest between organic matter and the sun, and the avoidance of a rottenness that would destroy the world. The random is systematized by the mere presence of Miles, as when he throws away the rotten meat; or when honey and tobacco are reconciled in Miss Emmett's brand of cigarettes, Honeydew; or when Miss Emmett attacks the double's genitals with scissors and there is, Miles notes, a rare collocation of three dual forms, scissors, trousers, ballocks. The wedding of Miles and his sister is accompanied by a charivari – an ancient European way of making an offensive demonstration against a marriage considered for some reason – disparity of age, or undue consanguinity – reprehensible. The same noises that signal a charivari are made at eclipses. Eclipses also signify a disruption, cosmological but analogous to the social; the unsuitable marriage and the eclipse alike interfere with the ordinary rhythmical processes of human life – with that cycle of season, love, friendship, and so on, which Fonanta squarely commends to the disgusted Miles, as preferable to the stinking chaos of Sib. Lévi-Strauss cites a myth, found, he says, all over America, that links eclipses, rotting meat, disease, and incest.[14] Without the tabu on incest (of which Miles's genetic arguments are merely a minor reinforcement) there could be no order, no human system-making.

I do not think we can dismiss this text as a mere fantasy on themes of Lévi-Strauss. Of course it is partly a matter of jokes – the naming of the hawks for English novelists is not only a private joke (who is Anthony?) but a comment on a passage in Edmund Leach's book which attacks the French anthropologist for being very un-English about the naming of animals.[15] But more serious questions arise. That the *structure* of the book makes sense only in terms of Lévi-Strauss's work must seem important. Lévi-Strauss thinks the transformations he describes are close to the essence of humanity: 'There is a simultaneous production of the myths themselves, by the mind which generates them; and by the myths, of an image of the world which is already inherent in the structure of the mind. By taking its raw material from nature, mythic thought proceeds in the same way as language, which chooses phonemes from among the natural sounds of which a practically unlimited range is to be found in childish babbling.'[16] We live in the world by making such systems of meaning; this involves things which have and things which have not significance, though in translating nature into culture man acts in such a way that the discrete and paradigmatic do not abolish the continuous. Does *MF*, by encoding material Lévi-Strauss decoded, naively endorse all that he says? Certainly its mythic universe sets us another problem: what to do with the material, sometimes deliberately planted, which we cannot on these terms encode (like the revelation that Miles is a black man, or that his solution of the first riddle was wrong)?

And this may only be part of a larger problem: what happens to this novel if we accept the quite common opinion that Lévi-Strauss is all wrong? Burgess seems to think of man as a being who 'hammers away at structures' – certainly *he* does, and so do other writers. His structures include much that deceives us in our attempts to read paradigmatically – some things which we may miss, others which he might have missed (since it is true that the reader speaks in the text, though perhaps not, as Barthes claims, the reader alone).[17] In this writer's text we may, if we choose, read a message. The speaking animal, condemned to the avoidance of incest, is constitutionally a system-maker. Zoon Fonanta invents language, Miles Faber invents homologous meaning-systems. The book in which they appear denies that it is a mere agglutination of random elements; it speaks of order and the threat to it of anti-cultural disorder. It could be called culturally conservative. It speaks of how structures arise; and it suggests a deeper centre from which they arise. The detail of the book is generated from this structure; to put this another way, there is a model exterior to the text which must be known if the book is to be explained or closed.

However, the rightness or wrongness of that model is not the point. The book is an example of ways of meaning-making, and yet strongly criticizes them; thus its structure is self-questioning. It is strongly implied that reading a novel is a process quite like, and sharing the dangers of, solving riddles: one finds the codes, distinguishes information from noise, plays the indeterminable game of syntagm and paradigm which is the origin of all plural readings. Playing the game, you may or may not come to agree that noise is intrusive on order, inimical to culture and to being human; that anti-art and mere galaxies of *signifiants* would be as fatal to our society as incest. But the ambiguous status of the riddles – and the whole book is one – must qualify the force of such conclusions. The speaking animal lives in nature by his power to create systems homologous with language. True or false? Lévi-Strauss himself describes as myths the transformations by which he illustrates this thesis. Burgess sees the point that books, like riddles, may best be left unanswered. And when you get through the apricot to the stone you find no hard organic substance, nothing unambiguous, but a riddle, a content at best dangerous and anyway problematical.

Here I am reminded of a lucid observation made by Barthes some years ago, before he developed his later method of analysis. 'A work of literature,' he said then, 'or at least of the kind that is normally considered by the critics (and this itself may be a possible definition of "good" literature) is neither ever quite meaningless (mysterious or "inspired") nor ever quite clear; it is, so to speak, *suspended* meaning; it offers itself to the reader as a declared system of significance, but as a signified object it eludes his grasp. This kind of *dis-appointment* or *de-ception* . . . inherent in the meaning explains how it is that a work of literature has such power to ask questions of the world . . . without, however, supplying any answers.'[18] Here we have the nub of the matter. Barthes's insight owes something to the *nouveau roman*; a consciousness that de-ception (in the French sense, 'disappointment') was an inherent property of narratives made Robbe-Grillet design his novels to demonstrate it, and the necessity of *déception* to the modern novel is an important theme of *Pour un nouveau roman*. Robbe-Grillet himself allowed that what he was doing was revolutionary only if one made the mistake of assuming that the 'rules' of the novel were established in Balzac's day. Barthes's developing mystique of *écriture* led him beyond the position; in 1963 he still, I think, had it right.

If he did, then of course it must be wrong to assume that a novel such as *MF*, for all its *lisibilité*, cannot exemplify 'suspended mean-ing', pose questions and disappoint the answer, constitute a world in which everything is *en jeu*, and in this way validate its relation-ship to a world elsewhere of which the same may be said. The difference between *lisible* and *scriptible* cannot be stated as simply as Barthes came to think, perhaps need not have been stated at all.

Perhaps some readers may have been induced, by the foregoing, to think of a more familiar book – one that contrives, without explicit advertisement, to raise the question of suspended meaning and ask questions which cannot be answered by an appeal to some incontrovertible, unproblematic structure. In *The Crying of Lot*

49, Pynchon's Oedipa, as her name implies, is also confronted with riddles and with the obligation to discover an order. The origin of these riddles is in doubt; it may be the nature of the human world, viewable as waste or as system; it may be a man called Inverarity, who in turn may be either untruth or *dans le vrai*.[19] The book is crammed with disappointed promises of significance, with ambiguous invitations to paradigmatic construction, and this is precisely Oedipa's problem. Is there a structure *au fond*, or only deceptive galaxies of signifiers? Like California itself, the text offers a choice: plenitude or vacuity. Is there a hidden plot concerning an almost Manichaean conflict, which makes sense, whether evil or benign, of the randomness of the world?

Consider the opening: we find Oedipa returning from a Tupperware party; I understand that on these occasions goods are sold outside the normal commercial system. She stands in her living-room before a blank television set (communication system without message) and considers the randomness she projects on the world: thoughts about God, a Mexican hotel, dawn at Cornell, a tune from Bartok, a Vivaldi concerto for kazoo. Soon we hear about the coded voices of Inverarity, the culinary jumble of a Southern Californian supermarket, her husband's life as a used-car salesman, systematising, giving meaning to, the trash in old cars. Now he works on a pop radio station, the communication system – without content – of another culture. Later he will start *listening* to Muzak, another type of the empty system. In a world where the psychiatrists provide material for paranoid fantasies, and lawyers are locked in imaginary rivalries with Perry Mason, everybody is tending toward his own dissident universe of meaning; Oedipa is Rapunzel, her own reality let down like hair from her head. Minority cultures, bricolaged from pop, old movies, astrology, coexist in a world whose significances, if any, relate to no conceivable armature.

But Oedipa has 'all manner of revelations', and a shadowy armature seems to be taking shape. Is it all in her head, or is the great plot real? If so, is it malign? To discover it may be the same thing as inventing it. What Peter Berger and Thomas Luckmann call 'the social construction of reality' proceeds because there are phenomena we cannot simply wish away; death is one, but there are others. The construction is what our social situation permits – say, the national limits, the limits of California, ultimately the limits of dissident groups and our protestant selves. As we plot against reality we comply with or deviate from the institutionalised plots; a great deviation is called a sect if shared, paranoia if not. There is always a way of coding the material, even that which on other views is simply waste. Having instituted a system one keeps it intact either by legitimating extraneous material or, if that is too difficult, or the threat too great, by 'nihilating' it.

Making sense of other somewhat arbitrary symbolic universes, understanding their construction, is an activity familiar to all critics. Certainly it involves choices, a limitation of pluralities. The activity of the critic, thus understood, is nomic. It seeks order, and is analogous to the social construction of reality. What Oedipa is doing is very like reading a book. Of course books can be read in very strange ways – a man once undertook to demonstrate infallibly to me that *Wuthering Heights* was an interlinear gloss on Genesis. How could this be disproved? He had hit on a code, and legitimated all the signs. Oedipa is afraid she may be like that man, or that she is drifting into paranoia, the normal hermeneutic activity in disease, and Pynchon's great subject.

She has contact with many sects: in advanced societies, such as Southern California, 'socially segregated subuniverses of meaning', as Berger and Luckmann observe,[20] tend to multiply. When she sees a way of linking them together Oedipa is conscious of other terrors than paranoia. She dreads the anomic, the world collapsed into filth and randomness; but she also dreads an evil order. Pynchon invents the Scurvhamite sect, who abandoned a very mechanical double predestinarianism ('nothing ever happens by accident') for the consolations of single predestination to damnation. Yet even on her wild San Francisco night Oedipa doesn't unambiguously believe in the patterns to which the evidence is apparently pointing. For instance, she dismisses the evidence of the children's rhymes. The entire structure is *à la fois posé et déçu*. We do not learn whether the dove, harmonizer of tongues, which would make all these meaning-systems mutually intelligible, descended with the auctioneer's hammer; *au fond*, the plot remains suspended.

What concerns us is precisely the existence of what seem to be systems that could transmit meanings, as in the account of San Narciso, the town which looks like a printed circuit, 'an intent to communicate. There'd seemed no limit to what the printed circuit could have told her (if she had tried to find out); so, in her first minute of San Narciso, a revelation trembled, just past the threshold of meaning.' The revelation would be of the kind that explains the whole of history, the present condition of America, Inverarity, Wharfinger's play, and so on; it would explain how waste has meaning, just as converted into an acronym, WASTE, it forms a sentence ('We await sad Tristero's empire'). But Oedipa is poised on the slash between meaning and unmeaning, as she is between smog and sun; interminably confronted with meaningless binary choices – artificial light in sunlight, the statue of the hooker/ nymph, which is both still and windblown – and by repetitions of the San Narciso situation: windows and bottles emptily reflecting the sun, messageless. The need of a revelation, the sense that such systems exist to transmit sense, drives us to find meaning in them, for we feel 'as if, on some other frequency . . . words were being spoken.' This is the sense in which Professor Mendelson is right in emphasising the pentecostal themes in the book; fifty may follow forty-nine, and if it were called we should all become competently polyglot, able to hear the words we think are being spoken but cannot quite hear.

This is why Oedipa continues her game of strip-Botticelli with the world. Her trial run with Metzger – merely on the plot of an old movie – sensitized her for a revelation; just as the flight of the rogue aerosol foreshadows a world which, though unpredictable, is determinate. And so she continues to spot the clues, though never sure where they are, in her head or out there. The text only says it is 'as if . . . there were a revelation in progress all round her.' Options remain naggingly and senselessly open, as when the naval action of Peter Pinguid, that ancestor of Inverarity, is described: 'off the coast of what is now Carmel-by-the-Sea, or what is now Pismo Beach, around noon or possibly towards dusk, the two ships sighted each other. One of them may have fired; if it did the other responded.' This niggling dubiety is Oedipa's, and the text's.

The messages sent by the illicit system are normally without content; this could be true of the novel. The clues pile up. *The Courier's Tragedy* (played in a theatre located between a traffic-analysis firm and a wildcat transistor outfit, circulation and communication) relates not only to the supposed history of Tristero but to incest, tongueless attempts to pray, an anti-Paraclete. The bones of the dead are turned into ink, a means of empty communication (or into wine and cigarettes, which belong to other systems). Ralph Driblette has heard a message in the system of the play; so could Oedipa, if she gave herself to it. Everything can be legitimated, systematised. But there are only clues, 'never,' we are told, 'the central truth itself, for if that should blaze out it would destroy its own message irreversibly.' If the systems are to work, and the book to work as a system, it will be because the reader can do what Oedipa could not when confronted with Maxwell's Demon: make the piston move, reverse the entropy of communication as that device reverses physical entropy. But if you make the eyes of this novel move, or if you believe in the original plot on which it depends, you risk a kind of madness, which is the ultimate human cost of holding everything together in a single design. The systems are there to be filled: the children's rhymes, the 'coded years of uselessness' in the mattresses of the poor, the societies of queers and failed suicides, all to be handled if you want a central truth, a word to reconcile your time with eternity. Nobody helps; Oedipa's friends drop away. The more she encodes the trash of America the more critical her isolation becomes. She is like the poor of whom she has heard, camping among telephone wires; she walks as if inside a digital computer, among either-ors, waiting for the systems to contain a message. Either there is a Tristero, or she is 'orbiting in the ecstasy of a true paranoia'.

We can't, of course, be told which, and we question the novel as Oedipa does the Tristero plot. That plot is pointed to as the object of some possible annunciation; but the power is in the pointing, not in any guarantee. One could talk for hours about this remarkable work, but at the bottom of all one said would be the truth that it imitates the texts of the world, and also imitates their problematical quality. If one coded *Lot 49*, its radical equivocations would be instantly evident – the cultural code, for example, is as little the inert congeries proposed by Barthes as the hermeneutic code is a progress to *dévoilement*. Its separation from its exterior and its totality are precisely what it is *about*. It is an invitation to the speaking animal to consider what he makes of the world into which he introduces his communication systems; and it asks him to read a text, to reread it, to produce it if that is a better word. In its totality it poses the choice: *plein/vide*, as it so often does in its texture. To seek an answer is to be disappointed, *déçu*. Deception is the discovery of the novel, not of its critics.

Needing sharp instances, I've chosen to write about two novels which refer more or less directly to a kind of world-plot prior to their own. But one could extend the argument to cover almost any book we think worth reading; the category of the *lisible* virtually melts away, since all such books assume that they will be competently read – 'produced' – not, of course, because they are complex riddles, but because they know, as if by introspection, that it is a property of narratives (doubtless often neglected) to be plural, self-examining, incapable of full closure, as indeed the history of interpretation confirms.

Let me add one more brief example, of a novel quite different from those I have discussed – a text which exploits without advertising its suspension of meaning. It is Henry Green's *Loving*. Edward Stokes, in the best available study of this neglected writer,[21] says he finds the book difficult because it offers no interpretative hints. There are unmotivated rhetorical shifts, sudden switches of level. Sometimes it sounds like fairy tale, sometimes like proletarian realism. Still, says Mr Stokes, Green must be talking about the disintegration of the class system, a theme he had handled in earlier novels. The decaying Irish castle, with its selfish, empty gentry and its evasive, quarrelling, draft-dodging servants, must have something to do with that theme. But why do patterns interfere with one another as they do? Why, for instance, does the coarse, seedy butler Raunce fall ecstatically in love with the implausibly beautiful housemaid Edith and why does he go back to England to join the army?

True, there are symbols – the peacocks especially, and their eggs; the doves; the weathervane stuck with its arrow pointing to a scene of adultery because a live mouse is caught in its cogs. Something might be made of all that. But 'the difficulty,' says Mr Stokes, is that 'there is no single, central, all-important clue,' and so 'the symbols remain . . . free and unassigned.' (Why then are they symbols?) He cannot reduce their 'perpetual cross-flickering . . . to any simple statement of meaning'; at best he can guess what some of them 'imply or insinuate'. The story about the loves and marriages of the doves, told by a nurse while before the very eyes of the children real doves mate and murder, is, says Mr Stokes, more hopefully, 'a microcosm of the whole novel'.[22] I think he was wiser when in doubt that anything could make this claim. The right reaction here is surely suspicion. The book is so shifty – the dialogue is particularly surprising, for instance, especially if we recall that Green is the greatest English master of working-class speech – should one not have doubts about so neat a contraption? Elsewhere *Loving* flourishes its 'symbols' only as if to trick us. The peacocks are something to do with lust, greed, and so on, but these equivalences are undermined. Green appears to be doing exactly as he pleases, with complete disregard for any desire we may have to extract the fruit stone. The game of blindman's buff among the statues, the girls dancing in the vast ballroom, they don't, except for the intrusions of Raunce, dyspeptic and venal, have much to do with anything else; or Paddy among the peacocks, or Mrs Jack taken in adultery, or the lisping insurance man, or the housemaids innocently lesbian in their room, or the conventional plot about a missing ring. All the gestures and tones warn us that it is risky to take the dove story as straight irony; and so does the narrative, for the maids arrive on the scene 'in long purple uniforms, swaying towards them in soft sunlight through the budding branches, fingers on lips. . . . All begin soundlessly giggling in the face of beauty.'

The simple closure is frustrated; so is Mr Stokes. In the concluding pages of the novel, after Raunce has decided to take Edith back to unsafe England, he lies, apparently ill, as peacocks extravagantly surround, and doves settle, on his girl. 'And their fluttering disturbed Raunce, who reopened his eyes. What he saw then he watched so that it could be guessed that he was in pain with his great delight. For what with the peacocks bowing at her purple skirts, the white doves nodding on her shoulders round her brilliant cheeks, and her great eyes that blinked tears of happiness, it made a picture.' It would be profitable, were there time, to analyse this extraordinary passage in detail; perhaps it is obvious that anything so rhetorically devious is unlikely to be straightforward in other ways. Mr Stokes thinks it leads directly to the conclusion, to Raunce's return to England, home, and duty, and the pleasures of marriage. Certainly the text ends, a few words later, by saying that they returned to England and 'lived happily ever after'; but it had opened thus: 'Once upon a day an old butler . . . lay dying,' muttering the name of Ellen while Raunce stole his office and his whisky. Yet Raunce could be dying. If we are not seduced by a naive desire for *dévoilement* we shall see that the text is not naively transparent. The evidence points in many ways, and Green simply allows it to do so. It invites structuration and strongly questions the notion of definitive structures. Without using the devices of the *nouveau roman*, it assumes that the problematical character of what may be *au fond* is a property of narrative; it accepts and exploits the pluralities that arise from this situation.

Once the problem of closure is stated in this more general way it becomes obvious that there is nothing new about suspending it. Think of James in *The Sacred Fount*, where it remains for ever uncertain whether there is anything at all *au fond*, or in 'The Figure in the Carpet', a comic handling of the whole question, though it emerges that the forces which prevent the critic (the narrator and us) from discovering the figure are love and death, the very powers which make us want legitimated life-plots and closures.

MF has a problematical content which itself forms the envelope of more content, consisting of solutions, right or wrong, to mythical riddles. It displays randomness subjected to human intentions and ideas of order. That it enacts the arbitrariness, the chanciness, of such order – there are texts everywhere but not everything is a text – validates not the explanations of Lévi-Strauss but its own status as a characteristic product of *homo faber*; it is aware of its own chimerical nature. As for *Lot 49*, it indicates the enormous absurdity of both assumptions: that there is a structure, and that there is not. Neither book endorses any simple requirement of full closure. Each knows, like James, that between such desires in the reader and the actuality of the text there is a gap that is dangerous to the point of madness, and that the reader must be responsible for what he does with it. And it is in this light that we should reconsider the view that the *lisible* text is a *naïve* chimera.

Finally the codes again. In some modified form they have use in textual analysis. As they stand they depend on an untrustworthy historical theory and a perverse valuation of the *lisible*, which is represented as nauseous except in so far as it has the luck to anticipate a meaningless modernity, and which is anyway a category of straw. Probably the basic issue is between those who think that textual simulacra of order and system must be ideological (nauseous) and those who take them to be responses to a more radical need for satisfaction, a need which the anthropology of *la pensée sauvage*, and the sociology of knowledge, each in its different way, confirms.

The pluralities of sense available to *zoon phonanta* appear to be indeterminate but none the less systematically limited. That suggests that we can have a humanly adequate measure of plurality without abandoning all notions of consensual interpretation. Perhaps we need once again to remind ourselves that the theory of infinite structuration is historically part of the continuing French reaction against an atavistic academic criticism. This has entailed the false assumption that flexible, productive, and plural reading is to be had only on the basis of new and revolutionary theoretical agreements. But these are circuitous routes to truths more readily accessible: the novel itself has long been aware of its chimerical potential; it is an authentic *faux-naïf*, expert in the limitations of its own pluralities. *That* self-consciousness, rather than an unwilling symbolic permissiveness, is what preserves the *lisible* as something more than an imperfect herald of the truly modern.

NOTES

1 From an interview with Stephen Heath in *Signs of the Times*, ed. S. Heath, C. McCabe, and C. Prendergast, 1971, p. 49.
2 Ibid., p. 51.
3 'Un roman est comme un archet; la caisse du violon qui rend les sons, c'est l'âme du lecteur.' (Stendhal, *Henri Brûlard*, quoted by Stephen Gilman, 'Meditations on a Stendhalian Metaphor', in *Interpretation: Theory and Practice*, ed. Charles S. Singleton, 1969, p. 155.)
4 'Ce qui bloque la réversibilité voilà ce qui limite le pluriel du texte classique. Ces blocages ont des noms: c'est d'une part la vérité et d'autre part l'empirie: c'est précisément contre quoi—ou entre quoi—s'établit le texte moderne.' Roland Barthes, *S/Z*, 1970, p. 37.
5 '. . . if up until now we have looked at the text as a species of fruit with a kernel (an apricot, for example), the flesh being the form and the pit the content, it would be better to see it as an onion, a construction of layers (or levels, or systems) whose body contains, finally, no heart, no kernel, no secret, no irreducible principle, nothing except the infinity of its own envelopes – which envelops nothing other than the unity of its own surfaces.' Roland Barthes, 'Style and Its Image', in *Literary Style: A Symposium*, ed. Seymour Chatman, 1971, p. 10.
6 Philippe Sollers, '*Reading S/Z*', in *Signs of the Times*, p. 40.
7 *S/Z*, p. 18.
8 Ibid., p. 12.
9 The theme of Barthes's essay, 'Le mythe, aujourd'hui', *Mythologies*, 1957.

10 Roland Barthes, *L'Empire des Signes*, 1970; Barthes's jacket note.
11 Claude Lévi-Strauss, *The Scope of Anthropology*, 1967, p. 30.
12 Ibid.
13 These have to do with phonology (see R. Jakobson and M. Halle, *Fundamentals of Language*, 1971, pp. 51ff). The justification for transposing phonological method to social anthropology is given in Lévi-Strauss, *Structural Anthropology*, 1958; 1963 translation, pp. 31ff.
14 Claude Lévi-Strauss, *The Raw and the Cooked*, 1970, p. 296, trans. J. and D. Weightman from *Le Cru et le Cuit*, 1964.
15 Edmund Leach, *Lévi-Strauss*, 1970, pp. 88ff. The reference is to a passage in Lévi-Strauss's *La Pensée Sauvage*, 1962.
16 *The Raw and the Cooked*, p. 341.
17 'Dans le texte, seul parle le lecteur,' *S/Z*, p. 157.
18 Roland Barthes, 'Criticism as Language', *Times Literary Supplement*, 27 September 1963, pp. 739–40.
19 Since I wrote this, commentators have offered many other interpretations of Inverarity and other names in the novel.
20 Peter L. Berger and Thomas Luckmann, *The Social Construction of Reality*, 1967, p. 85.
21 Edward Stokes, *The Novels of Henry Green*, 1959.
22 Ibid., pp. 162, 163, 164.

CHAPTER 4

RECOGNITION AND DECEPTION

I

This is a shot at expressing a few of the problems that arise when you try to understand how novels are read. I shall be trying to formulate them in very ordinary language: the subject is becoming fashionable, and most recent attempts seem to me quite unduly fogged by neologism and too ready to match the natural complexity of the subject with barren imitative complications. It may of course be asked why there should be theories of this kind at all, and I can only say that they are needed because of what we have missed by always meditating on what we *have* read and can survey, as it were, from a distance which allows us to think it's keeping still, rather than upon the ways in which, as we read, we deal with the actual turbulence of a text. Much of what I say will seem obvious enough, but it may throw some light on a fact that we all know so intimately that we don't bother to ask questions about it: the fact of plurality, of which the plurality of our own interpretations is evidence. There are interesting side issues: why do some novels seem to be more plural than others, and why, on the whole, do the ones that seem most plural so often turn out to be fairly recent, not to say modern? Also, perhaps, how do interpretations alter in time? And what's wrong with the sorts of theory we already have?

Some of the problems I can best open up by talking about the way novels begin. You may remember Ian Watt's brilliant exercise on the opening of *The Ambassadors* – the demonstration by grammatical and stylistic analysis of the multidimensional quality of that 'fairly ordinary' paragraph.[1] Watt shows how far it is from 'straightforward' telling, getting the story moving; how very different it is from the first words of *Roderick Hudson*. He develops his point by contrasting the opening of several other novels (all earlier). And indeed his point is simple enough. Look at the opening of Trollope's *Doctor Thorne*: 'Before the reader is introduced to the modest country medical practitioner who is to be the chief personage of the following tale, it will be well that he should be made acquainted with some particulars as to the locality in which, and the neighbours among whom, our doctor followed his profession.' This simple sequence would have been abhorrent to the polyphonic James; Fielding would of course have taken Trollope in his stride, might have been surprised though not confounded by the opening of *Our Mutual Friend* or *Bleak House* or even *Hard Times*, but would have boggled at the very title of *What Maisie Knew*. *Tom Jones*, you may recall, has two openings, one in the prefatory first chapter: 'An author ought to consider himself, not as a gentleman who gives a private or eleemosynary treat, but rather as one who keeps a public ordinary, at which all persons are welcome for their money'; and one in Chapter 2, which begins the narrative: 'In that part of the western division of this kingdom which is commonly called Somersetshire there lately lived (and perhaps lives still) a gentleman whose name was Allworthy, and who might well be called the favourite of both Nature and Fortune, for both of these seem to have contended which should bless or enrich him most.' We might say that the first of these openings establishes between author and reader a relationship which is that of producer and consumer in deeper senses than Fielding perhaps intended. What binds them is the cash that buys consumables; the diner at the ordinary will need another dinner, another novel, before long, and even if, as Fielding says, the provision is HUMAN NATURE, that merely confirms that this is a thing to be bought. The author's task is to cook and serve it well – in exact accordance with the customer's taste. This account of the producer's role, and the implied passivity of the consumer, is a fitting enough introduction to one kind of history of the novel. The second opening is the plain fare expressly promised by Fielding at the beginning of the feast: a reassuring statement that although the world of the story is fairly modern (this will later be made precise; he even worked, in 1749, with an almanac for 1745) it will not be difficult to relate it to more ancient expectations. Not only is the first character to appear given a morality name, to hint perhaps at a Bunyan-like moral transparency, but the twin goddesses of romance, Fortune and Nature, are at once invoked in a familiar trope. Novels are to be distinguished from romances by their novelty; but the reassurance of continuity and non-novelty is useful to the business of selling; so not only are the goddesses from stock – the whole cadence is. You might look for it in *Euphues His England*. Later Fielding claims 'historic integrity' for his work, and distinguishes it from 'idle romance', which shows he had both in his mind: romance schemata with modern corrections, if I may use a terminology I shall explain later.

Fielding is, of course, telling the reader how he expects him to proceed; the chef determines the order of the courses (though it is an expected order, one we have learnt), and within that order will arrange whatever surprises there are to be. There is an attempt to prescribe the imaginative action of the reader. Now it happens that even in these early days there were other estimates of what I shall call the reader's share – Sterne, for example, thought that 'the truest respect which you can pay to the reader's understanding, is to halve the matter amicably, and leave him something to imagine, in his turn.' More boldly, and a bit later, Clara Reeve: 'Perhaps there is not a better Criterion of the merit of a book, than our losing sight of the Author,'[2] which signals early a problematical abdication of authority and control – something you might find, long before the novel imposed its arbitrary rules, in Chaucer – as well as an understanding of the possibility, especially in novels – which ought to reconcile, she thought, the marvellous and the probable – of the voice as a nameless whisper or even as many whispers. How long before it may no longer seem necessary – no longer seem *decent* – simply to provide, at the outset, the plain fare, the simply presented information, which will start the reader off on a familiar and not very difficult task? After all, the audience at the Globe had learnt by 1601, in a short generation, to accept the deceptive challenge of the opening scene of *Hamlet*, and soon afterwards, the riddling overture of *Macbeth*. It seems that Mrs Reeve already understood that there might be a tougher conflict between narrative, which cannot help meaning more than it says, and the ability or need of the reader to ask it to comply with his habits and expectations; and that this conflict could itself be exploited. In other words, she knew intuitively what Wolfgang Iser weightily expounds in a recent article: 'The polysemantic nature of the text and the illusion-making of the reader are opposed factors.'[3] Out of the conflict arises the need of the reader to produce meaning.

I suppose that if we were asked to name the first modern critical treatment of such problems we should all think of Henry James. Of course he is more directly concerned with the delightful difficulties of the 'doing' than with those of the reader's share – though he does admit, like Sterne, that it should be 'quite half'.[4] But he was, notoriously, engrossed by the problem of narrative authority, and the need for authors to keep clear. There is a late essay in which he laments the low standard of criticism as the chief obstacle to the proper doing of fiction – accusing Bennett of a sort of *possession* in which mere 'affirmation of energy' did duty for 'treatment'. 'Is this *all*?' he asks. 'These are the circumstances of the interest – we see, we see; but where is the interest itself?' A book such as *Clayhanger*, he says, is not a monument *to* anything, but *of* 'the quarried and gathered material it happens to contain.'[5] He is arguing for the *dispossession* of the author by his own technical means; he makes an elaborate plea for novels of which the technical disposition is such that they *must* be read twice. So he applauds, among contemporary novels, Conrad's *Chance* – not his favourite Conrad, but at least a book which by the elaborateness of its method makes a gap between producer and product, a gap, as he puts it, to 'glory in'. The existence of that gap ensures another, between the text and its reader, whose expectations are no longer subject to the usual kind of authoritative correction. This gap, which may be called the hermeneutic gap, is of great importance to the late James, and some of his work might be said to exist primarily in order to characterise it: *The Sacred Fount*, *The Turn of the Screw*, 'The Figure in the Carpet' have in common that they create gaps that cannot be closed, only gloried in; they solicit mutually contradictory types of attention and close only on a problem of closure. The confounding of simple expectation – the *not* telling us what it was that Maisie knew – is a way of stimulating the reader to a fuller exercise of his imagination: to make him *read* in a more exalted sense (*not* 'devour'). Consequently the *affair* will not be grasped, even in its ambiguity, without many readings, and those readings will find senses which remain inexplicit. James is an historian of civilisation of quite a different kind from his admired Balzac; if Balzac is a secretary James is an oracle.

Ford's novel, *The Good Soldier*, though begun earlier, was written finally in 1914–15, and it was certainly an attempt to comply with the prescriptions of 'Notes on Novelists', by a writer who particularly admired *What Maisie Knew*. He knew that 'life does not narrate' and believed that to write novels as if it were otherwise was to tell lies. He wanted to be the historian of a civilisation, but in the Jamesian way. The dream of Flaubert – a shift of emphasis from story to treatment – is now at least half-realised; story is transformed into 'affair', telling into 'treatment'. Nothing in the text is to be classifiable as formal or inert, merely consumable; everything is capable of production. Fielding, master of the feast, quickly asserts a right to digress, to make piquant delays in the provision of consumables; Ford is a master of oracular digression ('of course you must *appear* to digress') but for him it is expressly a way of setting problems to the *interpreter*, who is as remote from Fielding's 'consumer' as he could well be. Ford once complained that James talked too much in his last novels because he was dismayed at the discovery that he had made stories 'capable of suggesting' what he had not intended; 'he was aiming at explicitness, never at obscurities'; as for him, he thought it right that his 'scenes' should 'suggest – of course with precision – far more than they actually express or project.' This is, theoretically, a step on from James, who thought he should keep more moral and technical authority over the reader than Ford wants; even 'precision' here means a precision of *means*, without implications as to the control of the reader's suggestibility. He accepts as right the surrender of a larger, less controllable, share to the reader. To get the full measure of the purpose of *The Good Soldier* one had better compare Ford with a writer of very similar *intentions* but wholly inferior technical resources, such as Galsworthy. That will have to await some other occasion. My purpose now is to ask about the kinds of suggestion and *deception* practised in the opening page of *The Good Soldier*, in contrast to the others we looked at earlier; and to ask what they imply about 'second readings' and the activity required of the reader.

This is the saddest story I have ever heard. We had known
the Ashburnhams for nine seasons of the town of Nauheim
with an extreme intimacy – or, rather, with an
acquaintanceship as loose and easy and yet as close as a
good glove's with your hand. My wife and I knew Captain
and Mrs Ashburnham as well as it was possible to know
anybody, and yet, in another sense, we knew nothing at all
about them. This is, I believe, a state of things only possible
with English people of whom, till to-day, when I sit down to
puzzle out what I know of this sad affair, I knew nothing
whatever. Six months ago I had never been to England, and,
certainly, I had never sounded the depths of an English
heart. I had known the shallows.

I don't mean to say that we were not acquainted with
many English people. Living, as we perforce lived, in
Europe, and being, as we perforce were, leisured Americans,
which is as much as to say that we were un-American, we
were thrown very much into the society of the nicer English.
Paris, you see, was our home. Somewhere between Nice and
Bordighera provided yearly winter quarters for us, and
Nauheim always received us from July to September. You
will gather from this statement that one of us had, as the
saying is, a 'heart,' and, from the statement that my wife is
dead, that she was the sufferer.

Captain Ashburnham also had a heart. But, whereas a
yearly month or so at Nauheim tuned him up to exactly the
right pitch for the rest of the twelvemonth, the two months
or so were only just enough to keep poor Florence alive
from year to year. The reason for his heart was,
approximately, polo, or too much hard sportsmanship in his
youth. The reason for poor Florence's broken years was a
storm at sea upon our first crossing to Europe, and the
immediate reasons for our imprisonment in that continent
were doctors' orders. They said that even the short Channel
crossing might well kill the poor thing.

When we all first met, Captain Ashburnham, home on
sick leave from an India to which he was never to return,
was thirty-three; Mrs Ashburnham – Leonora – was thirty-
one. I was thirty-six and poor Florence thirty. Thus to-day
Florence would have been thirty-nine and Captain

Ashburnham forty-two; whereas I am forty-five and Leonora forty. You will perceive, therefore, that our friendship has been a young-middle-aged affair, since we were all of us of quite quiet dispositions, the Ashburnhams being more particularly what in England it is custom to call 'quite good people.'

On a first reading the opening sentence of Ford's novel seems to tell you that what is to follow is a story, that it is very sad, and that it is going to be told by a narrator who was privileged to hear it. Later we discover that the story involves the suicide of two of the four main personages, the sudden death of another, and the hopeless insanity of a young girl, so *saddest* is a bit lame, perhaps, and certainly misleading. We also discover that the narrator is the deceived husband of one of the suicides and the keeper of the mad girl. It is not exactly some *anecdote* he's been told, and so *heard* is strikingly peculiar. Without going any further one can, I think, say that the opening sentence of the book is *deceptive*. You ask why. Perhaps you say, ah, we're not being told directly about the story because it's more important to know what sort of a chap this is; a bit dim, obviously. There he is, at the centre of the web of adulteries and deaths, talking about *hearing a story*. And as Character is a great thing, you may say that this book is obliquely announcing that it is really going to be about this evidently odd character. However, at this stage I think you would be wiser to make a more modest guess that the opening sentence is an indication that this narrative won't have the same pretension to authority as Trollope's, or the same steadiness of reference to types, whether narrative or ethical, as Fielding's. The speaker is a dropout from his own story. Later on he has a sort of apocalyptic vision of the principal characters, and there are only three of them. He will describe himself as an ignorant fool married to a cold sensualist, and repeat over and over again that what he is ignorant of is the human heart. In trying to find out he is as it were reading the story, as you are.

But it will not do to stick on the label 'unreliable narrator' and leave it there. He is certainly that; at one place he is simply wrong about his own story, speaking of the mad girl as dead, though she is in the same house as the writer, alive and babbling about the omnipotence of God. It is interesting that the book, so intently

98

organised, should contain this and other slips; they are indications that it is safer *not* to tidy it up prematurely with such slogans, but to work at the deceptive surface, the words which so often seem, perhaps often are, formal and inert, but which, in a text which abjures authoritative direction of the reader from the outset, may not be. Consider the second sentence, as an instance of what James thought the new novel ought to have, namely a 'baffled relation between the subject-matter and its emergence', and also as an instance of what Ford himself called the process of getting into the opening 'the note that suggests the whole book.' The word *know* in different forms occurs in this second sentence, three times in the third, twice in the fourth. In the second it is intensified – 'with an extreme intimacy' – but that qualification is at once withdrawn: 'or rather, with an acquaintanceship. . . .' This withdrawal is in-tensified by the simile of the glove, which professes closeness and warmth but betrays itself as the index of a trivial relationship dependent on a peculiar social usage of the word 'good'. That this is the first of a great deal of textual whispering about *know* is familiar ground; hence articles on the 'epistemology of *The Good Soldier*', and the like. But I don't think that is quite the point, either. *You*, like the narrator, have to decide about the word, and you can't do it yet. In the end you have to consider the ambiguities of knowing. There is the social sense: how are people known anyway? Are the English, and especially of this strongly marked period, the years before 1914, and especially the 'good' English, particularly hard to *know*? And the social merges into the sexual. Both marriages are *mariages blancs*, for reasons of ignorance, timidity, and later, adultery. How does Florence, the narrator's wife, whom he has never slept with, *know* so much: 'But how can she have known what she knew? How could she have got to know it? To know is so fully. Heavens! There doesn't seem to have been the actual time. It must have been when I was taking my baths, and my Sweedish [*sic*] exercises, being manicured'. So Dowell, in a complicated joke (conscious or not?) about the only kinds of exercise *he* ever took. When he says this, later in the first chapter, he is apparently talking about Florence's conversations with a wise friend, and not about her love affairs. But his not knowing Florence (who always locks her bedroom door, though capable of extremely coquettish behaviour in the bathing hut) is a complement of her knowing Jimmie and Edward all too well. His ignorance of her knowledge makes the text a sort of eunuch's report on passion, necessarily inaccurate, partial, fantasised. He knows *something*, of course; but the novel might have been called *What Dowell Knew*. The title Ford wanted really has the same force: *The Saddest Story*.

To finish with the second sentence let us not neglect 'We', expanded in the third as 'My wife and I'. We will find that the degree of intimacy between Florence and each of the Ashburnhams was so much deeper than her husband's that this has to be read as another *deception*; and the immediate withdrawal a qualification of the term 'extreme intimacy', correct for him but not at all for her, as another. So in the third sentence the first statement is true for Florence but not for Dowell; the further characteristic qualification that follows is true, but in quite different sense for each of them, so that the effect is again deceptive.

The fourth sentence suggests, and in doing so sounds another 'note that suggests the whole book', that the 'state of things' represented by all this semantic confusion can be generalised: the English, the people Dowell chooses to know, are especially unknowable; this particular affair, in its sadness, may be held to suggest the state of a nation, the condition of a culture that in all senses doesn't *know*. And later the text will allow us, if we wish, to see it as a figuration of the world tragedy of 1914, as 'the death of a mouse from cancer is the whole sack of Rome by the Goths.' But of course when Dowell *claims* that his subject is 'the falling to pieces of a people,' and develops this in a very passionate rhetorical way, a new voice enters which we may not want to accredit any more unequivocally than the others.

In the fifth sentence we discover, not only more evidence of the peculiar lack of qualifications in Dowell that makes for deception, but the first use of another difficult and deceptive word, *heart*. Hearts are what Dowell finds it hard to know. In the second and third paragraphs we find that his wife had a 'heart condition'. This condition imposes certain constraints upon them – 'perforce . . . perforce . . . we were thrown . . .' and later their condition is called 'imprisonment'. In the final sentence of that paragraph the reader is invited to draw a conclusion, namely that Florence had a 'heart'. This happens to be untrue in the proffered sense. Her fake heart condition was merely a way of keeping herself from her husband (not letting him *know* her). The death he supposes to have resulted from a heart attack was suicide; she knew her husband was about to find out that she had lovers. The phial contained not a drug prescribed for her condition, but prussic acid, to be taken if he should ever come to *know*. When we get to the end we reflect that if either of them had a heart it was Dowell himself, that he was the sufferer, or would have been had he *known*. The French title Ford gave the book was *Quelque chose au coeur*. It indicates the importance of this further semantic confusion.

This is confounded by the fact that having a heart also implies having a sexual life; only Florence and Ashburnham have this; the sport that gave him a heart was not polo (a second sense of 'approximately' and another joke about exercise), the storm at sea broke Dowell's years, not Florence's; if anybody was *poor* it was he. Yet of course they *are* sick, and their sicknesses are specified later; and they die of their heart conditions, as the bumbling meditation of the fourth paragraph lets us know. The word *affair* is another medley of whispers, and so is *quiet*, related not only to 'good' but to the secrecies of an adulterous affair continued over many years amid the meaningless decencies of a spa.

More might be said, and said differently, but I hope you'll agree that this text exploits characteristics of narrative that people tended, and still tend, to push out of their minds because of their long – but not necessarily perpetual – complicity in what is after all the rather special notion that narrative texts authoritatively establish a single standard of veracity, that deviations which amend this contract are obvious and may be simply identified. Terms such as *point of view* and its kin, and, much older, *irony*, may seem to come in handy here. But this book shows how inadequate they are. Authors can be dispossessed, as James thought they should be; he meant that a story can possess one demonically, make one dance to its tune. He thought the author should call the tune, contemplate the 'affair' and *do* it. Hence the gap; hence the deceptions, the multiple voices, the absence of a simple complicity, of a truth vouched-for and certainly known. The same things could be shown in the book as a whole. Nobody has yet discovered in *The Good Soldier* a hermeneutic series that ends in a discovered truth; to this, at any rate, the scholarly journals testify.

II

You see how many assumptions are here called into question. Vague talk of irony or of unreliable narrators won't do; the latter, as Wayne Booth's impressive book *The Rhetoric of Fiction* demonstrates, introduces ethics at the wrong moment. We are in a world of which it needs to be said *not* that plural readings are possible (for this is true of all narrative) but that the *illusion of the single right reading is possible no longer*. It is interesting that Ford himself seems to relate this state of narrative more or less directly to the state of the world, to the ignorance and narrowness of a leisured class, a nation in subtle decline. The point of calling something a novel, as Clara Reeve remarked, is that it has something new in it;[6] the need for some degree of contemporaneity is clear to Fielding also, but the requirement grows more exigent and also more obscure with time. Novels must always create gaps between their texts and narrative types, for otherwise they could not be new; all stories are banal and the redemption from banality must be, as Baudelaire remarked of *Madame Bovary*, and James in a different way of *The Golden Bowl*, a technical wager, a matter that is of treatment, a glorying in the gap between types and text; and this gap grows larger as it intrudes more and more on writer and reader.

This point, which can be made in various ways, is familiar enough. For myths that are in a narrow sense culture-specific, the narrative types have an authority agreed between teller and listener, and the telling is attended by a kind of communal affirmation rather than by questionings. Such stories are often difficult of access to anyone who does not belong to the culture; he may think them unfinished, for example, or he may seek in them only large, latent meanings of a vaguely universal kind. They belong to societies which change their social arrangements little, so that the passage of time creates no gap; the presentness inescapable from all views of the past is here virtually identical with the pastness inescapable from all views of the present. But the universality of allegorical reading in *literate* societies – the Stoics on Homer, the Alexandrian exegetes on the Bible – proves a need for updating which in its turn inescapably implies plurality of interpretation; and it is the next step to make texts which actually provide for such exegesis, as for example in the Gospels. In a sense the whole movement towards 'secretarial' realism – with its care for authenticating detail, its transparency, its passion for credibility and intelligibility – represents a nostalgia for the types, an anachronistic myth of common understanding and shared universes of meaning. At this level it is easy enough to see why the novel – the new – should try to cope with the fact that the new is puzzling, that we mortals stand alone, that to make sense of reality the mind must work with all its powers. In the lifetime of Ford there occurred the collapse of conventional narrative chronology, the attacks on 'the old stable ego of character' and on conventionalised notions of 'form' – on the whole concept, indeed, of a good read. Not surprisingly, some modern critics find the new kind of reading so difficult and so different from the old that they call it *writing*.

III

But now, before I find myself rushing towards the receding terminus of what the French call the *scriptible*, the text which the reader has virtually to write himself, there are a few qualifications I must enter. We can rattle on about hermeneutic gaps and traps, about the necessity for the reader to be always on duty and to avoid the assumption that this or that is formal or inert; but we need also to remind ourselves that the distinction, as among readers, between producer and consumer is not a simple one; however simple 'consumption' can be made, its techniques are the basis of those used in 'production'.

It may make us feel superior to speak of naive or incompetent readers who simply consume, as at Fielding's ordinary – who regard texts as disposable bit by bit; we may moralise about the alienation that underlies this habit. Yet to such readers stories are second nature; they can 'forget' they're reading a story, or anyway be unwilling to disinhabit it, put it down. It is hardly a figure of speech to say that they live in its world; if they ignore inconvenient clues, conflicts of interpretative possibilities, problematical verticals of interpretation which are not identifiable as the familiar ones of character, setting, cause, and so forth, so they do, and so we do, in the daily acts of life; where, as George Eliot said in anticipation of modern sociology of knowledge, we do well to be thickly wadded with stupidity against an intolerable chaos. But even so, it would be wrong to think of the activity of 'naive' readers as simply a consumption and a forgetting. For consumption, in this sense, is impossible without production. Let us see in what sense the consumer produces.

We might ask if there is any analogy with the way one looks at a picture. Constable remarked that art pleased by *reminding*, and not by *deceiving*; E. H. Gombrich quotes this in the course of his argument that we make sense of a picture by applying to it certain perceptual schemata, which we then correct – much as we look at the world in general. 'The picture,' he remarks, 'allows any number of readings, including the correct one.'[7] Producing the correct one is a delicate and complicated task, involving guessing and trying again – performing with skill and rapidity within the Popperian discipline of falsifying one's own hypotheses. Most people are intuitively disposed to accept this theory; they are familiar with the kind of ambiguity which proves its rules and understand without much difficulty Gombrich's epigrammatic 'the innocent eye sees nothing', which means that we see what we see only by carrying out learnt visual procedures. R. L. Gregory puts it thus: 'Perception must . . . be a matter of seeing the present with stored objects from the past.'[8] This applies to the perception of painting, but here, as Gregory remarks, there is a further difficulty, for paintings have 'a double reality', as objects in their own right and as some other thing. 'Pictures are paradoxes . . . pictures are impossible.'[9]

The 'other thing' is usually a representation of something the picture is not. Constable implies that although it is possible to deceive the beholder as to the nature of the representation, such deception is less pleasing than a reminder of something else would be. The skill he asks of the beholder is the choice of a reading the painter would authorise as correct, and which confers on the painting a kind of transparency. So his paintings are unlike those pictures of urns that might rather be two profiles, or those two-dimensional objects that encourage but reject attempts to read them in three dimensions, of which Gombrich had made such telling use; yet they have to be read skilfully for all that.

So the merest consumer of a Constable is doing something complicated in his head, adapting powers ultimately a part of his biological equipment for survival to cultural schemata he has learnt. And in some sense this is true also of the consumer of a story: the schemata exist, and can be corrected to conform with acceptable or reassuring versions of reality. The processing of a narrative into what may be passed over as formal and inert and what is, so to speak, subject and predicate – or, what is relevant to narrative and what merely indexes *le vrai* – this involves an intuitive performance of what Formalist critics do by intellectual effort. The difficulties they experience are an indication of the complexity of everyman's achievement. And here we might again remind ourselves of the differences between myth and novel: the reader's share in ensuring recognition rather than deception is a very much more active one in the novel, even when the text is arranged to facilitate recognition.

However, just as the impossibility of pictures is of interest to painters, so the impossibility of novels interests people who write them. What if, instead of doing the equivalent of what Gombrich[10] calls 'losing the surface', one insists on its presence? What if the illusionist insists on the fact of illusion? Then, whether we have a Cubist painting or an Escher trick, we can no longer speak of its having 'any number of readings including the correct one', but only say that it allows no reading that does not disappoint attempts to establish its conformity with the schemata. This can be done in novels, and, in some measure is often a feature of quite familiar texts; in every detective novel there is deception, for the best hiding place for hermeneutic secrets is the sequence that appears formal and inert; but I want to illustrate it more vividly by referring to a new book which offers a view of the matter directly opposed to Constable's.

In some measure Constable wants us to 'see through' a picture – we have the right 'set' to do so, and the result is 'recognition'. But Stephen Heath in his book *The Nouveau Roman* argues that novels ought to be 'a demonstration of possibilities and limits from the basis of a handful of received elements, a *mise-en-scène* of the production of narrative. This is to offer an experience of reading: to read a Robbe-Grillet text is not to pass through the text to some product (story, representation, sense) but to respond to the activity of the text, to its construction.'[11] When we are dealing with an art of non-illusion, says Heath, our job is 'to read, not recognise', so he argues, as it were, against Constable. What Robbe-Grillet does is to disappoint our expectations and techniques of recognition, changing and exploiting the reader's share; the key idea, both for the novelist and for his champion Roland Barthes, is *deception*, a necessity, they argue, of modern art, and connoting both the deception Constable rejected, and *disappointment*, which he would presumably also have disliked. The sense in which we, skilfully enough, see through a text has to be frustrated; we are checked at the surface; we see, as it were, the picture, the narrative, as an object in its own right. We examine the instrument of our deception, rather than the medium of recognitions.

One thing these opposed views have in common – the importance they attribute to the beholder's, or reader's, share. But for the new critics this share is much more the ability of an uninnocent eye to make an informed choice among possibilities; it means *production* by the reader, a performance equivalent to the creation of the text. The 'projective capacity' of the reader has no correlation with the intention of an artist – the text isn't a message in code from a source labelled 'Dickens' or 'Robbe-Grillet'. Nor has he any desire or power to penetrate the surface; writing that permits or encourages such penetration is given a new name, *écrivance*, to distinguish it from authentic *écriture*. Reading is not a matter of trying to get through, of guessing, abandoning or modifying the guess, and so on. Schemata are in bad faith, exist only to be confounded. There is, of course, no 'correct' reading: we are in a world of uncontrollable plurality, not divining structures but producing structurations that are all our own.

IV

So we are urged to see this kind of production as very different from the sort required by the processes of simple consumption. It is therefore interesting to note that just as those processes involve production, so the kind of production these theorists talk about involves consumption. There are two points to be made here, the first rather obvious. Deception, the disappointment of expectations as to referentiality and closure, cannot work unless there *are* expectations, and to entertain them is the act of a consumer. The second consideration is too often neglected when we are thinking about how we read novels: the importance of forgetting, which is another form of consumption. It was touched on long ago by Lubbock and it crops up again in Barthes, who asserts the value of *l'oubli* as an affirmation of the irresponsibility of the text and its transcendence of any single sense. It has effects comparable to what he calls *fading*, roughly the loss of one of the narrative voices of the text, which is one of the ways in which classic texts achieve tonal instability. Forgetting, in the reading of a consumer, consists of excluding from consideration all that is not relevant to a simple grammar of story, whereas in the reading of a competent producer it consists of the opposite exclusion, namely the neglect of such simplicities in favour of the more difficult possibilities contained in the elements the consumer forgets to consider. In so far as a novel approaches simple *lisibilité* it does so because the reader collaborates in smoothing out the continuum of temporally and causally related events: the *lisible*, says Barthes, admits of no joins.[12] But in so far as it is capable of being *produced* it allows of something approaching an anamnesis of the clues which encouraged continuous horizontal reading at the expense of a more speculative study of verticals.

So forgetting as well as remembering is necessary to the process of reading a deceptive text as well to a simpler one; to production as well as to consumptive reading, or, as Mr Heath would have it, to reading as well as to recognition. The study of the plane surface requires higher skills than those of simple recognition, but they seem to be skills of the same kind. I wonder whether an understanding of this might not reduce some of the moralistic heat that this question of varying degrees of competence seems to engender. Wayne Booth,[13] supported by John Harvey,[14] thinks there are dangers in books which confuse the simple reader by offering a text of uncertain authority; he calls the practice 'elitist' and fears that ordinary readers, getting 'less help than they should,' may go wrong in morally dangerous ways. Others see great danger in the resulting collapse of old values related to 'character'. On the other hand the protagonists of deception are also moralistic, as when Robbe-Grillet says that his books help their readers to make themselves and to live in the world as it is. The truth is that when we teach reading we don't, because that level of competence is early achieved, spend much time on recognition; the reading we teach, whatever our method, is not unlike what Mr Heath has in mind when he uses the word; but we are always clear that we are developing an existing skill and not implanting a new one. Production, given these senses of the words, is a development of the skill of the consumer, and if anybody behaves badly as a result of reading a text that can't simply be consumed, it is not because there is wickedness in such texts but because it is dangerous not to be able to read well.

V

I want now briefly to consider some of what, for short, may be called the problems of narrative opacity and plurality. Although there is no clear-cut division, it is easy enough to see that some narratives are of the kind that makes an ordinary reader either fret himself to death with impatience or make false attempts at recognition. His difficulties are those of falsified expectation or hermeneutic deception; of incomplete closure; and of a failure to understand the preferential treatment given to latent as against manifest significance. By the way, I do not think it profitable to erect the prejudiced expectations of the ordinary reader into rules, despite sophisticated attempts by Richard Ohmann[15] to develop such rules from those invented by J. L. Austin for illocutionary acts. Hermeneutic confusion and problematical closure are not breaches of contract but natural features of narrative; they are found in dreams, in romances, even in Gospels.[16] After a period in which they were somewhat ignored by practitioners, they were rediscovered and technically exploited. The exploitation requires an enhancement of the reader's share; we had an example of this in Ford's novel.

The revaluation of narrative calls, that is, for additional skills in reader as well as writer. This is obvious if you think about James's 'doing', which is a way of producing opacity by interfering with any simple application of culturally acquired schemata. A narrative called *What Maisie Knew* might be expected to tell you what it was that Maisie knew, but it does not, for the clues lead to no unambiguous *dévoilement*, and there is, in addition to the continuing problem of interpretation, a problem of closure. The exploitation of such opacities is familiar in such works as *The Turn of the Screw*, 'The Figure in the Carpet', 'The Beast in the Jungle', and, in the most exemplary instance, *The Sacred Fount*. It was James as theorist, meditating the achievements of James the technician, who narrowed the formulation of all the problems that arise from 'fading' to the single issue of 'point of view', and the difficulties we now experience arise in part from this, for we have bothered too much about the authority of the narrator and too little about that of the narrative. In the preface to *The Aspern Papers* James (speaking of *The Turn of the Screw*) asserted that 'all my values are positive blanks.'

Blanks and gaps: to read is to fill them on the evidence of conflicting and ambiguous clues. Once the technical discovery – or rediscovery – is made, it is not a long step to the narrative which at least tries, as in Robbe-Grillet, to be nearly all gap. All markers of temporality, character, closure, and so forth, are subject to a confusion thought to be beneficent, and the authority to interpret is transferred to the reader. The real difference in this respect between James, Ford and Conrad, and the *nouveau roman* is that the earlier writers retained – whether from an inheritance of inertia, or a need to sell books – more respect for the naive narrative and the naive reader. Yet the end of *Under Western Eyes* and the narrative gap in *The Secret Agent* are of the same technical order as the better advertised and more extreme innovations of recent years in France. In some senses those earlier inventions are still ahead of theory; Ford's book, and even *What Maisie Knew*, defeat the rules laid down for *lisible* texts. The linear codes are not continuous, and all the others are deceptive. These books cannot be read once and consumed; in every sense they close ambiguously, and possess a tonal instability much closer to atonality than Barthes would willingly allow.

As to latent against manifest, Freud made it commonplace that one class of narrative, which was very deceptive and resistant to 'recognition', could be interpreted only as concealing, not revealing, its sense. It seems that he was speaking truly of a larger class than dreams, and his discovery applies to all narrative, for even such texts as do resemble what Barthes means by *lisible* are held to say more than they appear to. The effect of 'fading' is to diminish the reader's ability to distinguish between those things that are significant and those which are there only for the sake of the things that are significant. Every part of the text must be granted equal, and possibly deceptive, status. After that is recognised the reader must develop hermeneutic skills appropriate to the new situation – hence our new ways with old novels. The fact that they respond calls into question the whole historical mythology of modern French criticism, the rationale of which is stated in this passage from Jacques Derrida.[17]

There are thus two interpretations of interpretation, of structure, of sign, of freeplay. The one seeks to decipher, dreams of deciphering, a truth or an origin which is free from freeplay and from the order of the sign, and lives like an exile the necessity of interpretation. The other, which is no longer turned toward the origin, affirms freeplay and tries to pass beyond man and humanism, the name 'man' being the name of that being who, throughout the history of metaphysics or of ontotheology – in other words, through the history of all his history – has dreamed of full presence, the reassuring foundation, the origin and the end of the game.

Yet this second kind of interpretation can be applied to narratives written well within the temporal limits of the ontotheological and humanist myths whose eclipse Derrida wishes to celebrate. One can read, for example, *The Scarlet Letter* with an orientation indifferent to origin or truth, concerning oneself only with its 'freeplay'. We can observe the novel hesitating between reality and emblem; we can follow its deceptions and its fading. We can note that Dimmesdale's Pentecostal sermon doubles the narrative, speaks to everybody in his own language. We have to allow that the narrative is not simply linear, and that plural interpretation is not merely permitted but enjoined, and that Hester's antinomianism is the novel's; the text even tells us that it may be fully realised in some possible future, explaining why it cannot be so at present. There is a deceptive contrast between two modes of interpretation: the old, Puritan, strict, limited, theocratic, radiating certainty about emblems and types; and the new, which depends on the activity of the individual creative mind, on the light of imagination which, like that of the meteor, or of the fire in the Customs House, falls on objects and makes their perception strange and different. To say that all this is accidental makes no sense; it is there, in the text, for the reader to manage, and that is all that matters.

Readings of such books are necessarily recursive. The best reader in the world cannot get much out of the beginning of *The Good Soldier*, or of *The Sound and the Fury*, unless he goes back to it and codes it in accordance with later discoveries. So good reading, even first reading, is recursive and can be required to be so in a high degree. The more self-reflexive that text, the more recursion

110

is necessary, and the harder it is to code information unequivocally. It is hard to believe that any novel, which must contain a lot of information that can be forgotten, cannot be reread in much the same way. Whatever the constraints of a particular culture or a particular period, plurality is in the nature of narrativity.

VI

Barthes, misled by his historical myth, deliberately limits recursiveness. His is essentially a left-to-right reading that has some of the disadvantages Chomsky attributes to left-to-right generative grammars which cannot account for relations between nonadjacent words. I do not think he could give an account of Ford's opening paragraphs which would on any reasonable view of the matter be adequate. He is of course emphatic about re-reading as a means of liberating the text from its internal chronology, from the naivety of the first reading, and he does accordingly make connections between non-adjacent lexies, but his objection to thematic organisation, and his preference for instability and dispersion, are so strong that he does so with diffidence and reluctance. Ford's opening paragraphs are a measure of the complexity of any really satisfactory coding system. Consider the verb 'to know'. It belongs, from the first, in the hermeneutic code ('what Dowell knew'), in the cultural (upper-class manners), in the symbolic (sexuality/impotence), in the semic (Dowell's character), and in the proairetic or action code; and to cross-reference all this in the necessary ways seems beyond the system that worked for *Sarrasine*. Furthermore, the simplicity of the hermeneutic code is constantly violated in ways which elude Barthes's machinery, and the *dévoilement* is beyond notation and not really a *dévoilement* anyway, any more than the end of *What Maisie Knew*. Nor does this book announce what it is about in such a way that it can only be about other things as the result of some accident.

My purpose, however, is not to argue with Barthes, whom in so many ways one admires – most, perhaps, for the bold specification, in *S/Z*, of a method that may well be improved and put to work. Some novel problems are now more sharply visible. We should be better now at handling the problems of recognition and deception that occur in productive reading, at understanding the nature of the reader's share. We shall no doubt pay less attention to other stock topics, such as intention and point of view, which for all their prestige seem to be wrongly formulated. We shan't, I think, despise the naive reading so completely; though we'll recognise that it involves an unconscious complicity with arbitrary authority, a training which forces the reader to find stability only, and ignore the evidence of instability, we shall understand that productive reading is a development and a correction of that variety, requiring a competence which cannot be achieved without it. No consumption, that is, can be wholly passive, no production wholly active. Recognition is an earlier stage of reading. By learning one passes from one to the other.

For the natural or naive way of reading – a matter of recognition, the medium being a virtual transparency – is neither natural nor naive. It is conditioned and arbitrary, a false return to 'story' – to the 'wisdom', as Benjamin calls it, of folktale, a pretence that everybody can agree on a particular construction of reality. It is, however, no more apposite to condemn this on moral grounds than to condemn texts that reject narrative, that reject story, theme, closure, authority, that trap us into contemplation of their own opacity, on the ground that this is deceptive. It seems right to allow into the plurality of readings the naive among the rest, though such a text as Ford's is so evidently not naive that naive readers of it would probably soon grow impatient. It calls for a virtuosity elaborately built on the basis of naive competence, a development in productive capacity. Even to think of what that virtuosity entails is to encounter novel problems. It is harder to describe it than to do it, like riding a bicycle. But it is worth trying, because of the errors that accumulate in the absence of serious discussion – false notions of plurality, a too simple view of the history of interpretation, even culpable negligence in the reception of new and difficult work. These are problems that arise from problems native to novels – they are the problems of modern criticism, its scope and responsibilities. We know them about as well as Dowell knew the Ashburnhams. But that is another sad story.

NOTES

1 'The First Paragraph of *The Ambassadors*: An Explication,' *Essays in Criticism* 10, 1960, pp. 250–74.
2 Clara Reeve, *The Progress of Romance through Times, Countries and Manners*, 2 vols., 1785, I, p. 25.
3 'The Reading Process: a Phenomenological Approach', *New Literary History*, 4, 1972, pp. 47–63.
4 Henry James, 'The New Novel', 1914, in *Selected Literary Criticism*, ed. M. Shapira, 1968, p. 366.
5 Ibid., p. 369.
6 Clara Reeve, op. cit., I, p. 110.
7 *Art and Illusion*, 1961, p. 278.
8 *The Intelligent Eye*, 1970, p. 36.
9 Ibid., p. 32.
10 E. H. Gombrich, 'The Evidence of Images', in *Interpretation: Theory and Practice*, ed. C. S. Singleton, 1969, p. 59.
11 Stephen Heath, *The Nouveau Roman*, 1972, p. 149.
12 Roland Barthes, *S/Z*, 1970, pp. 18, 48–9, 112.
13 *The Rhetoric of Fiction*, 1961, pp. 391–2.
14 W. J. Harvey, *Character and the Novel*, 1965.
15 Richard Ohmann, 'Speech, Action and Style', in *Literary Style*, ed. S. Chatman, 1971, 241–59.
16 See my *The Genesis of Secrecy*, 1979.
17 Jacques Derrida, 'Structure, Sign and Play', in *The Languages of Criticism and the Sciences of Man: The Structuralist Controversy*, ed. R. Macksey and E. Donato, 1970, pp. 264–5.

CHAPTER 5

ON READING NOVELS

I knew Gwilym James – not well, but well enough to wish, being a fellow-Celt, that I had some of his enchanter's skill, his expositor's passion. I have heard him read poetry and comment upon it, vividly alive to the complexities of interpretation and the need for lucid communication. I think he would have approved of my subject; and remembering that requirement of lucidity I have tried to keep my exposition simple – some might say misleadingly so. But however I fall short of his mark, I offer these speculations in homage to a man who was in so many ways a model to all who follow my profession.

It seems reasonable to begin a talk with such a title by reading a bit of a novel, so that we may all have in our heads some notion of what kinds of intellectual operation are entailed. In the circumstances it would be unwise to choose for this purpose a text noted for its obscurity, or for any special demands it makes; on the other hand it would be wrong to choose anything too simple or diagrammatic. In the end I walked to the shelf and without further deliberation took down *Adam Bede*, which everybody, whatever that may mean, has read, and which I dare say nobody regards as a major challenge to his ingenuity. *Adam Bede* was published in 1859. It begins thus:

With a single drop of ink for a mirror, the Egyptian sorcerer undertakes to reveal to any chance comer far-reaching visions of the past. This is what I undertake to do for you, reader. With this drop of ink at the end of my pen, I will show you the roomy workshop of Mr. Jonathan Burge, carpenter and builder, in the village of Hayslope, as it appeared on the eighteenth of June, in the year of our Lord 1799.

In these few words a considerable number of operations have been carried out with the reader's compliance. A narrator has been inserted into the text ('I undertake'). A reader has been inserted also ('you, reader') and with this figure you, reader, have been identified. The acceptance of the narrator's presence and your own implies on the part of both acceptance of a contract, or, if you prefer, signifies a willingness to play the ensuing game according to rules. Among these rules is one that says that the text is to be regarded as a magical means of making present what is absent. The absent that is to be made present is a past period, which the reader, who has agreed to read the clues accordingly, will not only regard as for certain purposes present, but scan for indications of difference; he will, for example, note that the *mise-en-scène*, the manners and dress of the personages, are different from those of the present. The chapter continues:

The afternoon sun was warm on the five workmen there, busy upon doors and windowframes and wainscoting. A scent of pine-wood from a tent-like pile of planks outside the open door mingled itself with the scent of the elder-bushes which were spreading their summer snow close to the open window opposite; the slanting sunbeams shone through the transparent shavings that flew before the steady plane, and lit up the fine grain of the oak panelling which stood propped against the wall. On a heap of those soft shavings a rough grey shepherd-dog had made himself a pleasant bed, and was lying with his nose between his fore-paws, occasionally wrinkling his brows to cast a glance at the tallest of the five workmen, who was carving a shield in the centre of a wooden mantelpiece. It was to this workman that the strong barytone belonged which was heard above the sound of plane and hammer singing –

'Awake, my soul, and with the sun
Thy daily stage of duty run;
Shake off dull sloth . . .'

Here some measurement was to be taken which required
more concentrated attention, and the sonorous voice
subsided into a low whistle; but it presently broke out again
with renewed vigour –

'Let all thy converse be sincere,
Thy conscience as the noonday clear.'

Such a voice could only come from a broad chest, and the
broad chest belonged to a large-boned muscular man nearly
six feet high, with a back so flat and a head so well poised
that when he drew himself up to take a more distant survey
of his work, he had the air of a soldier standing at ease. The
sleeve rolled up above the elbow showed an arm that was
likely to win the prize for feats of strength; yet the long
supple hand, with its broad finger-tips, looked ready for
works of skill. In his tall stalwartness Adam Bede was a
Saxon, and justified his name; but the jet-black hair, made
the more noticeable by its contrast with the light paper cap,
and the keen glance of the dark eyes that shone from under
strongly marked, prominent and mobile eyebrows, indicated
a mixture of Celtic blood. The face was large and roughly
hewn, and when in repose had no other beauty than such as
belongs to an expression of good-humoured honest
intelligence.

The reality of the pastness is guaranteed (why? how?) by the fact
that even then the sun was warm in June, and the elderbushes
scented, and planes made shavings. Its differences, which we are
expected to remember for future use, are indicated by the fact that
the carpenter is singing hymns as he carves a shield on a mantelpiece, wearing all the while 'an expression of good-humoured . . .
intelligence'.

The reader – this 'chance comer' who is willing to keep to the
rules in return for a certain reward – is in a sense the invention of
the author. One thing he will do is forget the elderbushes and
shavings as soon as they have done their work; they simply au-
thenticate this expenditure of ink as a representation of reality.

116

Another will be to remember the hymns and the good humour for future use, for they are indices of the type of the honest workman of an earlier age: pious, industrious, dedicated to his master's interests and the accuracy of the work, completely indigenous (Saxon and Celt). Sometimes the reader finds it quite easy to establish such distinctions; but occasionally he must make a choice. The sheepdog lying in the shavings may or may not be simply vouching for the reality of the scene – a detail incorporated merely as a form of reassurance that this is a novel and not, say, a romance. (But perhaps it is important to have the dog in here, he may have a part in the plot).[1] The shield Adam Bede is carving may suggest labour in the service of an institution of some kind, or of an armigerous contemporary; it serves not only to reinforce the registered reality (this is the sort of thing a good carpenter would be doing in the setting proposed) but perhaps also to establish the skilled workman as the essential but lowly instrument of social hierarchy. Before long we see that he has a relationship with a social superior, and that his strength and virtue as well as his social inferiority are germane to the story. Yet if we choose we may think of him as in some way of the true essence of manhood, for his name combines that of the first man with that of a pious Briton, and one who wrote the history of the English Church, so that the superior class of Arthur and the Methodism of Seth are both obscure deviations from a norm.

We see, then, that the reader whose role we have agreed to fill is at once constrained and, within limits, free to act. On the one hand it will benefit him nothing to make a fuss about the elder-bushes or the shavings, though the dog he had better place in a reserved category. On the other he has to decide about the shield and the hymn ('Shake off dull sloth,' 'Awake my soul,' and so on, may well be admonitions of more than merely historical or characterological force). However, he will only make the right choices with certainty if he possesses a measure of cultural and social conformity with the narrator; he is not free, or rather the rules of the game say he is not free, to conclude that Adam Bede is a running dog of the premonopolistic capitalist system, or even a bore or a hypocrite. In so far as he identifies himself with the reader inserted into the text his liberty is, in various ways, limited. On the other hand, it is clear why he was brought into the second sentence of the book; for without such collaborative acts on his part the text loses all sense; and if those acts were so constrained as to be uniform, if every reader at every reading made his decisions about the dog and the shield in precisely the same terms, the book would be that virtually impossible thing, a novel that can properly be read in only one way.

At this point, however, it is necessary to add that the prerequisite of cultural conformity between the 'I' that undertakes and the 'you' that reads must diminish with time. The first condition of substantial cultural agreement is contemporaneity. Given the heterogeneity of culture even in 1859 it may be true that no reader of *Adam Bede* ever enjoyed complete cultural uniformity with George Eliot, but it is certain that we have even less of it. We can, if we choose, make a special effort in this direction, and identify ourselves, in some measure, with the double proposed for us in that second sentence; we may even, by this means, make ourselves, for the moment, as industrious, obedient, and contented with our place in the scheme of things as Adam Bede himself. But all the evidence, and common sense as well, suggest that we cannot match the men and women of 1859. *The Athenaeum*, reviewing the book when it came out, demonstrated the effect of a totally obedient reading: the reader feels 'as though he had made acquaintance with real human beings: the story is not a story, but a true account of a place and people who have really lived; indeed, some of them may even be living yet, though they will be rather old, but that everything happened as here set down we have no doubt in the world.'[2] This is the perfect report on readerly compliance, but the publisher Blackwood, in a letter to his author, was more suggestive: 'The book is so novel and so true. The whole story remains in my mind like a succession of incidents in the lives of people whom I know.'[3] The requirement that a novel should, in accordance with its name, be new, and yet true, is as old as Clara Reeve; and in meeting those requirements most triumphantly it destroys itself, leaving readers with the impression that they have not been reading but meeting people and visiting places. Of course, what this really illustrates is the immense readiness of readers to be put upon; to find in a book the satisfactory operation of myths which always deceive us in life; and to forget their own contribution to the illusion upon which they congratulate the author. We should nevertheless remember that the reader-in-the-text of *Adam Bede* with whom Mr Blackwood so happily identified himself is as dead as the author-in-the-text, whom we identify with George Eliot. (An interesting question, which I shall not here try to answer fully, concerns the status of those of her contemporaries who found the novel shocking because Hetty gets seduced; the answer is presumably that they accepted the identification with the text-reader but then took improper liberties.)

Let us now look more briefly at another passage from *Adam Bede*, the opening of the sixteenth chapter. This is the conclusion of Book I, so we should remind ourselves that the book was originally divided into three volumes, each with two books. This purely physical consideration is not without importance, for it meant that further clauses were written into the contract; the author had to provide, and the reader to expect and interpret, the special kinds of clue which call for reading climaxes, temporary endings, breaks in the action; the next chapter is entitled 'In Which the Story Pauses a Little'. In fact this sixteenth chapter contains only a botched climax, being concerned with something that ought to have happened but didn't.

> Arthur Donnithorne, you remember, is under an engagement with himself to go and see Mr. Irwine this Friday morning, and he is awake and dressing so early, that he determines to go before breakfast, instead of after. The Rector, he knows, breakfasts alone at half-past nine, the ladies of the family having a different breakfast-hour; Arthur will have an early ride over the hill and breakfast with him. One can say everything best over a meal.
>
> The progress of civilisation has made a breakfast or a dinner an easy and cheerful substitute for more troublesome and disagreeable ceremonies. We take a less gloomy view of our errors now our father confessor listens to us over his eggs and coffee. We are more distinctly conscious that rude penances are out of the question for gentlemen in an enlightened age, and that mortal sin is not incompatible with an appetite for muffins. An assault on our pockets, which in more barbarous times would have been made in the brusque form of a pistolshot, is quite a well-bred and smiling procedure now it has become a request for a loan thrown in as an easy parenthesis between the second and third glasses of claret.

Still, there was this advantage in the old rigid forms, that they committed you to the fulfilment of a resolution by some outward deed: when you have put your mouth to one end of a hole in a stone wall, and are aware that there is an expectant ear at the other end, you are more likely to say what you came out with the intention of saying, than if you were seated with your legs in an easy attitude under the mahogany, with a companion who will have no reason to be surprised if you have nothing particular to say.

However, Arthur Donnithorne, as he winds among the pleasant lanes on horseback in the morning sunshine, has a sincere determination to open his heart to the Rector, and the swirling sound of the scythe as he passes by the meadow is all the pleasanter to him because of this honest purpose.

Chapter XV ends with a scene in which Hetty Sorel is given an opportunity to make Dinah her confidant or confessor. She refuses it. The present chapter shows Arthur failing to carry out an intention, formulated at the end of Chapter XIII, to use the Rector, Mr Irwine, as *his* confessor.

'Arthur Donnithorne, you remember. . . .' The verb has a touch of the imperative; it is the duty of the reader to remember when required to, to forget when required to. In return the author provides a bit more information about action and character, for it is assumed that the reader likes as much of that as he can get. He, for his part, must now do a simple piece of coding. Notice the sequence beginning 'The rector, he knows' and ending 'over a meal'. It is obviously necessary for Arthur to see the Rector alone; the author therefore explains that Arthur knows that Mr Irwine breakfasts alone, and why. The reader has legitimate expectations; one of them is plausibility. The author then adds: 'One can say everything best over a meal.'

But surely that is a mistake? Yes it is; for everything before that sentence reports what Arthur intended and what Arthur knew, and, as the sequel proves, knew accurately; now we are offered an opinion that happens to be wrong, but it is not the narrator's, it is still Arthur's. In other words, this sentence, though it lacks the usual markers, must be what people call *style indirect libre*, just as we know, from the tense of the verb, that 'Arthur will have an early ride' is in *style indirect libre*. It is, however, possible to disagree with this coding. Suppose we take the voice as that of the narrator, adding that it implies an appeal to the commonplace, a received opinion of the common culture ('let's have lunch and talk it over'). In that case there is a certain deception involved, since nothing of substance gets said over the meal at the Rectory. On the other hand, the passage that follows is apparently a straight-forward appeal to received opinion, to the shared cultural assump-tions of the implied author and reader; an appeal, as some now say, to the *endoxal* – referring to the unexamined assumptions of a common culture or class. Now the reader, with his tacit skill in text-linguistics, is perfectly well able to see these possibilities, even to entertain them both simultaneously. Since Arthur is an obviously endoxal figure you can say the next paragraph is simply an exten-sion of the *style indirect libre* as earlier used of him; it tells us what Arthur, and a lot of other people, believe at the time of writing. Of course it is all *doxa* anyway: '*we* take a less gloomy view, etc.' *We* are mid-century contemporaries of a certain class, drinking quite a lot of claret, possessing mahogany tables, and having special uses for facetiousness (mortal sin and muffins); all traits which incidentally, show that *we* have more in common with Arthur than with Adam.[4]

If you complain that we know irony when we see it, and that I have developed a very elaborate way of talking about something that seems perfectly simple, I can only reply that your reaction exactly conforms to my intention. I will therefore continue for a moment to complicate the issue. I think the French critics who taught us to speak of *doxa*, and very useful the term is, tend to forget that one of its characteristics is that each man thinks *doxa* is somebody else's body of opinions, not his; so that none of us genuinely thinks himself included in that *we*, substituting for it some such formula as 'People nowadays unconsideringly assume . . .,' and so forth. Consequently we are not very surprised by the concessive opening of the next paragraph: 'Still, there was this advantage in the old rigid forms. . . .' The old rigid forms are then described in a manner which might fool the slaves of *doxa*, but not us; for example, the confessional is reduced, by a kind of absurd synecdoche, to a mouth, a hole and an ear, but we may suppose that the grotesquerie of this is for others, while we our-selves understand perfectly well that a large truth is being insin-uated. Not only do we know that Arthur has already seen the need for confession, and that Hetty ought to have seen it. Extra-textual memories also affect us. We may remember, being well read, that George Eliot held fervently to the opinion that some religious institutions, including confession, ought to be preserved, though in a secularised form, and even that she had been reading Hawthorne, in whose novels there are not dissimilar preoccupations. Further-more the next chapter, as I've said, is a discursive one, and in it we are told that in novels that purport to be as truthful as Dutch paintings parsons must be human and fallible; the very virtues of Mr Irwine as a human being are responsible for his failure to create an opportunity for Arthur's secularised confession.

In short, it appears, even from these far from exhaustive obser-vations on the three paragraphs that come at the beginning of Chapter XVI, that a good deal is asked of 'you, reader'. Your activities could be variously described, but they include an under-standing that the frustration of Arthur's confession, as of Hetty's, is to be interpreted not only in terms of the action of the novel, but also in terms of its ideological, cultural and perhaps symbolic structures; and that interpretation requires an interpreter; and that, even if he is reasonably docile, the interpreter is likely to find space for activities beyond the immediate and obvious ones demanded. Having performed his obligatory tricks, he may find material for comment not only on the isolated passage before his eyes, but on large matters of structure, on a corpus rather than a single novel, on other works intertextually related to the one before him, and even on an entire culture and the opinions of the men and women within it. Over-interpretation (I use the word without pejorative implication, for reasons which will shortly appear) is merely a continuation of the processes we have all to master before we can read even the simplest tale.

E. M. Forster in *Aspects of the Novel* – a work first published in 1924, and one of which we should recognise the high merits as well as the 'period' limitations – thinks of story as very primitive. 'It is immensely old – goes back to neolithic times, perhaps to palaeolithic. . . . The primitive audience was an audience of shock-heads, gaping round the camp-fire, fatigued with contending against the mammoth or the woolly rhinoceros, and only kept awake by suspense. What would happen next? The novelist droned on, and as soon as the audience guessed what happened next they either fell asleep or killed him.' Anybody who looks at a modern analysis of folktale and myth, whether performed by Propp, by Lévi-Strauss, or by anthropologists of a less universalistic persuasion, will quickly abandon Forster's paradigm. It appears that the shockheads have mastered a complex grammar, to say the least; and have learnt that there is more to a narrative than what happens next. Their notions of causality and time may not be Forster's, but they are complicated enough.

It is surely extraordinary that these facts eluded our attention for so long, and the explanation can only be that the contract between the 'I' that undertakes and the 'you' that reads has acquired the force of a natural arrangement; we do not recognise its conventional or cultural aspect, nor enquire what it entails. What Forster was really describing was not the behaviour of palaeolithic shockheads, but the behaviour of modern readers, as they themselves understand it. That all readers need an ability to sense in the manifest that which is latent, leaving aside the question whether it was put there, is a fact that has come only recently to exercise those who speculate about narrative. It is now possible to say, quite seriously, that we need not histories of literature but histories of reading; a little while ago the observation would have seemed inane. The decisive role of the interpreter is now seen to be worth study.

Under what circumstances should we ever speak of *interpreting* a book? 'Have you interpreted any good novels lately?' does not seem acceptable. I shall now invent a spokesman for the view that the word is always out of place in this connexion. He could be practically any of the people who review fiction in our weeklies: witty, full of unillusioned common sense, well educated enough to know what makes a novel a good one, and what makes it tiresome or deviant, 'trendy' perhaps. He speaks: 'A book is a book; there it is, a solid object, perfectly all there; you can see where it begins and where it ends. All you have to do is read it. Interpreters are specialists who make it possible for Englishmen to converse with foreigners; or, perhaps, readers of entrails or tea leaves, or solvers of puzzles. What we do when we read a novel has nothing in common with such activities. We of course possess certain skills, the property of all educated men. I suppose you could say we have linguistic skills, possibly even rhetorical ones. But above all we have learned that what a novel must have, and what we must appreciate are the following: action, character and setting. From our knowledge of the matter we are able to see whether these requirements are met. If they are, the novelist is doing a good job. If they're not, he's no good.

'It would be ridiculous to say that this exercise of judgment, of common educated taste, had anything to do with interpretation. That word implies an activity both rarer and less interesting. I suppose you might say that a few writers, who go in for riddles and obscurities, require it. You might, with a tolerable, but barely tolerable, measure of affectation, announce that you were going off to your room in order to interpret a poem by Donne. But you couldn't in any circumstances say you were off to do a bit of interpretation of *Adam Bede*. Surely even you can see the difference: reading is only trivially related to interpreting. To all sensible men it is a different activity altogether.'

Now that *is*, it must be admitted, the opinion of most sensible men, and it has been so for a very long time. It survives enormous and obvious changes in what are regarded as the kinds of book worth reading; it survives in spite of the evident contempt in which it has been held by most of the most venerated novelists of the present century. It has great authority: *quod semper* (practically), *quod ubique* (except in Paris), *quod ab omnibus* (or anyway those most influential in the formation of opinion). Yet it is undoubtedly wrong, and deserves to be called *endoxal*. It is a cultural myth, and we have mistaken it for a fact of nature. How this myth took hold, and why it has persisted, are not part of our present business; but it is worth saying that it is attached specifically to the reading of fictional narrative. To argue that to read is to interpret is in other areas of intellectual activity a truism. Biblical scholarship two centuries ago reached the point where it was necessary to invent hermeneutics; the scriptural narrative could no longer be regarded as a simple historical report, nor as simply 'given', and a theory of interpretation was required. Once it began to develop there was, as Hans Frei observes, 'no going back to the precritical stance, for which the understanding process itself had no contribution to make to the object to be interpreted, or to the interpretive results, but was simply a picture of the normative subject matter. . . .'[5] And Frei further observes that the understanding of the need for hermeneutics coincides historically with the birth of the novel; only Germany got the hermeneutics and England got Fielding and Richardson.[6] Can it be that prose fiction was always somehow a *substitute* for critical thought about the interpretation of earlier narrative, especially sacred narrative? At any rate it must be said of the reviewer whose assured tones I tried to reproduce a moment ago, that his stance is pre-critical; he stands where biblical critics stood in the 1740s.

This archaism is all the more striking if you reflect upon developments in other disciplines in which our reviewer is more likely to be interested. *The Interpretation of Dreams* is dated 1900; it was published in 1899, but Freud understandably succumbed to *fin-de-siècle* superstitions. It is possible to hold that the application of the methods of the *Traumdeutung*, whether by Freud himself or by his followers, has been a bane to literary criticism; but only because he and they misunderstood the relation between reading and interpretation. Freud fought heroically against the *doxa* of his time – those cultural presuppositions and tabus were resisted only by the most obstinate intellectual effort – but because he was very well educated he succeeded less completely in matters of art than in psychoanalytic theory. That is why he was so given to analysing authors and artists rather than texts; he used the works as clinical data, or, at best, as evidence in support of his theory of cultural history as the phylogenetic parallel to what goes on in the individual psyche. But there are, nevertheless, among the insights of the *Interpretation*, some that imply a latent understanding of the problems that literary texts really do present.

Though Freud found himself on the side of peasant oneiromancy as against the scientific or cheese-for-supper explanations of dreaming, he wanted, as always, to be scientific. A desire to be systematic about the generation of dreams drove him towards language theory. For he was always sure that dream was a kind of language, though a strange kind. He compared this language to Egyptian hieroglyphics, he compared it to the traces left on a magic writing pad when the transparent top flap is lifted, he emphasised that it had to be learned, with all its idiomatic and grammatical peculiarities (for example, it lacks negatives). It was related to other languages – those of hysteria, paranoia and obsessional neurosis, but also to jokes and slips of the tongue. In all these forms of language there was no sense except that made available by the activity of an interpreter. Understanding the generative rules, he would discover in the manifest content of the dream its latent

125

sense; and an understanding of its regularities would enable him to focus the significant disturbances in what was *said*. The rules include those of displacement, condensation, considerations of representability. If you could see where and why an accent was displaced, or where and why several chains of association crossed, or why something had to be modified in order to be capable of being rendered as an image acceptable to the limitations of dream – if you could do this, and also remember that what is forgotten is more significant than what is remembered, you could read a dream. It could not be read otherwise, even if it were worth reading. Even jokes, which we interpret spontaneously, have to *be* interpreted. Reading a dream is interpreting a dream.

Freud takes great liberties of interpretation, indeed sets no limits to it; over-interpretation is necessary, and not only in dreams: 'Just as all neurotic symptoms, and, for that matter, dreams, are capable of being over-interpreted and indeed need to be, if they are to be fully understood, so all genuinely creative writings are the product of more than a single motive and more than a single impulse in the poet's mind, and are open to more than a single interpretation'.[7] If I dared I would rewrite that sentence, omitting the words 'and more than a single impulse in the poet's mind'; but the point is clear: in dreams as in literary language there is a need for interpretation and indeed for over-interpretation. 'There is no need to be astonished at the part played by words in dream-formation. Words, since they are the nodal points of numerous ideas, may be regarded as predestined to ambiguity.'[8] And he might have said the same about strings of words, about discourse, including narrative discourse. Condensation is a kind of punning. Later it was brilliantly observed by Roman Jakobson, in his essay on aphasia,[9] that condensation corresponded to metaphor, and displacement to metonymy, an insight with applications that have been regarded as profound for psychoanalysis, and might also be significant for narrative analysis; for as we have seen, in looking at the passage on Arthur's thwarted confession, a passage in a novel can exhibit the signs of condensation or metaphor or indeed symptom. There is, so to speak, a knot of senses in the horizontal thread of the fiction.

Freud, perhaps because he was a therapist, perhaps because he had no linguistics adequate to the purpose, was prevented from seeing that such knots are a characteristic of all discourse because of all language; he tended to seek their explanation in a subject, and to treat discourse as a message from a subject, just as George Eliot did. But he did see that 'a dream has form in the sense in which we speak of form or structure in a novel,' as Hadfield remarked;[10] and since he also saw that this structure emerged only as a consequence of the interpreter's operations, he would presumably have allowed the same to be true of novels: we, the interpreters, are, to a degree we find it hard to understand, responsible for their structure. In a sense it can be said that Freud, in researching the laws of dream narrative, was formulating principles applicable to the larger class that contains all narrative discourse.

Such are the persuasions of civility that we have for the most part allowed this consideration to escape our attention. But I had better insert a paragraph here for specialists; I had better show how modern literary criticism creeps cautiously towards a fuller sense of what the reader-interpreter has to do to a text. I can do so most economically by charting one line of progress, drawn between the works of three good critics. First, Wayne Booth, whose book *The Rhetoric of Fiction* was something of a landmark in 1961. Although Booth notoriously insisted that the author could not withdraw from his fiction, but always left a surrogate to control it, he did say that the author also 'makes his reader, as he makes his second self, and the most successful reading is one in which the created selves, author and reader, can find complete agreement'.[11] We have met this author and this reader before, in the opening words of *Adam Bede*; but Booth at least allows the reader some liberty, the liberty to agree with the author.

Some years later the English critic John Preston, in a book that seems to have been neglected, borrowed his title from Booth, and called his study of the eighteenth-century novel *The Created Self* (1970). Mr Preston finds the relation between the implied author and the implied reader more mysterious than Booth does, for 'the writer reaches out to an unseen and unforeseeable reader, and the reader wishes to respond to an absent writer who has already said his last word'.[12] Yet Mr Preston still sees the 'created self' of the reader as one that is somehow able to participate in the creation of meaning by obedience to these instructions from elsewhere; he speaks of the novelist keeping the form 'open', but still only to give the reader room to be obedient in.

The next step was taken by a German scholar, Wolfgang Iser,

in a book translated as *The Implied Reader* (1974) and in an essay entitled 'Indeterminacy and the Reader's Response', published in 1971.[13] Iser grants the reader a greater measure of freedom; for the text has, perhaps must have, a measure, which grows greater as we approach the modern, of indeterminacy. The reader is freely creative in the spaces between what the absent author has determined, in the 'indeterminacy gaps', or, if you prefer, *Unbestimmtheitsstellen*, the term Iser borrows from Roman Ingarten. A text with minimum indeterminacy is a boring text. Iser's view represents a clear increase in liberty for the interpreter; yet he continues to suppose that the author determines what is to be indeterminate and what not. My present purpose is not to ask how much beyond Iser we ought to go, but simply to sketch the slow expansion of interpretative freedom allowed us by critical theorists, always excepting the bolder spirits of Paris.

It might be reasonable to allow that literary theory has now caught up with common sense. Everybody knows that competent readers read the same text differently, which is proof that the text is not fully determined. Even professors know this; they give the best marks to the candidates who most diverge (without manifest foolishness, or error) from some 'normal' reading of a text. More accurately, literary theory has caught up with the practice of Henry James. For James was a specialist in indeterminacy, and wrote novels and stories which cannot be well read by an interpreter who will not accept its presence. On the other hand, he limited the reader's share to 'quite half',[14] was disturbed by over-interpretation, and asserted the right of the author to keep matters within his control. Conrad hated his readers for having expectations he was supposed to satisfy, which is to say he was sick of having to give the expected orders; the slave becomes the master.

In fact authors have for a long time been asking readers to use their interpretative freedom, even if it meant exceeding any limit of sense they themselves had detected in their work. In a letter to Melville (unfortunately lost) Sophia Hawthorne offered an interpretation of the 'Spirit Spout' chapter in *Moby Dick*. The gallantry of Melville's reply does not conceal a genuine pleasure in being over-interpreted:

> . . . you, with your spiritualizing nature, see more than other people, and by the same process, refine all you see, so that

they are not the same things that other people see, but things which while you think you but humbly discover them, you do in fact create them for yourself – therefore, upon the whole, I do not so much marvel at your expressions concerning Moby Dick. At any rate, your allusion for example to the 'Spirit Spout' first showed me that there was a subtle significance in that thing – but I did not, in that case, *mean* it. I had some vague idea while writing it, that the whole book was susceptible of an allegoric construction, and that *parts* of it were – but the speciality of many of the particular subordinate allegories, were first revealed to me, after reading Mr. Hawthorne's letter, which, without citing particular examples, yet intimated the part-and-parcel allegoricalness of the whole.[15]

Perhaps it is not surprising, since we ignored Melville for sixty years, that we paid no attention to such remarks as these. *While you think you but humbly discover them, you do in fact create them for yourself . . . I did not . . . mean it.* The licence to interpret is delivered by the author himself, whose shadow has always, in our fantasy, obscured our way to interpretative freedom.

As time goes on the author's need for freedom in his reader grows more insistent, and we are brought close to a situation in which we are commanded to be free on pain of making no sense at all. This happened in other arts; of Schönberg Adorno writes that his music 'requires the listener spontaneously to compose its inner movement and demands of him not mere contemplation but praxis'.[16] In other words, it's no use just sitting there listening; you have to work, to collaborate, not simply recognise a familiar landscape but help, by the exercise of an interpretive power which is essentially creative, to *make* it. And the markers and controls being much fewer than those liberally provided by George Eliot, even contemporaries find themselves uneasy with their necessary liberty – with their need to choose between many unsponsored possibilities, which is what liberty in practice amounts to.

We need not be amazed that a true understanding of the position was first vouchsafed to practitioners, who are daily confronted by the necessity of choice, and must understand the necessary indeterminacy of their text. James, situating the reader between two plausible but mutually contradictory alternatives, was conducting a demonstration of *limited* freedom. Modern practitioners go much further than Schönberg or James; the poetics of what is called 'open form' are now often studied, and sometimes related to changes in physics, and especially to the inclusion of sophisticated concepts of indeterminacy in the cognitive process.[17] But I hope one can put it reasonably simply, and say that by whatever historical process we are coming to understand it, there was always a requirement that the reader should be a more or less sophisticated interpreter; and the passage of time and the changes of history have brought about a situation in which not only are the older works we think worth preserving of necessity more open to interpretation, but many new works insist upon it, because to do otherwise would be in bad faith. Umberto Eco offers a stronger version of this proposition when he says that 'every work of art, even though it is produced by following an explicit or implicit poetic of necessity, is effectively open to a virtually unlimited range of possible readings, each of which causes the work to acquire new vitality in terms of one particular taste, or perspective, or personal performance.' Another word for performance is interpretation; and interpretation is another word for reading.

If I had time to dwell on some of the implications of Eco's position, which may strike you as rather extreme – licence, rather than liberty – I should be obliged to say that I believe in pleasure, and that it is possible to distinguish between at least two kinds of pleasure which are both proper to reading. One of them has it origin precisely in the gaps of which I have spoken – gaps which may have various causes, including error, but which are inescapably present in all texts. This is a private delight; it has even been described, by Roland Barthes, as an erotic and a perverse delight. The other pleasure is perhaps the only one people can be directed towards by friends and teachers; it consists in knowing what it is that 'holds a book together'; it involves the divination of generic expectations and structures; it requires you to know what educated people know, and is therefore a pleasure of conformity. Each of these pleasures is the product of interpretative activity, and there is no need, in this context, to say that one of them is higher than the other.

Our activity in reading *Adam Bede* is clearly rather heavily weighted on the side of conformism: what we had to do was to recognise that the text for the most part offered itself as a kind of transparency, through which we could see, as if by magic, what was absent; and we took orders about this, as about other matters. We needed skill to do so, but still we were doing as we were told. Some kinds of interpretation were clearly forbidden; we did not, for example, dare to think that by offering us an account of a series of events so intimately connected, so mutually significant, the author was behaving like a madman, though in real life, faced with a comparable construction of reality, we should at once diagnose paranoia. We were coded not to think such things. Nowadays this coding or conditioning process is quite frequently abandoned. To defeat our expectations of being mere recipients of a message, and our assumption that laws exist which ban certain inferences and enjoin others, is half the programme of the *nouveau roman*; and M. Robbe-Grillet will often, as they say, set us up, induce false expectations and then defeat them. You are always dealing with a piece of *writing*; it is not transparent, giving on to an absent reality; things do not in the ordinary sense *happen* in it, and if you try to make them they will disappoint you.

As I began with a quotation, let me end with one. I have lately been reading the novels of the young Austrian writer Peter Handke. Handke is obsessed by the notion that language is in its very nature an agent of human oppression and disappointment. He hates fiction with a puritanical fervour, loving the truth which language prevents us from telling. In his novel *The Goalie's Anxiety at the Penalty Kick* he expresses anxiety as a sort of linguistic disease. 'If the pressure of everything around him when his eyes were open was bad, the pressure of the words for everything out there when his eyes were closed was worse.' Bloch, the goalkeeper, is sick, and what makes him nauseated is language. His nausea affects the text of the novel, which, since it is a fiction made of words, cannot speak the truth. I quote one very brief and not particularly central passage. Bloch is posting some cards. 'Bloch dropped in the cards. The empty mailbox resounded as they fell into it. But the mailbox was so tiny that nothing could resound in there. Anyway, Bloch had walked away immediately.'

You see that our George Eliot exercise was child's play compared with this. The drop of ink that wrote it was no mirror; what you are shown is not something absent that magic makes present. It is an event impossible in itself, and mentioned only to be annulled; it is a language game, a problem about the present and the absent, words and things, the relation of that which signifies to that which is signified, which you cannot solve in any other terms than those dictated to you, as to the author, by language. And that is how – a little chilled perhaps by the implications of this new liberty – that is how we must now read novels.

NOTES

1 I am simplifying, of course, by considering only a *first reading*. A *second reading* makes some choices easier, some more complex. And the more competent the reader, the more the first resembles the second.

2 Geraldine Jewsbury in *The Athenaeum*, 26 February 1859; extract in Laurence Lerner and John Holmstrom, *George Eliot and her Readers*, 1966, p. 21.

3 Gordon Haight, *George Eliot, a Biography*, 1968, p. 272.

4 I should add that the study of *style indirect libre* or Free Indirect Discourse, has reached great heights of refinement in the hands of recent 'narratologists'. See, for example, Brian McHale, 'Free Indirect Discourse', *Poetics and Literary Theory*, 3, 1978, pp. 249–87, which has an extensive bibliography. Also Moshe Ron, 'Free Indirect Discourse', Mimetic Games and the Subject of Fiction, *Poetics Today*, 2, 1981, pp. 17–39.

5 Hans W. Frei, *The Eclipse of Biblical Narrative*, 1974, pp. 306.

6 Ibid., pp. 142 ff.

7 *Standard Edition*, iv, 1953, p. 266.

8 *Standard Edition*, v, 1953, p. 340.

9 'Two Aspects of Language and Two Types of Aphasic Disturbances', in Roman Jakobson and Morris Halle, *Fundamentals of Language*, 1956, pp. 69–96.

10 J. A. Hadfield, *Dreams and Nightmares*, 1954, p. 14.

11 Wayne Booth, *The Rhetoric of Fiction*, 1961, p. 138.

12 J. Preston, *The Created Self*, pp. 6–7.

13 In J. Hillis Miller (ed.) *Aspects of Narrative*, Selected Papers from the English Institute, 1971, 1–45. Iser was greatly to develop these ideas in his book *The Act of Reading* (*Der Akt des Lesens*, 1976), 1978.

14 The author, said James in an early essay, makes the reader: 'when he makes him well, that is makes him interested, then the reader does quite half the labor' ('The Novels of George Eliot', *Atlantic Monthly*, October 1866, reprinted in *Views and Reviews*, 1908).

15 Merrell R. Davis and William H. Gilman (eds), *The Letters of Herman Melville*, 1960, p. 146.

16 T. W. Adorno, *Prisms*, trans. S. & S. Weber, 1971, p. 150.

17 See Umberto Eco, 'The Poetics of the Open Work', *20th Century Studies*, 12, 1974, pp. 6–26.

CHAPTER 6

SECRETS AND NARRATIVE SEQUENCE

In the conduct of an invented story there are, no doubt, certain proprieties to be observed for the sake of clearness and effect.

Joseph Conrad, *Under Western Eyes*

Lucinda can't read poetry. She's good,
Sort of, at novels, though. The words, you know,
Don't sort of get in like Lucinda's way.
And then the story, well, you know, about
Real people, fall in love, like that, and all.
Sort of makes you think, Lucinda thinks.
George Khairallah, 'Our Latest Master of the Arts'[1]

The proprieties to be observed for the sake of clearness and effect are what enable Lucinda to get on sort of better with novels than with poetry. They ensure that words don't get in the way of story and characters ('real people') – characters, for example, by falling in love, are what enable the story to continue. 'And all' is sequence, also closure: plot, in short. These are the things that make Lucinda think; these are the things that are admitted (unlike words, which remain in perpetual quarantine) to Lucinda's consciousness; and what she is good at understanding is their message.

We are all rather more like Lucinda than we care to believe, always wishing words away. First we look for story – events sequentially related (possessing, shall we say, an irreducible minimum of 'connexity'). And sequence goes nowhere without his *Doppelgänger* or shadow, causality. Moreover, if there are represented persons acting, we suppose them to be enacting an action, as Aristotle almost, though not quite, remarked; and we suppose them to have 'certain qualities of thought and character' (*dianoia* and *ethos*), the two causes of action – as Aristotle really did remark (*Poetics*, 49b36).

Hence the first questions we like to ask resemble those of Keats: 'What leaf-fring'd legend. . . . What men or gods are these? What maidens loth? . . . To what green altar . . .?' There seems to be a *mythos*; these persons are acting, they seem to be trying to do something or to stop somebody else from doing it (the maidens are 'loth'), and they are heading somewhere. The *mythos* appears to have the usual relation to *ethos* and *dianoia*. But Keats, and we after him, are unable to discover the plot because the arrangement of the events (*synthesis tón pragmatón*) is not such as to allow us. Still, it must have some bearing upon our world, a world in which, as our experience suggests, there is evidence of sequence and cause; too much wine is followed by burning foreheads and parching tongues, sexual excitement is not perpetual and may be followed by sadness. Since matters appear to be otherwise on the urn, we are obliged to think that the contrast is the point of the story, for unless it has something to do with our normal expectations and beliefs, it can have no point. It lacks a quality we expect in imitations of our world, where heads ache and one may be disgusted. What it lacks is intelligible sequence, and this lack or absence must be the most important thing about it. That the young man will never stop singing, never kiss, implies a world in which the tree will never be bare nor maidens' beauty fade. Nothing in this sequenceless paradise has *character* – the ash, as Yeats put it, on a burnt stick. This utter eventlessness, this *nunc stans*, 'teases us out of thought,' which is not quite 'sort of makes [us] think.' We are nevertheless anxious that it should *say* something to us. What it says, we say, is that even in our world, the familiar world of chance and choice, it is an important though not self-evident fact that beauty is truth and truth beauty. The importance of the story on the urn, then, is that in its very difference it can tell us, by intruding into our sequence of scandal and outrage, intimations not obvious but comforting. We have, in the end, made it say something that suits us.[2]

I've been teasing Keats's poem into thought, into parable. Even if the *mythos* is incomplete and the characters so far above breathing human passion that we can infer very little about *ethos* or *dianoia*, we make them all relevant to a world in which we behave as if causes operated and matters came to an end. If the story on the urn does not observe the proprieties, we shall none the less consider it strictly in relation to those proprieties; and that will enable it to *say* something to us. Of course the poem encourages us to do these things by ending with the sort of message that seems possible and proper.

Obviously our task, and the author's, will be easier with a completed action, as Aristotle, with his talk of failure and success and of the progressive exposure of the agents' *ethos* and *pathos*, would agree. And since we are not here to talk about immobile urns, I shall hereafter consider only invented stories in which the proprieties (as to connexity, closure, and character) are better observed. The first thing to say, I think, is that stories of this kind have frequently, perhaps to all intents and purposes always, properties that are not immediately and obviously related to the proprieties I have mentioned. This might seem self-evident; we are always asking questions of well-formed narratives that are not altogether unlike those put by the poet to his urn – questions about the persons acting, questions about cause, questions about what the story *says*. And although we are all very good readers, we argue about the answers, even if we agree that the story under discussion observes the proprieties. This is partly because most of the stories we care to discuss in this way have properties not so directly under the control of propriety. Good readers may conspire to ignore these properties; but they are relevant to my main theme, which is the conflict between narrative sequence (or whatever it is that creates the 'illusion of narrative sequence') and what I shall loosely, but with pregnant intention, call 'secrets.'

Consider first the rather obvious point that a story is always subject to interpretation. Stories as we know them begin as interpretations. They grow and change on the blank of the pages. There is some truth in the theory of iconotropy; if we doubt the evidence that it happened in remote antiquity, we shall not trouble to deny that it happened in later versions of myth, in folk etymologies, in daily gossip, and perhaps even in daily newspapers. Creative distortion of this kind is indeed so familiar as to need no more words. So is the practice of deliberate, conscious narrative revision, whether in narrative midrash or by historians. There is a perpetual *aggiornamento* of the sense. Interference with the original project may begin at the beginning; as Edward Said might say, its authority is subject to primordial molestation.[3] We take this for granted in some matters, as New Testament critics assume that the parables had been distorted not only by the appended interpretations but even in their substance, before they were written down. Consequently the world divides between those who seek to restore something authentic but lost and those who conclude that the nature of parable, and perhaps of narrative in general, is to be 'open' – open, that is, to penetration by interpretation. They are, in Paul Ricoeur's formula, models for the redescription of the world; they will change endlessly since the world is endlessly capable of being redescribed. And this is a way of saying that they must always have their secrets.

The capacity of narrative to submit to the desires of this or that mind without giving up secret potential may be crudely represented as a dialogue between story and interpretation. This dialogue begins when the author puts pen to paper and it continues through every reading that is not merely submissive. In this sense we can see without too much difficulty that all narrative, in the writing and the reading, has something in common with the continuous modification of text that takes place in a psychoanalytical process (which may tempt us to relate secrets to the condensations and displacements of dreams) or in the distortions induced in historical narrative by metahistorical considerations.

All that I leave to Roy Schafer[4] and Hayden White. My immediate purpose is to make acceptable a simple proposition: we may like to think, for our purposes, of narrative as the product of two intertwined processes, the presentation of a fable and its progressive interpretation (which of course alters it). The first process tends toward clarity and propriety ('refined common sense'), the second toward secrecy, toward distortions which cover secrets. The proposition is not altogether alien to the now classic *fabula/sujet* distinction. A test for connexity (an important aspect of propriety) is that one can accurately infer the fable (which is not to say it ever had an independent anterior existence). The *sujet* is what

136

became of the fable when interpretation distorted its pristine, sequential propriety (and not only by dislocating its order of presentation, though the power to do so provides occasions for unobvious interpretations of a kind sequence cannot afford).

I do not know whether there is a minimum acceptable measure of narrativity. (On whom should we conduct acceptability tests? Wyndham Lewis's cabdriver? Philippe Sollers? The president of the MLA?) What seems reasonable, however, is the proposition that there will always be some inbuilt interpretation, that it will increase as respect for propriety decreases, and that it will produce distortions, secrets to be inquired into by later interpretation. Even in a detective story which has the maximum degree of specialised 'hermeneutic' organisation, one can always find significant concentrations of interpretable material that has nothing to do with clues and solutions and that can, if we choose, be read rather than simply discarded, though propriety recommends the latter course.[5] In the kinds of narrative upon which we conventionally place a higher value, the case against propriety is much stronger; there is much more material that is less manifestly under the control of authority, less easily subordinated to 'clearness and effect,' more palpably the enemy of order, of interpretative consensus, of message. It represents a fortunate collapse of authority (authors have authority, property rights; but they poach their own game and thereby set a precedent to all interpreters).

Whatever the comforts of sequence, connexity (I agree that we cannot do without them), it cannot be argued that the text which exhibits them will do nothing but contribute to them; some of it will be indifferent or even hostile to sequentiality. And although perhaps generated from some unproblematic ur-text, these nonsequential elements may grow unruly enough to be disturbing, even to the author. Such was the case with Conrad, to whom I shall return in a moment. He was certainly aware of the conflict between the proprieties and the mutinous text of interpretation. There is no doubt that sequence, *ethos*, and *dianoia* minister to comfort and confirm our notions of what life is like (notions that may have been derived from narrative in the first place) and perhaps even constitute a sort of secular viaticum, bearing intimately upon one's private eschatology, the sense of one's own life and its closure. Such are their comforts, and sometimes we want them badly enough to wish away what has to come with them: the treacherous text, with its displacements and condensations, its debauched significances and unofficial complicities. Because the authors may themselves be alarmed by these phenomena (but also because they need to please), we may enter into collusion with them and treat all the evidence of insubordinate text as mere disposable noise or use the evidence selectively, when it can be adapted to strengthen the façade of propriety.

Secrets, in short, are at odds with sequence, which is considered as an aspect of propriety; and a passion for sequence may result in the suppression of the secret. But it is there, and one way we can find the secret is to look out for evidence of suppression, which will sometimes tell us where the suppressed secret is located. It must be admitted that we rarely read in this way, for it seems unnatural; and when we do we are uncomfortably aware of the difference between what we are doing and what the *ordinary reader* not only does but seems to have been meant to do. To read a novel expecting the satisfactions of closure and the receipt of a message is what most people find enough to do; they are easier with this method because it resembles the one that works for ordinary acts of communication. In this way the gap is closed between what is sent and what is received, which is why it seems to many people perverse to deny the author possession of an authentic and normative sense of what he has said. Authors, indeed, however keenly aware of other possibilities, are often anxious to help readers behave as they wish to; they 'foreground' sequence and message. This cannot be done without backgrounding something, and indeed it is not uncommon for large parts of a novel to go virtually unread; the less manifest portions of its text (its secrets) tend to remain secret, tend to resist all but abnormally attentive scrutiny, reading so minute, intense, and slow that it seems to run counter to one's 'natural' sense of what a novel is, a sense which one feels to have behind it the history and sociology of the genre. That history has ensured that most readers underread, and the authors in turn tend to condone underreading because success depends upon it; there is public demand for narrative statements that can be agreed with, for problems rationally soluble. By the same token the authors are often suspicious of overreaders, usually members of a special academic class that has the time to pry into secrets. Joyce said he had written a book to keep the professors busy; but James would not have said so, nor would Conrad, in whom the struggle between propriety and secrecy is especially intense, nor Robbe-Grillet, who claims to write for the man in the street. This measure of collusion between novelist and public (his *de facto* contract or gentleman's agreement is with *la cour et la ville* not with *l'école*) helps one to see why the secrets are so easily over-looked and why – given that the problems only begin when the secrets are noticed – we have hardly, even now, found decent ways to speak of these matters.

If anybody thinks this is an exaggerated account of the matter, let him reflect that Forster's *A Passage to India* had a very unusual success on publication and gave rise to lively arguments about its account of Indian life and politics; yet it was a good many years before anybody noticed that it had secrets. What is more, I spend much of my time among learned men who were devoted colleagues and friends of Forster and who know *Passage* well, but they never seem to talk about its secrets, only about its message and what, in their view, is wrong with that message.

It is time, however, to consider a single text in more detail, and I shall henceforth be talking about *Under Western Eyes*. This novel was not, in 1911 or I think since, what could be called a popular success, though it offers a decent measure of connexity and closure (falling off a little, it must be allowed, from the highest standards of propriety). Its political and psychological messages are gratify-ingly complex; one can engage in an enlightened critical conver-sation about *ethos* and *dianoia* without talking about much else and so pass for an intelligent professional giving an effective 'read-ing.' Indeed that, until recently at any rate, was what the normal institutional game consisted of. Nor is it without interest; but the game is conducted within a very limited set of rules, in the estab-lishment of which the author as well as the institution has played a part. Under these rules it is not obligatory to talk of secrets. There are handier, more tangible or manageable mysteries.

Under Western Eyes wants to allow this game to be played, but it also gives due notice that a different game is possible; it indicates, by various signs, that there are other matters that might be con-sidered and that, though ignorable, they are detectable, given the right kind of attention. So it is a suitable text for my purpose, which is to consider the survival of secrecy in a narrative that pays a lot of attention to the proprieties which, according to its narrator, should be observed 'for the sake of clearness and effect.' Conrad took a high view of art and a low view of his public, which is why writing fiction seems to have been a continual cause of misery to him. It forced him into a situation sometimes reflected in his characters, a *dédoublement*. There is one writer who labours to save the 'dense' reader (one equipped, so to speak, with only Western eyes) from confusion, disappointment, and worry; and another dedicated to interpretation, to secrets, though at the same time he fears them as enemies of order, sequence, and message. There must be a strict repression of all that contests the supremacy of these features, 'else novel-writing becomes a mere debauch of the imagination,' as Conrad told Mrs Garnett, who was worried about the 'self-imposed limitation' of the method employed in *Under Western Eyes*.[6]

I am already operating, and will continue to operate, a crude distinction in the readership, actual or potential, of *Under Western Eyes*. There is a larger public which Conrad, although he despised it, wanted to read his book. To some extent he abrogates authority (which the common reader values highly) by interfering as usual with the 'normal' sequence of the story and by installing an unreliable narrator; all narrators are unreliable, but some are more expressly so than others;[7] the more unreliable they are, the more they can say that seems irrelevant to, or destructive of, the proprieties. They break down the conventional relationship between sequential narrative and history-likeness, with its arbitrary imposition of truth; they complicate the message. They are more or less bound to bore or antagonise the simpler reader, who feels that he has been left outside and cannot, without pains he is unwilling to take, gain access on his own terms, the observance of a due sequaciousness being one, and another the manifest presence of authority, so that he need not reason why. Some such explanation will suffice for the cold public reception of *Under Western Eyes*; it has not grown much warmer in these days, for all that the book is now regarded as a classic.

Saying what is a classic is the business of a second group of readers, the professionally initiate. They perform other tasks, of course. One is finding things out, in the manner of Eloise Knapp Hay and Norman Sherry. And I hope we should all rather know than be ignorant of what they tell us; it is a first principle of literary criticism that no principle should stand which prevents our being concerned with what stimulates our unaffected interest – for example, in what Conrad, when he was not writing *Under Western Eyes*, thought about Russia, Slav 'mysticism,' and Dostoevsky; or what Conrad originally planned to write, what he took to be the point of what he did write, and what, having written it, he cut. What he saw with his Eastern eyes is a legitimate subject of concern, though at present we are concerned with what he wrote in *Under Western Eyes*. And other members of this group assume the responsibility of saying what that was and how it is most profitable for us to think about it.

There are a great many books on Conrad, and I shall mention few of them. Albert Guerard's *Conrad the Novelist*, though it appeared in 1958, still seems to be a standard work, and not surprisingly, for it is a perceptive and resourceful book.[8] But it is characteristically uninterested in narrative secrets. On *Under Western Eyes* it makes plain that the author's first interest is in the psychopathology of Razumov; and it would have been possible to quote Conrad in defence of this preference. Razumov, the loner, the man of independent reason undermined by the shocks of Russian despotism and anarchy, is 'psychologically . . . fuller' than Lord Jim (p. 232). The design of the story (*synthesis tón pragmatón*) is commended because Razumov is enabled to keep quiet during his long period on the rack of guilt and fear, but to confess when every threat to his security has been removed. 'It would be hard to conceive a plot more successfully combining dramatic suspense and psycho-moral significance.' *Mythos, ethos, dianoia*: all present and sound.

Even the dislocated narrative sequence is said to have some advantages: by concealing what a more straightforward rendering of the fable would have revealed, it enables us to observe Razumov in Geneva before we find out that he has accepted employment as a spy for Mikulin. Such are the rewards of entrusting the narration to an observer who is not only limited and prejudiced but pretends to neither omniscience nor omnicommunicativeness. But these rewards are obtained at a cost, for the old language teacher 'creates unnecessary obstacles by raising the question of authority' (p. 248). He is a clumsy device for ensuring fair play to the Russians by reminding us that their actions are being reported through a rather 'dense' medium. On the other hand, first person narration, in the extended form here employed, gives 'eyewitness credibility and the authority of spoken voice' (p. 249).

Here is a contradiction, interesting though perhaps only apparent. Authority doesn't normally 'raise the question of authority.' They have it very oft that have it not. Yet there is a sense in which Conrad does both claim and renounce authority. Having it makes for clearness and effect; Conrad admired Trollope.[9] Not having it is to risk a debauch of the imagination. The contradiction of the critic replicates a conflict in the author. Writing under conditions even more agonising than usual, Conrad said that 'following the psychology of Mr Razumov' was 'like working in hell.' The point to remember is that following the psychology required him to do many other things at the same time, or it would not have been so hellish. When a critic devoted to clearness and effect argued that *Chance* should be cut by half, Conrad replied sarcastically that yes, given a certain method, it 'might have been written out on a cigarette paper.'[10] Clearness and effect he sought, out of need, and desire too; but there was also the pursuit of interpretations. Hence the doubling I spoke of. In the hell of composition we see one writer committed to authority, another involved in debauch.

What is the critic to say when confronted with the evidence of debauch committed behind the back of authority? Guerard is not like Lucinda, the words do get in his way to some extent. Early in the book Razumov sees the phantom of Haldin lying in the snow. He tramples over it. Gaining from this act an intuition of Russia's 'sacred inertia,' he decides to give Haldin up to the police. The phantom crops up from time to time in the course of the novel but can always be disposed of by reference to the psychological difficulties arising from the first hallucination. Or can it? When Razumov and Sophia Antonovna, in the garden of the exiles' villa at Geneva, are discussing whether there will be any tea left for her indoors, Razumov remarks that she might be lucky enough to find there 'the cold ghost of tea.' Guerard finds this odd and describes it as 'mildly obsessive.' So it is, but fortunately it can be got rid of, psychologized as 'hallucination, psychic symbol, or shorthand notice of anxiety.' In such ways are the ghosts and phantoms subjected to the needs of clearness and effect, buried in the psychology. I shall dig them out in a minute or two.

There are other ways of exorcising secrets. Near the end of the book Razumov says he had been in a position to steal Natalia's soul. Guerard speaks of the Dostoevskian power of this moment of diabolism but is anxious to be rid of it, for it does not comply with what Roy Schafer might call his 'guiding fiction,' his interpretation principle. Guerard dismisses Razumov's remark by arguing that Conrad, here, writing for the first time in Razumov's person, 'returned imaginatively' to his original plan for the novel, in which Razumov was to marry Natalia, so stealing her soul. The diabolism is, therefore, an irrelevant intrusion, a fault, a vestigial survival. Also near the end of the book, Razumov has the notion that the old language teacher is the devil. Of this second diabolistic conjecture Guerard says nothing, which is the more usual way of dealing with these awkwardnesses.

To attend to what complies with the proprieties, and by one means or another to eliminate from consideration whatever does not, is a time-honoured and perfectly respectable way of reading novels, especially when it is quite a task (as it often is in Conrad) to establish within proper bounds all the tricks and deviations which interfere with one's view of the fable. It is therefore not surprising that good readers, sensing that there is more going on than they have accounted for, show signs of strain. Guerard admires *Under Western Eyes* but admits that, having such a narrator, it lacks 'the rich connotative effects and subtly disturbing rhythms of *Lord Jim*' (p. 252). On the other hand, this 'self-effacing and more rational prose has the great merit of not interfering with the drama of ideas or with the drama of betrayal and redemption.' *Under Western Eyes*, that is to say, is unsubtle but clear and effective.

This is an extraordinary notion, and for a good critic to hold it is evidence of a strong though uneasy desire not to let the words get in the way – it is, after all, a refined version of Lucinda's view of the matter. To an eye undimmed by, or awakened from, the proprieties, this novel positively flaunts the 'irrationality' of its prose. It becomes 'readable' in the way Guerard wants it to be only when, by every possible means, attention to its secrets is repressed. Guerard's psychologising of the phantom and his exorcism of the devil are of a piece with his decision that the prose is self-effacing and rational, lacking in resonance and connotation.

If you're looking out for this kind of thing, you find it almost anywhere. Eloise Knapp Hay, for example, rightly asks why Razumov's cover story, during the preparations for his visit to Geneva, should include an eye disease and a visit to an oculist (so far as simple plotting goes, any non-ocular meeting-place would have done just as well; indeed, no specification of this sort was, strictly, needed at all).[11] What Hay, having noticed this, makes of it is that Razumov, during these visits, is being commissioned 'to use his own eyes to spy for the state' (p. 294), and she mentions the young man's earlier discomfort at the stares of the goggle-eyed general who interviewed him on the night he betrayed Haldin. But to leave it at that simple allegorical level is precisely to refuse the kind of covert invitation of which this text has so many. Another of Hay's interesting observations is that behind the description of Russia as 'a monstrous blank page awaiting the record of an inconceivable history,' there may lie an observation of Mickiewicz's to the effect that Russia was 'a page prepared for writing' – an alarming thought, since one could not know that the devil would not cover the page before God did (pp. 287–8). But she is content to observe that in Conrad 'the question is posed differently,' without allusion to God and the devil. Here again, properly interested in the relation of Conrad's figure to its presumable source, she omits to ask what that relation is doing in the book and what it may have to do with the elements of diabolism. So too, she quotes the famous letter to Cunninghame Graham, in which Conrad says that to serve a national ideal, however much suffering it may cause, is better than to serve the shadow of an eloquence that is dead, a mere phantom (p. 20). We may think of Conrad as painfully finding out in the writing of *Under Western Eyes* what the novel was; he did so by writing it, black on white, as if it were Russia, and by meditating on eyes, phantoms, and devils, as surely as by deciding to cut all the American material from the final version; it was Russia he was writing on.

The secrets to which these words and ideas are an index have no direct relation to the main business of the plot; as some analysts would say, they are not kernels but catalysts or, as Seymour Chatman calls them, 'satellites.' But they form associations of their own, nonsequential, secret invitations to interpretation rather than appeals to a consensus. They inhabit a world in which relationships are not arranged according to some agreed system but remain occult or of questionable shape. There is a relatively clean, well-lighted plot – rectangular like the room in which its climax occurs, almost without shadow, having, like Switzerland, no horizons, for they are cut off by crude and impassable barriers like the Jura, by conventional closure.

Such a plot may be suitable for the citizens of a tedious democracy, either Switzerland, where they sit colourlessly uncouth, drinking beer out of glittering glasses, obvious in an obvious light, or England, which has made its bargain with fate, so much liberty for so much cash, knowing also that it is entitled to the obvious. Such a nation deserves novels like the view of Geneva on which Razumov turns his back in contempt, finding it 'odious – oppressively odious – in its unsuggestive finish; the very perfection of mediocrity attained at last after centuries of toil and culture.' But this novel contains another plot, misty, full of phantoms, of which the passage about the blank page of Russia forms a part, as would be manifest if anybody considered it in relation to the large number of allusions (they even look, when one is looking for them, obtrusive) to blackness and whiteness, paper and ink, snow and shadow – and to writing itself.

These are secrets from which, by a curious process of collusion, we avert our attention. It was a welcome surprise to find in an excellent paper by Avrom Fleishman proof that an effort of attention is after all possible.[12] Fleishman observes that the 'artlessness' of the narrator is not a guarantee of factuality so much as a hint that the text is extremely artful; he sorts out the interrelations between the various documentary sources the old man is supposed to be using, notes the hints of falsification and omission, and emphasizes the abnormal interest of the novel in the acts and arts of writing, as when Razumov, prompted to write by Laspara, composes his first (Russian) spy report in the shadow of the statue of the (Genevan) writer Rousseau. He also argues that the novel moves out of writing into speech, as indeed it does: the inspiration mentioned in the last off-key conversation between the narrator and Sophia is drawn in with the breath, Razumov is no longer a writer but a beloved speaker. Fleishman draws back finally (perhaps needlessly) from his own proposal that the book suggests an 'ultimate despair of written language, and of the art of fiction. . . .'

And indeed it is obvious that *Under Western Eyes* (rather than any character in it) is obsessed with writing and also with deafness – deafness not only of the ears but of the eyes (Ivanovitch seems to speak from his eyes; Sophia Antonovna seems to receive 'the sound of his voice into her pupils instead of her ears'; at the grand climax the narrator is blinded by his own amazement, but the slamming of a door restores his sight). There is a hint that we may, though we probably won't, read for more than mere evidence of Razumov's psychological condition. If we are willing to do so, we shall find over the plot the shadow of a secret that has resisted being made altogether otherwise than it is for the sake of readers who want the work to be throughout like beer in a glittering glass. I have been giving instances of subtler, more learned modes of inattention; even good readers find means to dispose of the evidence rather than work upon it. It would be easy to give more: for example, the explanation of all the souls and phantoms of the text as part of a refutation, or parody, of *Crime and Punishment*. This can be used to sterilize larger portions of Conrad's text. I do not mean to argue that no such observations ought to be made. Like the psychological and political readings, they belong squarely to a tradition of ordinary reading that may be perfectly intelligent; a person might run his life in accordance with what he concluded from such readings, as Lawrence claimed he might do from his reading of *Anna Karenina*. I object only to their use as means to purge secrets from the text.

Let me now give one or two more detailed instances of the way in which this novel advertises and conceals its secrets. As the story of Razumov's treachery reaches its crisis, the narrator pauses to note that his job is 'not in truth the writing in the narrative form a précis of a strange human document, but the rendering ... of the moral conditions ruling over a large portion of this earth's surface; conditions not easily to be understood, much less discovered in the limits of a story, till some key-word is found; a word that could stand at the back of all the words covering the pages, a word which, if not truth itself, may perchance hold truth enough to help the moral discovery which should be the object of every tale.' He stops, scans Razumov's journal, then takes up his pen again, ready to set down 'black on white.' Then he says that the key word is 'cynicism.'

Even in a novel so benignly disingenuous from the preface on (but perhaps it is not benign; in a sense it hates its readers), this passage is remarkable. Playing the role of straight narrator, the old man repeatedly veers close to the position of his occult double. 'A large portion of the earth's surface' is a periphrasis easily divested of its originating notion, Russia; the case is more general. He sees that the point of the narrative is not solely or primarily psychological but wanders away from the insight to speak of 'moral conditions.' He speaks of a key word; pauses, as it were, unwittingly speaks one of the key words of the book he is in ('black on white'), then lapses into the obvious or irrelevant 'cynicism.' For a real secret he substitutes a pseudosecret, though in doing so he cannot help telling the attentive reader that there is a secret there. Readers as 'dense' as he himself is will be happy with 'cynicism.' They will get on with sequence while the double busies himself with secrets and key words such as 'soul,' 'eyes,' and 'black and white.' Indications that these words have a special function are various. They occur with quite abnormal frequency; they are used in such a way as to distort the plausibility of narrative and especially of dialogue. Some instances may be explained away as evidence of Razumov's stressed condition ('what I need is not a lot of haunting phantoms that I could walk through' is the kind of remark that certainly suggests stress of some kind). But in others it is simply astonishing that anybody capable of reading could fail to observe the gross distortions in what they think of as 'self-effacing and rational prose.'

Let us look at a continuous passage; it is ripped from the midst of a longer one, so one must allow for an even greater measure of eccentric insistence in the context of the whole: 'We shall get some tea,' says Ivanovitch, leading Razumov to his mistress's drawing-room. They cross a black-and-white tessellated floor. Ivanovitch's hat, black but shiny, stands outside the drawing-room which is 'haunted, it is said, by evoked ghosts, and frequented, it is supposed, by fugitive revolutionists.' (We may remember that the villa itself 'might well have been haunted in traditional style by some doleful, groaning, futile ghost of a middle-class order.') The white paint of the panels is cracked. Ivanovitch, from behind his dark spectacles, speaks of the true light of femininity. His mistress has brilliant eyes in a death's-head face, they gleam white but their pupils are black. Ivanovitch speaks as if from his invisible eyes. The lady 'ghoulishly' eats the cakes Ivanovitch brought in his hat. Razumov gives a moment's thought to Tekla, the *dame de compagnie*: 'Have they terrified her out of her senses with ghosts, or simply have they only been beating her?' He is aware of having to come to terms with phantoms, with the ghastly. His interlocutors

147

appear to understand nothing of what he says; Ivanovitch is as if deaf. The purpose of the revolutionary movement, it seems, is to 'spiritualise discontent,' and the lady declares herself, in matters of politics, a 'supernaturalist.' She can see Razumov's soul with her 'shiny eyes.' What does she see? asks Razumov. 'Some sort of phantom in my image? . . . For, I suppose, a soul when it is seen is just that. A vain thing. There are phantoms of the living as well as of the dead.' He then tells them he has seen a phantom. Soon he leaves, passing the top hat, 'black and glossy in all that crude whiteness,' and looks at the chequered floor below.

I'll pause there and admit that this is a very partial account of Razumov's visit, meant to bring out what a 'normal' reading largely ignores. The easiest thing to notice is the unidiomatic quality of the writing. 'Haunted . . . by evoked ghosts'; 'Have they terrified her out of her senses with ghosts, or simply have they only been beating her?'; 'Some sort of phantom in my image?' How are we to explain these oddities? I suppose the 'evoked ghosts' might be put down to Conrad thinking in French; possibly also 'simply have they only been beating her'; but however they got there we are, I think, obliged to read them, not wish them away. Both the remark about Tekla's scared appearance (was it caused by evoked ghosts?) and the character of the phantom the second-sighted lady might see in Razumov are, one might have thought, almost intolerably odd if one is reading this as a sequence-advancing, psychology-investigating dialogue. But our reading may be so sequence-connected that we can screen them out by thinking of psychology rather than the words. Conrad helps us to psychologise them out of the way by making Razumov enter into a dangerous, though censored, account of his encounter with Haldin's phantom. But only our recollections of anarchists of the period, their flirting with the occult and with feminism, can explain the interest in seeing souls coming to terms with phantoms; unless we decide, as we ought, that the emphasis on eyes and seeing is otherwise, and occultly, related to the virtually uncontrolled dispersion of souls, spirits, phantoms, ghosts, ghouls, and so forth. Here, against the repetitive black and white (against ink on paper, against the page we are *seeing*) are crowded the evidences of things unseen and the huge variety of eyes that may or may not see them. It is not an easy thing to talk about such a constellation of irrational figures, but it must somehow be done if we are to read secrets as well as sequence – to avoid attributing all these phenomena to Razumov's 'nervous exhaustion.'

What I ask you to believe is that such oddities are not merely local; they are, perhaps, the very 'spirit' of the novel. If one follows Razumov a little way from the encounter just described, one finds him talking to Tekla with her striped cat and terrified eyes and then with Sophia Antonovna, whose black eyes and white hair are mentioned almost as often as she is. It is in this interview that the ghost of tea occurs. Razumov has just mentioned that his mind is a murky medium in which Haldin appears as a featureless shadow. He adds that Haldin is now beyond the reach of feminine influence, except possibly that of the spiritualist lady. 'Formerly the dead were allowed to rest, but now it seems they are at the beck and call of a crazy old harridan.' 'Let us hope,' says Sophia humorously, 'that she will make an effort and conjure up some tea for us.' The figure arises naturally from the talk about the spiritualist lady. But it continues. 'There has been tea up there. . . . If you hurry . . . instead of wasting your time with such an unsatisfactory sceptical person as myself, you may find the ghost of it – the cold ghost of it – still lingering. . . .' And two pages later Razumov again tells her that she risks missing 'the mere ghost of that tea.' In her reply Sophia uses the figure yet again. Then they speak of ghouls, ogres, vampires. She denies that she is a materialist; she is described as Mephistophelian. Finally Razumov tells the story of his escape; it is in truth the story of Haldin, gliding from Razumov's room as if he were a phantom, at midnight; the flame gutters as he passes. She listens but as if with her eyes not her ears – with her black impenetrable eyes glowing under the white hair. At one point Sophia tells him to 'wait until you have trodden every particle of yourself under your own feet . . . you've got to trample down every particle of your own feelings.' These are words private to Razumov, not possible to her; only he, and perhaps Councillor Mikulin, knows about that trampling. Are we inclined to seek, in the body of the plot, a reason why Sophia should use such an expression? No, for any notion that she had access to secret police information about Razumov would extravagantly spoil the plot. No; here an expression private to Razumov (if we stick to conventional characterization) – evidence as to his peculiar psychological state – has bled into the texture of the book and attached itself to Sophia. I wonder if anything quite like it can be found in the English novel till Virginia Woolf. Note, too, the repetition ('trodden' . . . 'trample'): it is an indication that we are to pause and take note of it.

I have mentioned elsewhere[13] the oddity of Natalia Haldin's remark – that when she went to the villa she didn't at first see a soul, but then Tekla came in, and she *did* see a soul. Perhaps Conrad was not aware that the idiomatic expression 'I didn't see a soul' is incapable of a positive transformation. That doesn't matter; 'seeing a soul' is another important key word. The oddity of the expression is a way of directing attention to it; it must not be swept away by talk of Conrad's English. So with the other key words, the repetitions – four ghosts of tea are surely beyond a joke. The frequency with which 'soul,' 'ghost,' and related words are used has not altogether escaped attention; but if one reflects that they occur (if one allows not only 'spirit' but 'inspired') well over a hundred times in the novel (sometimes in grotesquely thick concentrations), besides several ghostly apparitions, people appearing as if they had risen from the ground, and so on, it becomes obvious that the attention has not been very sustained. Of course, all these usages are somehow related to the appearance of Haldin's phantom in the plots of action and psychology; but they must not be totally subsumed in them. Indeed, on any reasonably minute and careful reading they cannot be, for they distort the dialogue and are incompatible with any psychology that could be thought appropriate to Razumov, who is always sane. Nor should one forget the frequency of associated key words. I have counted well over sixty references to eyes – the eyes of all the principal characters are incessantly mentioned or described – and to seeing. Black on white occurs twenty-four times expressly and many more less directly – in references to snow and darkness, light in dark rooms, and, as I have said, ink on paper. All this adds up to a quantitatively quite large body of text which on the face of it contributes nothing to sequence – clogs it, indeed.

It would be to inflict even more laborious reports on you to specify at any greater length the character of the 'secret' material in *Under Western Eyes*. My purpose is to supplement the 'straight' reading, which irons out such considerable quantities of text. Conrad, when he began the book, called it *Razumov*; but when it was done (on the last page of the manuscript, in fact) he changed the title to *Under Western Eyes*. He had found out what he was doing. Most readers silently restore the old title, being readier to think about Razumov than about eyes. They want something clearly seen, a message to be apprehended with civilized ease. Let us look at the underside of one more scene, Razumov's confession to Natalia.

Razumov's face is pale, his eyes dark. The inner room is dark by contrast with the well-lit anteroom; Mrs Haldin's face is white against the undefined dark mass of her chair. Razumov has been writing and stopped to come and talk, so entering the writing, the black on white, of the narrator. He is safe; the phantom on the snow has been walked over, though the phantom's mother is white as a ghost. Natalia enters, like a ghost ('her presence ... was as unforeseen as the apparition of her brother had been,' with a pun on two senses of 'apparition').[14] She had done the same in the garden of the villa; she 'had been haunting him.' They stand in the rectangular box of a room with its white paper and lack of shadows. They are trapped, we might say, in a rational plot – the narrator has them captive 'within the boundaries of his eyes.' Razumov says that he was born clear-eyed but has seen apparitions. Natalia's eyes are trustful, as always. She says that her brother's soul is in Razumov, reason benignly possessed by spirit. There they stand, boxed in a Western room, brought out of a 'confused immensity' for the benefit of Western eyes. They do not see the old man. Natalia removes her veil. Her eyes are lustrous; he listens, as if to music rather than speech. She explains that her mother expects to *see* her dead son. 'It will end by her seeing him.' 'That is very possible,' says Razumov. 'That will be the end. Her spirit will depart.' He speaks of the phantoms of the dead. Natalia's veil lies on the floor between them. 'Why are you looking at me like this ...? I need ... to see. ...' He begins the confession: more phantoms. The old man intervenes; Razumov stands with the veil at his feet, 'intensely black in the white crudity of the light.' He seems to vanish. He goes home and writes more in his journal. In its pages, we are told of eyes, phantoms, his temptation to steal Natalia's soul. Was the old Englishman the devil ('I was possessed')? Natalia has saved him; she is an apparition ('suddenly you stood before me'), and the old man a 'disappointed devil.' He wraps the writing in the veil.

At midnight (when spirits walk) he runs down the stairs into the storm, the rain enveloping him like a veil. Later, deafened, he again runs into the storm, which has transformed the dull civility of

Geneva. Lightning blinds him; he 'puts his arm over his eyes to recover his sight'; he wanders into a drift of mist, walking 'in a phantom world.'

This is of course psychological disclosure, but if it is *only* that it is full of irrelevant information, of redundancies, of what, if its business consists of sequence and psychology, is a feebly bloated rhetoric. I have spoken of secrets; but they are all but blatantly advertised. The book has a semblance of Geneva, but in the end it yields to Russia, misty, spiritual, its significance occulted; it is without horizon, only by trickery and collusion got into a square, well-lighted box. The writing of the book, the covering of the monstrous blank page, is a work of 'strange mystic arrogance'; it gives the western eye its box, its civilized mediocrity, but keeps its secrets also. It is a controlled 'debauch'; we may ignore this aspect if we choose and read it as Genevans or Englishmen would read it. It is a question of the form of attention we choose to bestow; of our willingness to see that in reading according to restricted codes we disregard as noise what, if read differently, patiently, would make another and rarer kind of sense. And the text, almost with 'cynicism,' tells us what is there, confident that we shall ignore it.

'The illogicality of its attitude, the arbitrariness of its conclusions, the frequency of the exceptional, should present no difficulty to the student of many grammars. . . . There is a generosity in its ardour of speech which removes it as far as possible from common loquacity; and it is ever too disconnected to be classed as eloquence.' I adapt these words from the passage near the beginning of the book in which the old language teacher speaks of the Russian character and the Russian use of language. He apologises for the digression, which we should know is not a digression, exactly as we know it is not 'idle to inquire' why Razumov should have left his written record. He is telling us (or rather the double is telling us, ventriloquially) that a large part of what he says is precisely what we are not willing to attend to. He, who claims a professional mistrust of words, is talking about the book he is in, the black on white. He is necessary; for, as Razumov remarks, 'there may be truth in every manner of speaking. What if that absurd saying [that he himself might be a "chosen instrument of Providence"] were true in its essence?' What if the old Englishman should be the father of lies?

152

It seems to be the case that there is in this book a 'manner of speaking' that is horizonless, misty. Is there some great idea that unites all the key words, the language with which the text is obsessed? One could make shift to discover such a truth, perhaps. Black on white is the manuscript or the book; the reading of black on white (including the seeing into its soul or spirit) is a hearing with the eyes of what is said rather than written, since it is not seen. It is in the veil that covered Natalia's eyes that the manuscript is wrapped. The secrets of the book are phantoms, inexplicably appearing, ignored, trampled down, turned into lies by the father of lies, a diabolical narrator. For the reading of such a book we have the wrong kind of eyes. It despises its Genevan readers, with their requirements of brightness and obvious structure, their detached, informed interest in alien 'mystery.'

And at this point why should we not add some biographical evidence? Conrad was in one of his greatest crises as he turned *Razumov* into *Under Western Eyes* and had a severe breakdown when he finished the book. Part of the trouble was poverty; not enough people read his books. They were not sufficiently obvious. So this book provides an accurate prophecy of its own reception which is the reception of all such works; like the language teacher, like Lucinda, we distrust words, think it better to ignore them if they seem wild or misty. And like the language teacher, we are surprised at the book's end, which is the ending of another story than the one he had seemed to be in charge of. The actual black on white defeats the narrator's attempt to achieve parsimony of sequence, squareness, limit. It seems that a god and a devil wrote simultaneously, another *dédoublement* if you like, and one that, somehow, the good reader must emulate; for if he does not he will, by concurring in the illusions of limit and authority, deny the god (the hidden god of secrets) his due. Thus may a novel complain against the commonsense way we read it, though this is the kind of reading it seems also to solicit by appearing to respect the proprieties and to aim at 'clearness and effect.'

NOTES

1 From *Academe*, 1979. My thanks to Alexander Baramki, who sent me this book.

2 After this was written, I read Jurij M. Lotman's 'The Origin of Plot in the Light of Typology, *Poetics Today*, 1, nos. 1–2, 1979: 161–84. Lotman speaks of two primeval kinds of plot. The first is 'mythic' and has no 'excesses or anomalies'; it is timeless and motionless. The second is the linear tale about incidents, news, 'excesses.' The two exist in dialectical interaction, and the result is a 'fusion of scandal and miracle.' A secret motivation arising from the 'eschatological' plot intrudes into the linear plot; 'mythologism penetrates into the sphere of excess.' It is from such combinations that we have learnt to interpret reality as we do, plotwise. Keats's poem foreshadows this theory. The mythic event is injected into scandal and outrage; beauty subsumes a version of truth which represents it as calamity, decay, and consequence; the assurance that there is a timeless and motionless transcendent world reduces to insignificance the *faits divers* which seem to constitute the narrative of ordinary life.

3 Edward W. Said, *Beginnings*, 1975, p. 83.

4 Not forever, I hope; his essay and its 'refined common sense' have powerful implications for a more general narrative theory. [The essay, first presented at the Chicago Symposium on 'Narrative: the Illusion of Sequence', which was also the occasion of the present chapter, is called 'Narration in the Psychoanalytic Dialogue'. It is reprinted in *Narrative*, ed. W. J. T. Mitchell, 1981, pp. 25–49. For Hayden White's essay, see *Narrative*, pp. 1–23.]

5 See Chapter 2 of the present volume.

6 Joseph Conrad, *Letters from Joseph Conrad, 1895–1924*, ed. Edward Garnett, 1928, p. 234.

7 The trouble is not that there are unreliable narrators but that we have endorsed as reality the fiction of the 'reliable' narrator.

8 Albert J. Guerard, *Conrad the Novelist*, 1958; all references to this work will be cited in the text.

9 See Frederick R. Karl, *Joseph Conrad: The Three Lives*, 1979, p. 68 n.

10 Conrad, preface to *Chance*, 1920, p. viii.

11 Eloise Knapp Hay, *The Political Novels of Joseph Conrad*, 1963; all references to this work will be cited in the text. See also D. C. Yelton's *Mimesis and Metaphor*, 1967 which sees a connection between the 'motif of vision' and the phantom but treats it only psychologically.

12 Avrom Fleishman, 'Speech and Writing in *Under Western Eyes*,' in *Conrad: A Commemoration*, ed. Norman Sherry, 1976, pp. 119–28. After this paper was written, there appeared Jeremy Hawthorn's *Joseph Conrad: Language and Fictional Self-Consciousness*, 1979, which contains interesting remarks on Conrad's play with English tenses and argues that when the language teacher tells Miss Haldin

that he has understood 'all the words' but without understanding, he is speaking for the reader as Conrad imagined him (see pp. 102–28).

13 See 'The Structures of Fiction,' in *Velocities of Change*, ed. R. Macksey, 1974, p. 198.

14 The pun is actually French, since English 'apparition' = 'appearance' is virtually obsolete.

CHAPTER 7

CAN WE SAY ABSOLUTELY ANYTHING WE LIKE?

'There was a student once who wrote a paper saying that a couplet by Alexander Pope, "no Prelate's Lawn with Hair-shirt lin'd, / Is half so incoherent as my Mind" (*Epistle* I.i. 165–6) ought to be read in the light of a couplet in another poem by Pope: "Whose ample Lawns are not asham'd to feed / The milky heifer and deserving steed" (*Moral Essays* IV. 185–6). Since I believe in the force of puns and all sorts of other resemblances in poetry, I do not know quite how to formulate the rule of context by which I confidently reject that connection.'[1] So writes W. K. Wimsatt; he adds a note in which he tentatively proposes the kind of explanation a structural linguist might offer but, instead of endorsing or developing it, quotes I. A. Richards on the way in which 'the semantic texture' of a poem might be held to forbid certain interpretations; Richards goes on to lament the state of affairs in which a prospective teacher of literature, such as the one whose reading of Marvell he is rejecting, should show so little sense 'of what is and is not admissible in interpretation,' and display 'a reckless disregard of all the means by which language defends itself.'

But when it comes to defining the means by which language and poems and plays defend themselves, most of us are in trouble. How, then, does it come about that in the absence of known and certain rules we are, like Mr Wimsatt, confident in our rejections?

Here is my subject. That we do reject confidently is not to be disputed. Even the nomoclastic Roland Barthes allows it, for he remarks, in the course of defending himself against the *ancien régime* and M. Picard, that '*le critique ne peut se dire "n'importe quoi"*,' and speaks of constraints, '*les contraintes formelles du sens: on ne fait pas du sens n'importe comment (si vous en doutez, essayez).*' He does add that '*la sanction du critique, ce n'est pas le sens de l'oeuvre, c'est le sens de ce qu'il en dit,*' which moves the problem away from the site upon which Wimsatt and Richards thought to examine it.[2] But it does nothing at all toward the solution of the problem as to how *we* know constraints are being violated, whether these constraints are in the 'semantic texture' of the text or in the semantic texture of what we say about the text. It is assumed that *we know* what they are. And the matter that needs considering is therefore expressible as two questions: who are *we*? And how do we *know* what can be said of a poem and what cannot? We must find some tentative answer to these general questions before turning to the special case of Shakespeare. We shall then have to ask in what sense that case *is* special, and whether whatever speciality it has makes a difference to the way in which we know, whoever *we* may be, and whatever *know* can here mean.

First, the more general issue. Let me first put a view which is on the whole reassuring rather than dismaying; it is an application to our questions of the thought of Michael Polanyi. Simply as persons we each exercise considerable cognitive power without being aware of doing so, as for example when we recognise a face. Such tacit knowing works in combination with more readily identifiable operations of intellect. We combine knowing-what with knowing-how. Polanyi might agree with Barthes that in textual as in other matters we create by our ways of knowing an anamorphosis of the object attended to, he expressly states that meticulous attention to a text ought to provide material for the fuller understanding of it that comes only when we switch from 'proximal' to 'distal,' that is, from a concentration on the detail to a remoter survey of the whole. In fact he argues that excessive concentration on the first stage can destroy the object for us. We have to move it into the phase in which our more subliminal intellectual powers can work on it; into what he calls the 'tacit dimension.'

Here, of course, it is not a matter of accepting or not accepting the whole Polanyi theory, which in any case I've hardly begun to expound. The point is simply that he is clearly talking about a state of affairs of which we each have personal experience. And I think we are even less likely to accuse him of talking about a situation unfamiliar to us when he turns to the question of how a professional body *knows*. Take for example the case of the paper published in *Nature*, in which the author observed that 'the average gestation period of different animals ranging from rabbits to cows was an integer multiple of the number π.' 'The evidence he produced was ample,' says Polanyi, 'the agreement good. Yet the acceptance of this contribution by the journal was meant only as a joke. *No amount of evidence could convince a modern biologist that gestation periods are equal to integer multiples of the number π*' (my emphasis). Polanyi then gives instances from physics; revolutionary claims ostensibly of the most exciting order are simply ignored, not because anybody at the time of their announcement can disprove them, but because they are tacitly and instantaneously known to be wrong. Nobody would bother to disprove them even if he could, and there is even an implication that if their authors had been real physicists they would have known better than to propose them, 'correct' though they be.[3]

One might here insert a caution: the process can go wrong. Mendel was ignored, but it turned out that his hypotheses were tacitly unacceptable only in the existing conditions of science; and we could doubtless develop critical parallels, Whiter for example. But although one can know that one does not know enough, one cannot know what it is that one does not know; and tacit knowledge is founded in the only *epistème* available.

So we now have some notion of what *know* means in this connection, and of what *we* are. *We* who *know* are the possessors of an institutionalised competence. We make mistakes, but on the whole we know that it is better not to confound the senses of the two *lawns*, and we might even say that it was an indication of incompetence to do so; and this condemnation might extend from cases in which it seems to be the semantic quality of the text that justifies the rejection, to others in which we tacitly resist an anamorphosis less obviously open to detailed criticism. The institution has a hierarchy, since competence has to be acquired; and so it rejects not only unqualified material that issues from outside its own limits, but also the efforts of catechumens within. This we do when we examine, say, doctoral dissertations – not without disagreement, but with the sense that agreement is always possible, even if it means calling in a third member of the hierarchy to mediate.[4] With these few words I must leave the whole subject of institutionalised competence, though it is worth many more.[5] The important fact is that if we ceased to behave as if it existed we should be quite useless as teachers and quite incapable, save in what Donne calls 'unconcerning things, matters of fact,' of deciding upon the value of contributions to the subject. It is, and we have to believe it, *we* who *know*.

The problems inherent in this situation are complicated by the consideration that there are special cases like Shakespeare. I must omit to consider many possible reasons why this should be so and mention only one: Shakespeare is the focus of an inveterate institutional rivalry. Or, the institution Shakespeare is not coterminous with the institution of professional literary scholarship. This is of course true in different ways and lesser measure of other literary institutions, Burns for example, or Blake, or diminishingly, Wordsworth; but none of these is so solidly founded outside the academy, and in respect of none of them is there so much criticism which has so little to do with *our* sense of what may or may not be usefully said.

Shakespeare has acquired some but not all the characteristic cultural differentiae of a sacred book, and with them has imposed upon his interpreters exceptionally difficult tasks. For these the history of the interpretation of the Bible suggests certain partial parallels. The Roman Catholic Church, for example, has maintained the view that as an institution possessing a valid oral tradition it provides a privileged and authoritative interpretation of Scripture, rather as, I am told, the reading of the Jewish Bible is regulated by the Mishnah. One hothead at the Council of Trent even suggested that the time had passed when it was necessary for anybody to read Scripture at all. But extreme Protestant theology believed that the text, accepted by a grace-illumined mind, was in itself enough; and here the text becomes very 'open,' as, I am told, the text of the Koran is. It is the presence or absence of a *church*, and the hierarchical rigor of that church, that makes the difference. So within the biblical tradition you have an institutional interpretation full of constraints, and anarchically individual interpretations proposed by independent minds assured of grace and of course hating the institution which claims such privilege and authority. The institution will characteristically be concerned with such matters as canon, and with anathematising incompetent, that is, heretical or unorthodox, interpretation. The individuals will characteristically do whatever the spirit moves them to do.

Since Shakespeare is, originally at any rate, an English institution, we may expect a good deal of muddle or compromise; and indeed we find a mixture of interpretative traditions, which could if one had the time or desire to develop the parallel at length, be likened to Roman Catholic, Anglican and all the other Protestant traditions of biblical interpretation down to the extremest forms of antinomianism. Anybody can be directly illuminated by Shakespeare and will claim the right to express his sense of the text.

Consequently we have, in addition to degrees of competence and variations of doctrinal adhesion within the hierarchy, further degrees of antinomian and incorrigible speculation outside it. It may be that a good deal of this lawless speculation derives unconsciously and corruptly from intra-institutional doctrine that has been superannuated, as for instance when entrance examiners are pained to discover the schoolboys think like a Bad Quarto of Bradley. But that is by the way. The real difference between the outside and the inside is marked by the insistence of the outsider that he can say what he likes about Shakespeare and the tacit knowledge of the institution, which he therefore hates, that nothing he says is worth attending to.

We are all familiar with this situation; an obvious but tedious example would be the energetic contempt of all anti-Stratfordians for the academic establishment, and the cruel joy with which they announce in their newsletters that some academic (never one of *us*; usually a stray historian) has expressed some painful doubt about the conventional view. However, I shall briefly illustrate the hostility and lack of communication of which I speak by referring to a book entitled *Othello: Time Enigma and Color Problem*, by Ernest Bloomfield Zeisler, published in Chicago in 1954 in an undated limited edition of two hundred copies. I know nothing of Mr Zeisler, except that he was kind enough to send me a copy of his book. He is clearly not one of *us*, though; and I do not know whether *we* took any notice of his book when it appeared. My purpose is not to examine the argument of the two essays it contains, but merely to draw attention to Mr Zeisler's tone. On the question whether Othello was a black man he takes violent exception to the views of some of our institutional colleagues: 'Mr Coleridge's nonsense is so utterly dishonest and vicious that it must be answered in detail,' he says; and having done that, concludes that Mr Coleridge as an arguer has the 'razor-sharpness of melted butter.' And indeed it must be said that Professor Coleridge was below his best in his comments on this topic. As for Mr Bradley, he is, like all the rest of us, an 'intellectual pygmy' and 'a cerebral castrate.'[6] It has the ring of a Milton castigating his Catholic opponents.

It would serve no purpose to complain to Mr Zeisler that we no longer bother our heads about the views of Coleridge and Bradley on this subject. To him the academy is an institution homogeneous, timeless and infamous. Nor is he alone in so believing, for it is only too obvious that a great many people hypostatise our institution in precisely this way, as a sort of transcendental eunuch. But we took no notice of Mr Zeisler. Institutionalised tacit knowledge assured us that he could be safely ignored, and we no more thought of answering him than the physicists did of responding to Lord Rayleigh's well-formed demonstration 'that a hydrogen atom impinging on a metal wire could transmit to it energies ranging up to a hundred electron volts' – a demonstration which, Polanyi assures us, implied a discovery 'far more revolutionary than the discovery of atomic fission.'[7] In so far as he was one of *them*, Rayleigh ought to have known better; and not to be one of them is to be outside the ranks of the competent.

As I have suggested, the law of tacit exclusion can also operate within the academy, being applied by the more to the less competent. I take, as an instance of this, a totally neglected book called *Caliban: The Missing Link*, published in 1873 by Sir Daniel Wilson, who was a Doctor of Laws and an important professor at Toronto. One could make out a case for this as a book of some importance; so far as I know, it is the first modern reading to attend to Caliban as a Wild Man, relating him to the *homo sylvestris* of Linnaeus, and finding useful parallels in Purchas. The work Wilson began had to be begun all over again, because nobody except Furness, who had a special license to include what all others excluded, paid the slightest attention to Wilson's book.

Why? First because at the time, which was two years before the first edition of Dowden's *Shakespeare: His Mind and Art*, nobody, as they say, wanted to know. Dowden does not mention Wilson, nor does Arthur M. Eastman, author of the latest history of Shakespearian criticism. We do not want to know either, though for the different reason that Wilson has nothing to tell us that we don't know already, having access to later scholarship that superseded him without taking any notice of him.

There is, however, a second and perhaps more interesting reason for institutional inattention. Wilson's research into the Wild Man was done in the service of a critical discourse, an anamorphosis of *The Tempest*, which tacit knowledge instantly rejected; and now we can see why. He had been reading *The Descent of Man*, and Huxley; and it occurred to him that Shakespeare had, by a purely unconscious process, got there first and created in Caliban, the beast endowed with speech, the equivalent of 'the so-called "brute progenitor of man" of our latest school of science.' Assuming that Caliban had at least as much brain as a gorilla, and accepting Huxley's statement that the brain of that animal measures thirty-five cubic inches as against the fifty-five of the human brain, Wilson concludes that 'twenty inches is the whole interval to be bridged over'; though that interval contains a qualitative change. 'As water at two hundred and twelve degrees passes beyond the boiling point into vapour: so at some undetermined degree in the cerebral scale, between thirty-five and fifty-five, the point is reached at which the irrational brute flashes into the living soul.' Intuiting this, Shakespeare created Caliban right, so to speak, on the flash- or boiling-point, and put him on 'an imaginary island in the cainozoic world,' warm and furnished with abundance of suitable food. Darwin chose Borneo, but Shakespeare remembered the travellers' tales and borrowed for his Mediterranean island certain Caribbean features, even endowing his missing link with a name that is an anagram of 'cannibal,' which is the same as 'Carib.' He further gave him certain fishlike qualities because he had a premonition of Darwin on our aquatic origins.

This is the anamorphosis of an infatuated amateur of the science of the seventies. Wilson of course insists that he is discussing an unknowable process, by which the supreme poet could anticipate the supreme biologist; but in fact he is simply fitting the play into a contemporary fashion. The whole thing was tacitly rejected, and for good reason. Now, if we cared to spell it out, we could say why Wilson made such peculiar blunders, and so forfeited the attention some of his inquiries deserved. Despite his reference to Linnaeus, he was incapable of conceiving the Wild Man within a static framework of scientific reference, the only one in which he has a place. The confusion that results from trying to fit the old *homme du bois* into a dynamic evolutionary theory is such that *we* refuse to attend to the attempt; and the assertion that supreme poets can do and can anticipate *everything* is merely to attribute to Shakespeare the omnipossibilism of the heretical individual, which the institution exists to deny.[8]

Henceforth I shall stay with *The Tempest*. The works of Colin Still are probably more familiar, at least by name, than Wilson's, because they were warmly commended by T. S. Eliot and G. Wilson Knight; but in this respect at least *we* regard these distinguished critics as aberrant. Still was convinced that Art resembled the mystery religions not only in the general sense that both provided access to Ultimate Reality, but in the more particular sense that certain very great works of art, notably the Gospels, the *Aeneid* and *The Tempest*, recapitulated with some exactness the ritual of those mysteries. He who would interpret such works therefore must become, in the expression of Aeschylus, *krites enuptiōn*, interpreter of dreams. He must learn the universal language of symbolism, which would give him 'the key to every enigmatic utterance in the sphere of art.' We note in Still a recurring feature of this kind of interpretation, its absolute inclusiveness; not only will it explain everything, but nothing can be explained in any other way. The academy is by comparison genteel, Anglican, and pluralistic.

Like Wilson, Still postulates that Shakespeare could very well have performed his act of recapitulation in entire ignorance of the rites enacted and the texts cited. The court party of *The Tempest* makes a passage through Purgatory, which constitutes the Lesser Initiation; Ferdinand ascends to the Celestial Paradise (the Greater Initiation) and Stephano and his crew undergo the Psychological Fall. Identifications tend to be peremptory: Miranda is Wisdom, and 'if the reader be unconvinced let him ask a Freemason of very high degree (of the rank of Most Wise Sovereign, for example) how far the foregoing argument reflects the more recondite ritual of the Craft. . . .' But explanation also descends to minute particulars. The dogs that are set upon the conspirators have an occult source; even the 'Mountayneeres / Dew-lapped' *must* come from a place identifiable as Dante's Mount of Purgatory and Bacon's Hill of Truth. When Sebastian suggests (II.i.87) that Gonzalo might 'carry this island home in his pocket, and give it his son for an apple,' the reference must be to Avalon, thought to mean paradise as an apple-garden (*aval*, apple, *yn*, island). When Prospero uses the word 'revels' he must mean *orgia*; 'for nowhere else in his works does the Poet use the word "revels" in any but its popular and debased sense, as riotous festivity. He must, therefore, have used it on the present occasion with a special and purer meaning.' There are also occasions, adds Mr Still, when the text seems fatuous, and only to be rescued by 'drastic interpretation,' such as he provides for the foolery about the clothes on the line.[9]

When we reject this interpretation of *The Tempest* we reject some good things, notably some of the detail of the parallel with the *Aeneid*. But we reject it all the same. It is not simply that we can show the detail to be sometimes wrong, though it is so, for example in the passage on the word 'revels,' or trivial, as in the part about the apple; but rather that it is sectarian to the point of desperation. It is perfectly possible to argue for a Tradition, even a Tradition which establishes some affinity between *The Tempest* and the Eleusinian Mysteries, without going overboard in this way (I think this is the point where Eliot and Knight must have exercised their charity). Mr Still does not appear to mention *The Magic Flute* in either of his books, but the existence of that work, its analogues with *The Tempest*, and its undisputed Masonic elements, raise issues *we* should probably regard as worth serious attention; but we should want, I think, something much more 'scientific,' much less dependent on the inexplicable intuitions of Shakespeare. And we should no more ask a Most Wise Sovereign Freemason to interpret Miranda for us than we should ask a Shriner to interpret Stephano.

But whatever we do we shall not accept or even test Mr Still's thesis, or even invite him to explain all that his total explanation appears to exclude. Unless we belong to a particular sect we simply reject him tacitly, with at least as much confidence as Mr Wimsatt exhibited in the matter of the lawns.

Let me, in conclusion, repeat that it is no part of my argument that the institution is infallible. The biologists have their Mendel, we our Whiter. The 'routinisation' of our studies can make it difficult for us, however keenly we feel we need new and perhaps revolutionary departures, to admit the case which challenges our tacit knowledge. Allow me a moment of autobiography. When I began, twenty-seven years ago, to edit *The Tempest* for the Arden series, I looked into Daniel Wilson's book, and, like Mr Brooke in *Middlemarch*, saw that it would not do. I therefore missed his points about Purchas and the Wild Man, and had to go into it all again. When the edition appeared in 1954 it was reviewed with hilarity by the late John Crowe, who remarked that if the pages on Caliban were representative of the new approach to Shakespeare we might as well head straight for the madhouse and give ourselves up. (I quote from memory, having no intention of looking up *that* review.) A little while ago, in 1974, I was reading a new article on the play which began with a brief account of the conventional views it was about to destroy; the author added a footnote to say that these views were usefully summarised in my introduction, access to which he had perhaps obtained in a late edition.

I speak, I assure you, not out of injured merit, having little pride in my insignificant priority. The point is simply that what a highly respected academician thought extremely silly in 1954 had become tediously conventional by 1974. We must not suppose that in judging our exclusions according to our institutionalised and tacit knowledge we are always referring to the same criteria.

Which conducts me to my last paragraph. There are periodic alterations, sometimes sharp enough to be thought of as quasi-revolutionary but more often consequent upon small changes and adjustments, in the ways in which we judge men or discourses to be competent. But it is upon the current basis of that corpus of tacit knowledge, supposed to be held more fully by those in the upper ranks of the hierarchy, that we allow or disallow criticism or interpretation.[10] Obviously if it comes from a position which denies our competence and privilege, as it does more often than usual when Shakespeare is the text, we spend very little time on it. In general we act, and must act, as if omnipossibilism were a heresy. We may say, with Richards, that the language of the text excludes certain interpretations as impossible (which is sometimes clearly the case, but usually clearly the case only when the error is so obvious and trivial as to leave nothing much to discuss); or, perhaps more often, we may reject an anamorphosis as counter-intuitive – the intuition being, whether we are aware of it or not, institutional in character and founded on a probably unformulated theory of competence.

NOTES

1 W. K. Wimsatt, 'Battering the Object,' *Contemporary Criticism*, Stratford-upon-Avon Studies, 12, eds Malcolm Bradbury and David Palmer (London: Arnold, 1970), pp. 75–6.

2 Roland Barthes, *Critique et Vérité* (Paris: Seuil, 1966), pp. 64–5.

3 Michael Polanyi, *The Tacit Dimension* (London: Routledge & Kegan Paul, 1967), pp. 4, 19, 64–5. I have quoted from this short book because Polanyi regards it as providing 'a correct summary' of his position (x). But see also the opening section of *Personal Knowledge*, rev. edn (London: Routledge & Kegan Paul, 1962). Polanyi's theory of 'commitment,' expounded later in *Personal Knowledge*, is specifically Christian, but has a bearing on the personal effort one makes within a scientific institution, or an institution resembling such an institution in some ways, as ours does. One hopes that this remark could truthfully be adapted to our situation: 'While the machinery of scientific institutions severely suppresses some suggested contributions, because they contradict the currently accepted view of things, the same scientific authorities pay their highest homage to ideas which sharply modify these accepted views' (*The Tacit Dimension*, p. 68).

I should add that this point could be made in varying ways by reference to other philosophies of science; see, for example, a fairly recent account of the situation in *Criticism and the Growth of Knowledge*, ed. Imre Lakatos and Alan Musgrave (Cambridge: Cambridge University Press, 1970); and Michel Foucault, *Les mots et les choses* (Paris: Gallimard, 1966) (*The Order of Things*, London: Tavistock Publications, 1970).

4 For succinctness I must here omit to discuss the view that agreement is possible only in the branch of the subject called by the French 'science de la littérature' and by Northrop Frye 'criticism,' as distinct from 'critique' or 'history of taste.'

5 By far the best account of 'competence' in this sense is Jonathan Culler's in *Structuralist Poetics* (London: Routledge & Kegan Paul, 1975), Chapter 6.

6 Zeisler, *Othello*, pp. 54, 56, 60.

7 *The Tacit Dimension*, p. 65.

8 Daniel Wilson, *Caliban: The Missing Link* (London: Macmillan, 1873), pp. xii, 21, 25, 36, 72–3.

9 Still first wrote *Shakespeare's Mystery Play* (London: Cecil Palmer, 1923), and then *The Timeless Theme* (London: Ivor Nicholson and Watson, 1936). The argument of the first book is somewhat

expanded, and placed in the context of a larger theory of art, in the second, which I have therefore quoted. See pp. 19, 173–4, 189, 206.

10 Here again I must omit to consider the formation of warring parties within the institution, the conflicts, as it were, of theologians and canon lawyers. They are of course important, not only for whatever interest the debates have in themselves, but because in some form they do, in the long run, reach the ears of the parish priest (the instructor in the schoolroom) and affect his pastoral work.

CHAPTER 8

INSTITUTIONAL CONTROL OF INTERPRETATION

A very large number of people, of whom I am one, conceive of themselves as interpreters of texts. Whoever expounds a text (no matter at what level) and whoever castigates a text, is an interpreter. And no such person can go about the work of interpretation without some awareness of forces which limit, or try to limit, what he may say, and the ways in which he may say it. They may originate in the past, but will usually be felt as sanctions operated by one's contemporaries (this will be true whether or not one opposes and resents them). There is an organisation of opinion which may either facilitate or inhibit the individual's manner of doing interpretation, which will prescribe what may legitimately be subjected to intensive interpretative scrutiny, and determine whether a particular act of interpretation will be regarded as a success or a failure, be taken into account in licit future interpretation or not. The medium of these pressures and interventions is the institution.

In practice, the institution with which we have to deal is the professional community which interprets secular literature and teaches others to do so. There are better-defined and more despotic institutions, but their existence does not invalidate the present use of the expression. If we wanted to describe its actual social existence we should get involved in a complex account of its concrete manifestations in universities, colleges, associations of higher learning; and if we wanted to define its authority we should have to consider not only its statutory right to confer degrees and the like, but also the subtler forms of authority acquired and exercised by its senior and more gifted members. But we need not at present bother with these details. It can surely be agreed that we are talking about something quite easily identified: a professional community which has authority (not undisputed) to define (or indicate the limits of) a subject; to impose valuations and validate interpretations. Such are its characteristics. It has complex relations with other institutions. In so far as it has, undeniably, a political aspect, it trespasses on the world of power; but of itself, we will agree, it has little power, if by that one means power to bind and loose, to enforce compliance and anathematise deviation. Compared with other institutions, that is, the one we are talking about is a rather weak one. But it has none the less a family resemblance to the others.

Such a community may be described as a self-perpetuating, sempiternal corporation. It is, however unemphatically, however modestly, hierarchical in structure, because its continuance depends on the right of the old to instruct the young; the young submit because there is no other way to the succession. The old, or senior, apply at their discretion certain checks on the competence of those who seek to join, and eventually to replace them. Their right to do this is accompanied by an assumption that they possess a degree of competence, partly tacit, partly a matter of techniques which may be examined and learnt; that one has acquired these latter is of course a claim that can be straightforwardly tested, but the possession of interpretative power, power of divination, is tested only by reference to the tacit knowledge of the seniors, who nevertheless claim, tacitly as a rule, that they can select candidates capable of acquiring these skills, and have the right to certify that they have achieved them. I am describing the world as it is or as we all know it, and am doing so only because its familiarity may have come to conceal from us its mode of operation.

The texts on which members of this institution practise their trade are not secret and the laity has, in principle, full access to them. But although the laity may, unaided or helped only by secondary or sub-institutional instruction (radio talks, Sunday newspapers, reading groups or literary clubs) acquire what in some circumstances might pass for competence, there is a necessary difference between them and persons whom we may think of as licensed practitioners. It is as if the latter were 'in orders'. Their right to practise is indicated by arbitrary signs, not only certificates, robes and titles, but also professional jargons. The activities of such persons, whether diagnostic or exegetical, are privileged, and they have access to senses that do not declare themselves to the laity. Moreover they are subject, in professional matters, to no censure but that of other licensed practitioners acting as a body; the opinion of the laity is of no consequence whatever, a state of affairs which did not exist before the institution now under consideration firmly established itself – as anyone may see by looking with a layman's eye on the prose its members habitually write, and comparing it with the prose of critics who still thought of themselves as writing for an educated general public, for *la cour et la ville*.

However, my concern here is to explore a little further the means by which the institution controls the exegetical activities of its members. Though it does so in part by fairly obvious means – for example, it controls the formation and the subsequent career of its members (who decides whether one is to have one's PhD?) – it has subtler resources, such as *canonical* and *hermeneutic* restrictions, and these are more interesting. By the first of these expressions I mean the determination of what may or ought to be interpreted, and by the second the decision as to whether a particular means of doing so is permissible. Of course canons change, especially in a 'weak' institution; and so do styles of interpretation. How these changes occur is another part of my subject, and a subdivision of that part is the question of heresy.

In Chapter 7 I raised the question, how do we know an interpretation is wrong? We claim this knowledge, obviously; if a student in reading 'my love is fair / As any she belied with false compare' construes 'she' as a personal pronoun and not as a noun we have no compunction about saying he is wrong; though if William Empson said the 'wrong' sense was present, as an instance of one or other (fourth to seventh) type of ambiguity (a 'verbal nuance . . . which gives room for alternative reactions to the same piece of language') most of us would be less ready with our pencils. I. A. Richards, who did so much to encourage liberty of interpretation, has always been exercised as to the moment when this liberty becomes licence; he deplores people who have no sense 'of what is and is not admissible in interpretation', and sees in some of Roman Jakobson's work means by which poetry may be defended against such 'omnipossibilists'. Yet it seems clear that the necessary decisions are rarely if ever arrived at methodically. What happens is rather that the institution requires interpretations to satisfy its tacit knowledge of the permitted range of sense; the requirement operates very simply when the disputed interpretation is the work of a novice, and may be harder or even, in the long run impossible, to apply if the author is known to be competent – one reason why the institutional consensus changes. But there clearly is a sense in which a professional body *knows*; how it does so was a preoccupation of Michael Polanyi's. There is an institutionalised competence, and what it finds unacceptable is incompetent. It does not, as a rule, have to think hard about individual cases – there is no guarantee that this tacit knowledge is infallible; it is founded on the set of assumptions currently available – the paradigm, if you like, or, if you like, the *epistème*, and a revolution may change everything. But the immediate point is simply that it is upon the basis of a corpus of tacit knowledge, shared – with whatever qualifications – by the senior ranks of the hierarchy, that we allow or disallow an interpretation.

There is nothing astonishing about this conclusion, which might even be regarded as trite by members of other institutions no less quarrelsome though possibly more self-conscious than our own. In the psychoanalytic community, we are told, 'the experience of insight results from the construction of a perspective most satisfying to the present communal initiative.'[1] That is, what is found is the sort of thing it is agreed we ought to be looking for. True interpretation is, in fact, what Jürgen Habermas calls it: 'a consensus among partners'.[2] How else shall we judge its truth? Yet we should not altogether omit to mention that the institution also values originality; if there is agreement that some contribution has the force to modify or even transform what was formerly agreed, then that contribution is honoured and may become the staple of a new pattern of consensus. Yet even such rare and revolutionary departures depend upon the consent of the hierarchy.

Of institutions having a primary duty to interpret texts, and to nominate a certain body of texts as deserving or requiring repeated exegesis (interminable exegesis, indeed) the Church is the most exemplary. Self-perpetuating, hierarchical, authoritative, much concerned with questions of canon, and wont, as we are, to distinguish sharply between initiate and uninitiate readings, it is a model we would do well to consider as we attempt to understand our own practice.

It is, of course, difficult to make such brief generalisations stick, and the Church has been prone to fission on precisely the issues I am discussing: authority, hierarchy, canon, initiation, and differential readings. But if it has something to teach us we must do what we can to overcome this difficulty. Let us first consider the canon. The word means 'rod' or 'rule' or 'measure' and we all know, roughly, how it applies to the Old and New Testaments, or to Shakespeare: *Hamlet* belongs to the canon, *The Yorkshire Tragedy* to Apocrypha, *Two Noble Kinsmen* is still among the latter, but many think it should belong to the former. Apocrypha meant 'hidden ones', but came to mean 'spurious ones', and now just means 'uncanonical ones'. The canon possesses an authenticity which the Apocrypha lack. But to say in what that authenticity resided or resides is a very complicated matter.

The canon seems to have begun to crystallise in reaction against an heretical attempt to impose a rigorously restricted list of sacred books on the church of the mid-second century. Marcion rejected the whole of the Old Testament, accepted one gospel (Luke, much reduced) and added ten purged versions of Pauline letters to complete the canon. Marcion's canon may remind us at once of some rigoristic attempts to purge our own. He certainly knew what he wanted. In abolishing the Old Testament he was acting on a belief that its types and prophecies were false. This was a bold way of solving a difficulty of the early Church. The establishment of a narrow canon eliminated, among other awkwardness, the problem of the status of the Old Testament. The first Christians had no scripture except the Old Testament, but as the Law ceased to be of prime importance to them their relation to it grew problematical; rejecting the Gnostic rejection, they instituted a new way of reading it, as a repertory of types prefiguring Christianity. In so doing they virtually destroyed its value as history or as law; it became a set of scattered indications of events it did not itself report. But the correspondences between what was to be the New Testament and the Old were very important, since they were held to validate the Christian version. Marcion thought the Old Testament wrong and wicked, and he accepted the conclusion that Christianity up to his time had been erroneous, the true words of the founder adulterated.[3]

Marcion was certain that he knew what the original tradition was in its purity; he is the first in a long line of protestant reformers who enjoyed the same assurance. The magnitude of the crisis he brought upon the church is well described by Von Campenhausen. And he was for a time very successful. His was the first canon. The counter-offensive had to include the provision of a canon more acceptable to the consensus of the Church. There is much dispute about the criteria employed. The Old Testament was defended, and out of a mass of gospels four were chosen as 'authentic' (the rejected included of course Marcion's). All this took time; and the idea of closing the canon took more time, and was prompted by the threat of another heresy, namely Montanism, which used innumerable apocalyptic books. Thus was the canon achieved; and eventually the habit grew of thinking of it as two books, or two parts of one total, comprehensive book.

Later came further benefits. For at various moments the institution, protecting its text, conferred upon it the virtues of apostolicity, infallibility, inexhaustibility and inspiration. Indeed, it took centuries of scholarly research and dispute to reach the point where the text was believed to possess all these qualities; the canon was not finally closed, even for Roman Catholics, till the Council of Trent, in 1546, when it was also pronounced equally authoritative in all its parts. The Lutheran tradition opposes this doctrine still. It is among Protestant theologians that one notes a tendency at present to re-open the canon – and perhaps admit the Gospel of St Thomas, discovered at Nag Hammadi in 1945.[4]

The brief allusion to the history of the canon is meant simply to demonstrate the nature of the operations conducted by the institution which formulates and protects it, and the close relation between the character of an institution and the needs it satisfies by validating texts and interpretations of them. The desire to have a canon, more or less unchanging, and to protect it against charges of inauthenticity or low value (as the Church protected Hebrews, for example, against Luther) is an aspect of the necessary conservatism of a learned institution. An interesting example of this conservatism is the history of Erasmus's edition of the Greek New Testament, which was for three centuries the *textus receptus*.

Erasmus hardly began the editorial job, even in terms of the manu-
scripts and editorial techniques then available; for some parts of
the book he had no Greek text at all, and himself translated it
from the Latin. His errors were obvious enough, but his successors
dared not alter his text, reprinting the mistakes and putting the
better readings in the notes. So it remained until Lachmann; and
the vast editorial effort which he began still goes on. The institution
had its own sources of truth, and purposes best served by claims
of inerrancy, even in a text that could not (like vernacular translation) seduce the unlearned, or free interpretation from the control
of Tradition held to be more authoritative even than the text itself.

It is obvious that control of interpretation is intimately connected
with the valuations set upon texts. The decision as to canonicity
depends upon a consensus that a book has the requisite qualities,
the determination of which is, in part, a work of interpretation.
And once a work becomes canonical the work of the interpreter
begins again. For example, so long as the institution, assuming
inerrancy, desires to minimise the contradictions and redundancies
of the gospels, a main object of interpretation must be the achievement of harmony – 'the concord of the canonical scriptures,' as
Augustine proclaims it in *The City of God*. There is a very long
lapse of time between the first known 'harmony' and the first
known 'synopsis', made in the nineteenth century under a new
impulse to explain rather than explain away the discrepancies.
They had been noted from the earliest times, and either elided (as
in the *Diatessaron* of Tatian) or discounted (as by Origen and
Augustine). Scrutiny of the gospels never ceased to be intense; but
the attention they got was controlled by the desire of the institution
to justify them as they were and find them harmonious; until, in
the long course of time and under the pressure of changes in the
general culture, a more secular form of attention prevailed.

The acceptance within the institution of the position that there
is no separate discipline of sacred hermeneutics was very slow and
is still incomplete. But one thing is true, whatever the measure of
secularisation achieved: at all stages the interpretation of the scriptures is primarily the task of professionals. The position that they
are openly available to all men, yet in an important sense closed
to everybody except approved institutional interpreters has been
maintained from the beginning (in Mark, 4:11) and is far from
fully eroded. The work of the early interpreters was intended not

only to establish harmonies between canonised texts, but also to elicit senses not available to persons of ordinary perceptions. Interpretation of the Old Testament was required to deal with its peculiar relation to the new established faith, to make it part, as Clement said, of the 'symphony of senses'.[5] Whatever seemed not to suit the institution's requirements had to be glossed into conformity. Gaps which opened between the apparent literal sense and the sense acceptable to doctrine or later-established custom had to be filled by interpretations, usually typological or allegorical. And always there were the secret senses, protected by the institution itself. At first these were oral, part of a tradition for which the institution was responsible; later there might be two texts, one generally available, the other reserved for initiates. And even of the public text there might be private interpretations. The Roman Catholic Church preserved at Trent (and I suppose in theory continues to preserve, though restrictions on Catholic exegetes have been much reduced) the position that it alone has the right, in the light of tradition, to determine interpretation. It was at Trent – in violent reaction against the enemy's bibliocentrism – that the inutility of scripture was seriously proposed; for since scripture was always subject to the superior traditional knowledge of the Church, it could be called redundant and, in the hands of ignorant outsiders, a source of error.

Yet despite the success of Protestants in contesting this institutional position, and despite the availability of the texts to a laity of much increased literacy, the interpretation of the works of the canon continued to be the duty of the clergy. Between the layman reading his Bible and the modern exegete disintegrating the Pauline epistles or performing newly-validated hermeneutic operations – form-criticism, redaction-criticism, structuralist criticism – on the texts, there is as great a gulf as ever. The extent of it can be judged by anybody who looks at a modern gospel commentary written for professionals with one written for laymen – say, the Cambridge commentaries on the Greek New Testament, and the Cambridge commentaries on the New English Bible. The difference is astonishing, and cannot be explained in terms of the relative inaccessibility of the Greek text; the nature of the discussion is wholly altered.

It is clear, then, that there is, in the canonical texts, a reserve of privileged senses which are accessible only to people who in some measure have the kind of training, and are supported by the authority, of the learned institution to which they belong. And even in the most disinterested forms of interpretation – those which depend on historical enquiry or editorial techniques – there is, practically always, some effect from a prior doctrinal commitment. The practitioners believe, that is, in the religion whose doctors have instructed them in scholarship. This is not in the least surprising, but its obviousness ought not to prevent our taking it into account. It is a very important aspect of the sociology of interpretation. There are senses beyond the literal; but to divine them one needs to know where they are, how they relate to doctrine more broadly defined, and how it is permissible to attain them. Changes occur, certainly; a very radical change began in the late eighteenth century, and we have still not seen the last effects of it. For though they occur, they are slow and complicated; and they are attended by comparable changes in the institution itself, some of them signalled by public announcement and demonstration, as in Vatican II, some of them less obvious. A neat instance of the relation between the desires of the institution and the kinds of interpretation undertaken is this: after Leo XIII proposed the philosophy of St Thomas Aquinas as a subject of neglected importance, there was a neo-scholastic revival. After Vatican II Catholic scholars acquired a new freedom in exegesis; disciplinary threats removed or diminished, they were able to do the kind of speculative research and commentary that had been largely forbidden them, so that modern biblical scholarship had been overwhelmingly non-Catholic. Of course we should remember that changes in different parts of the institution occur at very different speeds; the new liberty of Catholic scholarship is one thing; the fact that there are in the modern world many fundamentalisms, some merely popular but others belonging to highly organised institutions with control over interpretation, is another.

To labour the matter no further, let me turn to the literary institution and its canon. The points of comparison are that like its senior, though much less effectively, it controls the choice of canonical texts, limits their interpretation, and attends to the training of those who will inherit the presumption of institutional competence by which these sanctions are applied.

Can one really speak of a canon of literary-academic studies? It has perhaps grown a little more difficult to do so, but I think the answer is still yes. The only serious attempt at a description of its formation is, so far as I know, the sixteen-page essay by E. R. Curtius in his *European Literature in the Latin Middle Ages*.[6] Curtius shows that the ecclesiastical canon grew in importance, not only as a measure of the sacred writings, but also in the liturgical and juristic activities of the institution. So there was a canon of Fathers, a canon of Doctors; the notion that there was a set scheme for everything took hold. The medieval schools evolved a blend of pagan and Christian authors which also became canonical. It changed between the Middle Ages and the Renaissance, and it has changed again since then. The Renaissance also saw the first vernacular canon, which was Italian; other vernaculars followed suit, the French in the seventeenth, the English in the eighteenth centuries. I suppose we could say that the American canon is a formation of the present century. Curtius is somewhat impatient with these nationalistic canon-formations, and wants a canon of world literature which will put an end to such local conceptions.

The formation of a secular world canon is, however, outside the scope of existing institutions; the success of 'comparative literature' in the academic world has been real but limited, partly because it does not work easily within the bureaucratic systems that give force to institutional decisions. The interest of Curtius's valuable and learned but inconclusive essay lies in his understanding of the fact that the relation between a canon and the historical situation of the institution which establishes it is close and complex; and he gives some support to the view that the formation and control of the secular canon we are now considering are historically related as well as analogous to the forces that have formed and monitored the ecclesiastical canons.

Of course we must not look, in an institution which lacks formal creeds and has no conceivable right to discipline a laity, for anything resembling that ecclesiastical rigour of which Trent is the image. The canon we are now discussing will necessarily be a more shadowy affair, even more subject to dispute than the ecclesiastic. The contenders for inclusion, and the apocrypha, will be more numerous, and it is impossible for us to settle the question by burning either the books or those who support their claim to inclusion.

Our institution is relatively new, and it is not so long since the question of the canon was simpler. It was defined, in a manner familiar to us from ecclesiastical history, by attacks upon it, which usually included moves to replace some member of the canon with another brought in from outside it. When did Donne become canonical? With Grierson's edition? Not quite; probably only with Eliot's essay of 1921, or even later, when that essay (itself a very late move in a campaign which had been going on intermittently for the best part of a century) gained academic support. Eliot was very much a canonist; the argument of 'Tradition and the Individual Talent' presupposes a canon, though one to which works can be added in a timeless mix, the new affecting the sense of the old, much as the New Testament altered the sense of the Old.

As everybody knows, the accession of Donne was the cause of major alterations in the canon, or at any rate of attempts to change it radically. For example, the doctrinal changes which enabled that accession also implied a new valuation or even the extrusion of Milton, not to speak of the rewriting of the history of poetry in accordance with the law of the Dissociation of Sensibility. I myself was taught by enthusiasts who believed that Milton had been 'dislodged', to use Dr Leavis's celebrated word for it. The Chinese Wall had been outflanked. This movement began outside the academy, but was taken up within it. In the long run Milton stayed in; but great changes in the method of interpreting his texts became necessary, as anybody can see who compares the Miltonists of the early part of the century with those now dominant – say M. Y. Hughes with Stanley Fish, or Walter Raleigh with Christopher Ricks, whose book on Milton is indeed a splendid example of the ways in which a need to defend a canonical author may call forth new critical and exegetical resources. Meanwhile the motives of the anti-Miltonists were scrutinised with hostility.

Sociologists of religion suggest that institutions react, broadly, in two ways to threats from outside. Either they 'legitimate' the new doctrine or text (the reception of Donne) or they 'nihilate' it (the defeat of the attempt to dislodge Milton). In our institution the first of these is the more usual course, partly because of a relative lack of power, partly because of a looseness of organisation, and partly because the tradition in which we work is predominantly Protestant. There is a measure of tolerance in all that we do. What we value most in work submitted to us by those who would like to join us is an originality that remains close to the consensual norms. Moreover we are, in general, inclined to pluralism and none too systematic, as scholars who take method seriously are often willing to tell us. And yet there is some rigour somewhere in the institution.

If you look at any recent MLA December programme you will see what looks like total licence in regard to canon, or, to put that more liberally, an openness to innovation, a willingness to respond to legitimate pressures from the (political) world outside. There are sessions on Black literature, on neglected women writers, and the like; there are also discussions of relatively avant-garde critical and theoretical movements which have certainly not won their appeal to the senior consensus. On the other hand, the MLA Bibliography shows a solid concentration of interpretative effort on the canonical figures.[7] One concludes that here, as with the national and regional variations of canon that everybody is aware of, we have evidence of the ability of the institution to control marginal innovation and unrest. A few years ago the MLA suffered something that looked for a moment like a revolution; but it was only a saturnalian interlude (appropriate to the season of their meeting), an episode of Misrule, tolerated because in the end reinforcing the stability of the institution. The boy bishops had their day, and the more usual, more authentically prelatical figures have resumed their places. We can tolerate even those who believe the institution should be destroyed. As Thoreau remarked, 'They speak of moving society but have no resting place without it.'

I have digressed from the question of our canon to speak of the forces within the institution which operate to change it, usually slowly. Over a period we can see marked differences. When I was a student nobody taught Dickens; we can trace his acceptance (in England, anyway) by the stages of Dr Leavis's slow change of mind (he is the Marcion of the canon, unless that role is reserved for Yvor Winters). Few of my teachers even mentioned George Eliot. Blake hovered on the canonical margin, Joyce was still an outsider, though we read him. At Oxford all these problems were simplified somewhat by the decree that studiable, judgeable literature came to an end in 1830; nothing after that was licenced for exegesis.

How do changes in the canon occur? They usually depend on the penetration of the academy by enthusiastic movements from without. This is not always so; for example, there seems to be in progress at the moment an academic revaluation of early American literature; Cotton Mather is suddenly full of interest, Charles

Brockden Brown is readable and capable of interpretation. But however the changes originate, there is still a rule which says that the institution must validate texts before they are licensed for professional exegesis. After that there seems to be no limit, the exegetical progress is interminable. *Ulysses* is a good instance of this; a more remarkable one is Melville, ignored for sixty years or more and now fully canonical and endlessly explicated. George Eliot is another interesting case. The laity had probably gone on reading her, as it went on reading Dickens; but only lately, in my own time, has she become the subject of an apparently infinite series of interpretations, which are of quite a different kind from those which for years served as standard, say those of Leslie Stephen and Henry James.

Licensed for exegesis: such is the seal we place upon our canonical works. How do we license the exegesis itself? The intrusion of new work into the canon usually involves some change in the common wisdom of the institution as to permissible hermeneutic procedures. Thus the admission to American faculties of New Critics from outside the academy was a complex phenomenon, involving a quasi-political victory over the older philologists, a change in the canon (acceptance of Donne, Eliot, etc.) and a new hermeneutic, popularised by Brooks and Warren, and formalised by Wimsatt. The more evangelical success of Leavis resulted in the penetration of the English system of literary education by his followers; at the pastoral level they are still, probably, the most powerful teachers of reading in the country, and their moralistic contempt for non-believers – the unargued certitudes of the conventicle, the easy sneers of the epigoni – still makes its lamentable contribution to the tone of English literary debate. They hold to a rigorous canon (the line of wit, the great tradition, the wheelwright's shop) into which, from time to time, there are furtive insertions (Dickens, Tolstoi), uneasy candidatures (Emily Brontë), apocryphal appendices (L. H. Myers, Ronald Bottrall, Hawthorne).

From the institutional point of view the New Criticism and *Scrutiny* were (and still are) pretty successful heresies. They revised the canon and they changed the methods. The people initiated into reading by the institution began to read differently. Other attempts to alter canon and doctrine – those of Winters, Pound, James, Reeves – had markedly less success. But we are now observing the progress of what may be more radical heresy. Unlike the theologians, we are not good at finding distinctive names for hermeneutic fashions; this is another New Criticism, or *nouvelle critique*, though it has moved a long way on from the French innovations of the 1960s. The revival of Russian Formalism, the development of a new semiology, a new Marxism, a new psychoanalysis, a new post-Heideggerian anti-metaphysics, with new forms of cultural history – all the developments we associate with such names as Barthes, Lacan, Derrida, Foucault – have had some success within the institution, and may have more. A certain ideological fervour accompanies these manifestations, and they undoubtedly alter the shape of institutional interests in interpretation. Indeed they are avowedly subversive. They alter the limits of the subject, propose new views of history, institutions and meaning. This is not the place to enter into discussion of the validity of such new doctrine; I should, to keep within the boundaries of my topic, merely ask how we may expect the institution to contain or control it.

The fact that interpretation, under these new auspices, has a different sociology is not, in the end, subversive at all; it was probably necessary to move away from the aesthetic or iconic mode in which we spent a generation, and to view literary texts as texts among texts, all perhaps requiring 'deconstructive' interpretation to give them another span of life. Certain kinds of literature, what the Germans call *Kleinliteratur*, or 'trivial literature', and also film, are accommodated in a sort of deuterocanonical sense. The institution, by hierarchical consensus, will try to protect itself against barbarism, but it will do so by control of appointments and promotions more than by working on the canon. For there is a risk that new hermeneutic procedures can be taken up by people interested only in new procedures, methodological mimics whose gestures seem empty, and who care nothing for any canon. They will have to be controlled in some other way. New modes of interpretation, seriously practised, are less of a problem than 'wild' practitioners, there is always an underlying continuity between them and the traditional modes.

It would be wrong to press too far the analogy between the institution of literary and critical scholarship, and ecclesiastic and scientific institutions. As we have seen, the scientists may not even bother to examine notions that are institutionally counter-intuitive; a demonstration that the average gestation period of mammals is an integer multiple of the number π is ignored or treated as a joke. But this example comes from the annals of an institution far more sure of itself than ours – far more so indeed than the Church, which, in its present uncertainties, lets all manner of things through the gate that would have been firmly dismissed a generation ago. Control over interpretation varies with the social stability of the institution. On the other hand, thousands of relatively unimportant findings, made within the confines of what Kuhn calls 'normal science', are tested and approved, though not greatly applauded. In between are the works, very rare, which, in Polanyi's words, 'sharply modify accepted views' yet are themselves accepted; to such works the authorities 'pay their highest homage.'[8] The men who make them – Einstein, Dirac, Gödel – have a security of fame beyond the dreams of critics, whether secular or biblical.

The implication must be that the scientific institution, though it admires change more than anything, monitors it with very sophisticated machinery; judgments of the value of proposed changes must depend on an accumulation of knowledge and experience that has been so thoroughly learned that its application is almost automatic. Our practices are less decisive; they must be, for the art of interpretation is not a natural science. Yet they too depend upon acquired skills and assumptions. It is assumed that the senior members of the institution impart to their juniors not only information but the power and authority to make valuations, to say that one thing is trash, or that another is sound; finally, that some proposed major change of focus is acceptable. It is true that this assumption is subject to question; for example, it was by asking discriminating questions about it that Northrop Frye arrived at his negative theory of value, his view that what can be taught is literary taxonomy. But most of us suppose that we are doing more than that (if indeed we are doing that at all). And in practice we do indeed do more than that. We wean candidates from the habit of literal reading. Like the masters who reserved secret senses in the second century, we are in the business of conducting readers out of the sphere of the manifest. Our institutional readings are not those of the outsiders, so much is self-evident; though it is only when we see some intelligent non-professional confronted by a critical essay from our side of the fence that we see how esoteric we are. And in this respect we have to think of ourselves as exponents of various kinds of secondary interpretation – spiritual understandings, as it were, compared with carnal, and available only to those who, in second-century terms, have circumcised ears, that is, are trained by us.

And here we may reflect on the resemblance between ours and the psychoanalytical practice. Our concern, when we depart from the merely descriptive, is with latent sense. We learn, and teach others, to be alert to condensation and displacement in the text; we develop a strong taste for, and a power to divine, overdeterminations. That is why my reading of a Conrad novel, say, is different from an undergraduate's, though his will grow more like mine; and even more different from a layman's. The layman, we like to think, sees without perceiving, hears without understanding. He who has ears to hear, let him hear.

The continuity of the newest criticism with earlier forms of interpretation licenced by the establishment testifies to the perpetuity of such assumptions. Poets may have a third eye, analysts a third ear, exegetes a circumcised ear; these additional or purified organs are figures for the divinatory skills acquired within institutions. The deconstruction of a text is a bold figure for what exegetes *de métier* have always claimed the right to do. In the early enthusiastic stage the techniques employed may seem overbold, and attract the censure of the hierarchy – this is what happened to Empson, and to the anti-historical element of the New Criticism. But in the end the fate so much dreaded by the newest critics, who are conscious enough of history and of the cultural forces of inertia, will overtake the enthusiasts; they will be 'recuperated' or, if they are not, they will be nihilated. I do not offer an opinion as to whether this is right or just, but merely argue that when the charismatic becomes institutional some 'routinisation' is bound to occur; and if it does not become institutional it falls into neglect. As it has, in not too fanciful a sense, been institutional all along, and as nobody outside the institution has much chance of understanding it, I do not think there is much doubt about the outcome. How the experience will alter the future 'tacit knowledge' of the institution it is impossible to guess.

I wonder whether some among my hearers, the younger perhaps, may not find what I have said a little cynical and gloomy. I believe that institutions confer value and privilege upon texts, and licence modes of interpretation; and that qualification for senior membership of such institutions implies acceptance, not total of course, of this state of affairs. And I suppose one might well look upon this as an unhappy situation. Such institutions as ours do reflect the larger society which they somehow serve, and it may be an unjust society. But how else shall we protect the latent sense? The mysteries, said Clement, were not proclaimed openly, 'in such a way that any listener could understand them'; they were spoken in parables, riddles, requiring exegesis.[9] And exegesis has its rules, on the foundation of which has been built the whole structure of modern hermeneutics. It is by recognising the tacit authority of the institution that we achieve the measure of liberty we have in interpreting. It is a price to pay, but it purchases an incalculable boon; and for my own part I cannot bring myself to say that my conclusions concerning the power of the institution to validate texts and control interpretation are sad ones. They might even be a reason for moderate rejoicing.

NOTES

1 David Bleich, 'The Logic of Interpretation', *Genre* 10 (Fall, 1977), p. 384.
2 *Knowledge and Human Interests* (1968) translated by Jeremy J. Shapiro, 1972, p. 193. This remark is not inconsistent with the view of Habermas (*Knowledge and Human Interests*, p. 175) that 'the hermeneutical art remains tied to "personal virtuosity" to a greater measure than does the mastery of operations of measurement'.
3 See Hans von Campenhausen, *The Formation of the Christian Bible* (1972) trans. J. A. Baker, pp. 147 ff.
4 See David L. Dungan, 'The New Testament Canon in Recent Study', *Interpretation*, 29 (1975), pp. 339–51; Albert C. Sundberg, 'The Bible Canon and the Christian Doctrine of Inspiration', *Interpretation* 29 (1975), pp. 352–71.
5 Quoted by Von Campenhausen, p. 304.
6 Translated by Willard R. Trask, 1963 [1953], pp. 256 ff.
7 I owe this observation to a remark in conversation by E. D. Hirsch.
8 Michael Polanyi, *The Tacit Dimension*, 1967, p. 68. The example of the paper on gestation periods is also from Polanyi, p. 64.
9 Von Campenhausen, p. 303.

CHAPTER 9

INSTANCES OF INTERPRETATION: DEATH AND SURVIVAL

Some, though not all, interpretations die, which is why we are always having to make new ones. Narratives keep better, though they are themselves interpretations, and so must vary. I shall discuss two examples of stories which vary and persist and carry a changing freight of interpretation. Both are from the Gospels.

The first is the Temptation in the Wilderness. It is told in the three synoptic Gospels but not in John; there its place in the sequence is taken by the first miracle at Cana and the Cleansing of the Temple. The space between the Baptism and the beginning of Jesus's ministry is an important one, and Matthew, Mark, and Luke agree as to how it should be filled; but they differ considerably in the manner and detail of their filling it. Mark is brief: 'The spirit immediately drove him out into the wilderness. And he was in the wilderness forty days, tempted by Satan; and he was with the wild beasts.' He then hurries into the main narrative, with the arrest of John the Baptist and the beginning of the Galilean ministry.

Matthew is more extensive. After forty days in the wilderness, Jesus is tempted by the devil. First he is invited to turn stones into bread. He declines, with a quotation from Deuteronomy: 'Man shall not live by bread alone. . . .' Secondly, the devil sets him on a pinnacle of the Temple and suggests that he throw himself down, reminding him of the Psalmist's promise: 'he will give his angels charge of you . . . on their hands they will bear you up, least you strike your foot against a stone.' Jesus counters with another text from Deuteronomy: 'You shall not tempt the Lord your God.' The third and final temptation, in Matthew's order, takes place on a high mountain. Offered the kingdoms of the world and their glory, Jesus again declines, once more citing Deuteronomy: 'You shall worship the Lord your God and him only shall you serve.' Then the devil leaves him, and angels minister to him.

Luke also specifies three temptations, but with differences. He spreads them over the forty days instead of putting them together at the end. More important, he changes the order of the second and third, so that the temptation of the kingdoms precedes that of the pinnacle. Luke does not mention the service of the angels, but he says more than Matthew about the devil's departure from the scene: 'when the devil had ended every temptation, he departed from him until an opportune time' (so runs the Revised Standard Version; the New English prefers 'biding his time,' and the idea of the original Greek is that there is to be, at some important moment in the future, another contest, another trial or testing).

Of the three versions Mark's is obviously, in one sense, the simplest – hardly a narrative at all; yet it is also the most enigmatic because it is inexplicit and inarticulate. There are many guesses at his intention. Why does he say 'drove' (the original Greek word is even more forceful)? Are the wild beasts hostile, or are they subject to Jesus, as the beasts of Eden were to Adam? Is the wilderness here to be thought of as an abode of demons, or as the place from which the Messiah will come, or as both? And so forth. All that can be said with certainty is that Mark's Temptation, placed between the Baptism, with its announcement that Jesus is the Son of God, and the beginning of his mature work or quest, stands for some kind of initiation, some *rite de passage*. And some commentators speak, as commentators will, of a lost myth or a ritual here crudely or obscurely recalled.

Mark, we know, has a taste for mystery – he alone uses that word as a synonym for 'parable.' With Matthew we are conscious of moving out of that ambience; but we shall see that his way of filling out the story creates interpretative problems of another, though perhaps a more familiar kind: they resemble those that may confront us in other *narratives*. Of course we aren't to think of Matthew as given to free fictive invention. There were certain constraints upon – or perhaps they were aids to – his imagination. This narrative, like others in his Gospel, is governed by a previously existing one. For Matthew understands story and history in this way: what may be said to happen now must comply with what has already happened, and significantly, happened, with an earlier and divinely sanctioned narrative. For him the truth of fiction always depends on its being an interpretation, an updating.

As we've seen, all three replies made by Matthew's Jesus were direct quotations from Deuteronomy. One reason why they were appropriately so is that Matthew's Jesus is the New Israel. The first Israel was tempted in the wilderness, so the second must be tried or tempted in the same way. The three replies relate to the testing of Israel by his father, God. The scene of the original temptation was a desert place named Temptation, or Testing, and we may suppose that the second Israel was tried at the same place, in the same allegorised geography. This time God does not do the testing himself, but uses Satan as his agent; the precedent here was the Book of Job. Otherwise the tempting of Jesus is rather precisely founded upon that of Israel in the wilderness. Of course such a testing must be one-sided. A covenant is to be established, and the father must test the son, but there could be no reciprocal testing, for that would defeat the object of the trial, which is 'to humble you, and to prove you,' and 'to know what was in your heart, whether you would keep his commandments or no,' as Deuteronomy explains.

Given this parallel between Israel and Jesus, other features of Matthew's narrative may be seen to be relevant to the theme of the test. The nature of history and of providence is such that the establishment of this new covenant will follow the pattern of the establishment of the old one. The wilderness setting, the view of the kingdoms from the mountain top, the length of the ordeal – forty days – and the angelic service, can all be thus explained: Moses had such a view, forty was the number of years spent by Israel in the wilderness, and the number of days Moses and Elijah fasted. The service of the angels recalls manna. This is how Matthew invented. To invent is to find, in the light of the way things must be.

As for Luke, we might say quite simply that he thought it a narrative improvement to change the order and place the most violent of the temptations, the temptation of the pinnacle, last.

With the same instinct he forged a link between this episode and the longer story in which it is embedded; this he did by saying that the ordeal of the test is related to a more decisive encounter that must follow in due season. Thus he planted a narrative enigma to be solved later in the sequence, a familiar device of the storyteller; and he neatly avoided the suggestion of closure, of sealing the episode off, that was given by Matthew's angelic service. Of course, in doing so he blurred Matthew's clear typological parallelism. His story obeys different structural rules. In fact Luke was less interested in this typological kind of narration than Matthew; if that is where one's interests lie. Matthew's is certainly the better order.

However they differ from each other, Matthew and Luke have it in common that unlike Mark they wrote formed, articulated narratives, and sought in varying ways to relate this episode to the larger structure in which it appears. Mark's beasts do not belong to the theme of testing as they understand it, so they are dropped. In describing three temptations they choose, as has often been said, a number associated with religious mysteries; but it is also a number immemorially associated with the folktales of our tradition. The evangelists often observed this 'rule of three'; it is a stock way of increasing narrative tension, and it also implies a sort of totality. Two sisters fail; the third, young and oppressed, succeeds. Two brothers blunder, but the third and youngest completes the quest. Three travellers see a wounded man in a ditch, but only the third stops, and he is an outsider. The owner of the vineyard sends three emissaries to the Wicked Husbandmen, and the third, his only son, is killed. Peter's denial of his master is threefold and therefore total. So we may say that the pattern recurs in biblical narrative whether it is parabolic or 'historical'; though it is fair to add that Mark bothers less about it than the others.

All narrative (and especially when it has this folktale character) possesses, or may have read into it, some quality of parable. Augustine would not have called the Desert Feedings parables, but he allegorises them just as he does the story of the Good Samaritan. Modern historical discourse tries to distinguish itself sharply from the kind of narrative that is susceptible of such reading, but it cannot ever quite do so (especially since Freud); and there are of course varieties of modern narrative – Kafka's, most obviously – where a blurring of the types is essential to the effect. This is certainly true of New Testament narrative, which is why the narrative orders conferred by Matthew and Luke on the topic Mark left as a brief, inarticulate myth create interpretative possibilities of a different kind from his. They write neither myth nor history, and Origen noticed this when he declared that there is no mountain top from which you can see all the kingdoms of the world, so that this part of the story at least invites allegorical interpretation.

The invitation to interpret, once issued, is never revoked, though it is never unconditional. Broadly speaking, two forces control its history. Texts certified as canonical by a competent institution are regularly credited with literal inspiration and inexhaustible meaning; but the same institution that establishes the canon also controls its interpretation and issues more or less powerful hermeneutical fiats and restrictions. Liberty of interpretation accordingly varies through time and from place to place. The freedom of Alexandrian patristic allegory was bitterly opposed by the scholars of Antioch, for whom Paul was the only authentic model for allegorists, and for whom history was more important than Alexandrian fantasy. Over the last two centuries the Antiochan view has on the whole prevailed; the tradition is historicist, seeking to discover what was originally intended, and how the first readers understood the texts. But however stoutly the principle of the 'single correct interpretation' may be defended, few interpreters now actually behave as if this interpretation will ever be found, and of late there has been a curious peripeteia, for strict historical enquiry has persuaded many scholars that the process of imaginative reconstruction began with the evangelists themselves, so that the historian is compelled to study not a definitively historical document, but an interpretation dependent on another interpretation which has itself no firm historical status. Thus Matthew, writing in the manner of a learned first-century scribe, would assume that his account of the testing of Jesus must adapt existing accounts of the first testing of Israel; he would update Deuteronomy and change it, so that the second initiate passed the test which the earlier one had failed. The true old story provided the materials for a true new one; otherwise the new one simply would not be true.

That is why Matthew placed the mountain-top temptation third. He was, perhaps, thinking of the Jewish *shema*, which is supposed to be recited daily by all male Jews. It contains a triple commandment, to love God with one's heart, soul, and might. The pinnacle temptation related to loving with one's soul, which implied a readiness to give up one's life. The third entails a rejection of the world with one's whole mind and strength. When Moses saw the kingdoms from a mountain top (such places were associated with idolatry), what he surveyed, according to the rabbis, was *mamón* – the world, its riches, glory, and power. To worship Mammon is to be idolatrous, and that temptation must be resisted with all one's might. So Matthew (it is said) puts the temptations in his order because he wants to reconcile the triple scheme of the narrative with the triple scheme of the *shema*.

Luke, on the other hand, seems indifferent to this reconciliation. (Elsewhere, in the debate on the Great Commandment, he gives the three elements of the *shema* prayer in a different order.) He seems to have had something quite different in mind. As we've seen, he further reduces the typological interest by omitting the service of the angels. Instead – and this is a very important difference – he makes explicit what Matthew merely leaves us to infer: the *totality* of the temptations. He thus gives the episode an *exemplary* force that powerfully affected later interpretation of the story. He also emphasises the connection of this with the greater testing that is to come. Thus he recapitulates the myth of an earlier and partial defeat of the demonic powers which in time will be completed by a total victory.

The priority of Matthew over the other Gospels, which was more or less taken for granted from early times till about a century ago, ensured that Matthew's order was the favourite of the commentators; but Luke's insistence on the totality of the experience was not neglected. It had the powerful support of the Epistle to the Hebrews, which maintains that the Son of God was tempted in all things, not only for the sake of a better covenant and the cancellation of Israel's former failure, but so that he might afford succour, and an example, to his tempted followers.

So Matthew and Luke offer, at the very outset, different interpretations of the story, each with its own theological, historical, and narrative shape. Of course propositions of that kind themselves fall under the rule that they are likely to be distorted by temporal distance; but at least they take account of the fact that stories survive interpretations and become elements in different discourses. The history of the interpretation of this episode is naturally as various as it was in the beginning. Some early commentators stress the typological interest, others the exemplary. Gnostics saw the narrative as an account of the contest with evil demons that assailed the newly baptized, and invented their own initiation rituals to match. Irenaeus stresses the point that the triumph of Jesus reverses the defeat of Adam, and the importance of the Temptation as a preparation for the Passion. Tertullian affirms that Jesus here complies with two types, Adam and Israel in the wilderness. Origen makes the passage the basis of a hermeneutical principle, as we have seen, but also reads it in the light of Hebrews. He regards it as the first important victory, to be completed by the Passion and Resurrection, and (most interestingly) he links it with John's story of the Cana miracle and Jesus's saying, on that occasion, 'My hour is not yet come.' Much that Origen said was remembered, and persists in the tradition to this day.

Yet if some interpretations are persistent, others are forgotten. So far as I can discover, the early Fathers say nothing about Matthew and the *shema*. The story survives, but its original interpretative freight may at any time be unloaded into oblivion. The tradition preserves some interpretations, loses others, and acquires new ones instead. We are always having to explain not the story, but why it counts. Of course one reason is that it has always been the vehicle of urgent but mortal interpretations.

We noticed Origen as an early inventor of hermeneutic rules, and also the historicism of Antioch. To make rules is the function of interpretative institutions. But interpretation may continue outside their immediate scope, for example in poetry. Canonisation may restrict clerical freedom, but poets continue the more inventive tradition of the apocryphal gospels. They rewrite stories, as the evangelists did and as the exegete must not. They place them in new contexts of story, perhaps embedding them in the machinery of pagan epic, or making them fit other genres valued at the time. Interpretation by poems began in antiquity and has hardly stopped since; the nineteenth century offers distinguished examples, and they are not lacking in our own time. In the seventeenth century there was a clash between biblical topics and classical kinds, and new varieties of religious poetry came out of the argument, but it is probably true to say that none of it is now much read except for Milton's. His *Paradise Regain'd* (1671) is a poem about the Temptation. It was long thought (though not by Milton) to be an anticlimax after *Paradise Lost*, but of late we have been learning more about how to read it.

Milton was aware of the existing interpretative tradition, which he wanted to preserve in a new kind of discourse; he took Job as his model for 'brief epic' and within the generic context thus established assumed the right to do rather as the evangelists them-selves had done, and give the old story new detail and frames of reference. He departs from custom in preferring Luke's order of temptations; Luke's 'every temptation,' and his allusion to a future conflict, are important to Milton, though he keeps whatever he chooses of Matthew's account, including the angelic service. He rewrites freely, and attributes long apocryphal speeches to Jesus and Satan. He makes a bow to the canonical first temptation, but prefers in its place an elaborate Satanic banquet, a table set in the wilderness, appealing to all the senses. Yet despite this freedom of treatment, Milton is firmly in a tradition continuous with that in which the evangelists themselves were working. As they made the first Temptation the foundation of the second, so he (well aware of that relationship) transferred both stories to an appropriate later context, which included interests remote from those of the original writers – a later theology, a concern for the poetry and the philo-sophy of a pagan world. These last were part of what, in the totality of rejection, must be rejected; but it seemed that they ought nevertheless to be considered.

The advantage of Luke's scheme to Milton is manifest, but the preference naturally entailed the loss of Matthew's triple scheme; however, if stories survive there need be no lack of interpretations, and reasons for there being three temptations are never far to seek. Modern commentators on Milton have found plenty more, most of them mortal. For example, we have had to unearth a scheme Milton probably borrowed from Spenser, whereby another triple scheme is imposed on the existing one: the banquet represents sensual temptation, the power of Rome and Parthia temptations of the active life, the philosophy and poetry of Greece those of the contemplative, specified here as the temptation of forbidden know-ledge. (Spenser had worked to a similar design in cantos vi and vii of *The Faerie Queene*, Book II, and his Mammon may somehow reflect a knowledge of the rabbinical tradition that included not only money but all other forms of earthly power in the temptation of *Mamón*. Certainly his Guyon, having faithfully imitated Christ in his rejection of all the temptations, is ministered to by angels at the end of his ordeal.)

So Milton uses a good measure of interpretative freedom, but still he preserves, in this new discourse, such elements of the tradition as satisfied him. There is continuity as well as novelty; that is the way with interpretative traditions. Above all, Milton sets his story of the Temptation firmly in the Lucan scheme of the rest of the hero's life. His Jesus is being tested, undergoing initiation. God says he will 'exercise' his son in the wilderness:

> There shall he first lay down the rudiments
> Of his great warfare, ere I send him forth
> To conquer sin and death, the two grand foes
> By humiliation and strong sufferance . . .

When he has overcome all the temptations, Jesus will proceed to 'the great work before him set.' That, of course is Luke's second, decisive encounter. In a sense, Milton's poem is an elaborate gloss on Luke's word 'all' (*panta*). The exegetical tradition handed him this reading, but he expanded it – he wanted to make even plainer what it means to say that the Christian must resist all temptation, and he does it by specifying the testing in all its variety, and by demonstrating that the heroism of renunciation is superior to that of the active Roman heroes, and even to the contemplative Greek heroes. By choosing Luke's order he was able to make the violent final test sum up all the others: in refusing to test the God who is testing him, Jesus, invited to act with conventional heroism by jumping, acts more heroically by simply standing still.

> Tempt not the Lord thy God, he said, and stood.

Above all we should remember that all these new glosses and explanations subjoin the old tale of the triple test. Milton can put more in – he can draw upon the Old Testament, like Matthew, but unlike Matthew he also knows the New Testament, and a great deal more besides – centuries of commentary, much of it typological in character, new ethical formulations, the whole non-Christian classical tradition, the work of sage and of serious poets like Spenser. Yet vast as are the differences in culture and circumstance, his poem still depends, like Matthew's, on a story, the story of the triple test. So must all modern interpretations, however learned and historical.

My second narrative, which is that of the Entry into Jerusalem ('Palm Sunday'), should enable me to make a rather different point. Most of us could give an account of it from memory; but which of us – experts apart – could distinguish offhand between the four versions, or say whether one more than the rest informs our casual recollection? In fact that honour probably goes to John, to whom we owe the whole notion of Holy Week. He alone mentions palms – Mark and Matthew have branches merely, and Luke has no vegetation at all. There are indeed many discrepancies in these four brief narratives, but in our memories we mix them up into a paste, just as we do with the two Birth narratives. Of course it is true that we often favour one over another, perhaps because it is in some detail more vivid, or perhaps because it is continually re-peated in church. Only Matthew has 'Hosanna to the son of Dav-id,' and he alone explicitly connects the story of the ass's colt (or, as he puts it, the ass and the colt) with a particular prophecy, though Mark seems to have known about it, and John introduces an interesting narrative complication by telling us that the disciples didn't get the prophetic point until thinking back on the event after the Resurrection. John alone identifies the accompanying crowd with the people who witnessed the raising of Lazarus or wanted to see him. And so on.

Yet from these discrepant discourses we infer without difficulty a single fable. Our desire to do so is apparently stronger than any anxiety we may feel about the failure of the narratives to confirm one another. This may seem a deplorable atavism, or mere laziness. But perhaps we need the unanxious story. Forgetfulness can be an important asset; it enables us to give an intelligible account of, say, *Middlemarch* though we have not read it for years, and although we shall omit many characters and many incidents; and we can even do something of the same sort for novels designed to prevent such simple recapitulations, like those of Robbe-Grillet. In so far as stories give assurances we prefer them to conflicts of detail or interpretation.

Still, the variants exist, and on proper occasions we ought to give them a different, more anxious kind of attention. Like the Temptation, the Entry is a necessary part of a longer narrative. It has an intimate relation with all that follows: the Last Supper, the Betrayal, the Passion. And in this perspective the variations grow in importance. They affect the mechanics of the story. For example,

Matthew's crowd does more than the others; only in his version is the whole city stirred up, and only he makes the children cry out in the Temple. Since feeling in the city runs so strongly in Jesus' favour, his enemies are inhibited from present action against him, for they fear a tumult. So there has to be another narrative move to enable them to do so. First he is attacked with tricky questions, and that attempt fails. But the Cleansing of the Temple gives the opponents their chance. What is necessary to the narrative is the conversion of a faceless crowd, at first favourable to Jesus, into a mob demanding his execution. It is the kind of change Shakespeare knew well how to motivate; here the method is not the same, but it works very well none the less.

John has already used the Cleansing of the Temple at the beginning of his Gospel, and must therefore go about his task differently. The hostility of the chief priests is now related to Lazarus, and the change in the mood of the people, to their failure to read correctly the signs of a Messiah different from the one they expected. Change there must be, though its means may differ. What we remember, though, is the change, not the means; or, as I say, we may remember also some vivid detail. Thus our unanxious story of the Entry would almost certainly place it before the Cleansing of the Temple, which is where it comes in the synoptics; yet we might well, in describing the Temple Cleansing, say that Jesus made and wielded a whip, though John alone has that detail, which we remember as El Greco did, though we mix it with the synoptic account.

It is the interpretation-bearing story, not a particular variant, that sees us through. And it must be said that there is a rightness in this forgetfulness. For however the machinery works, all the versions are really interpretations of a single fable. Characteristically, it derives from the Old Testament prophecy of the Royal Entry of the Messiah into Jerusalem, which each evangelist in his different way updates and actualises. In John, the Cleansing, a messianic act, occurs immediately after the miracle at Cana, which is virtually a parable alluding to the provision of wine at the coming of the Messiah. The others place the Cleansing after the Entry, which is a narrative development of a central messianic prophecy in Zechariah: 'Rejoice greatly, O daughters of Zion! Shout in triumph, O daughters of Jerusalem! Behold your king is coming to you; he is just and endowed with salvation humble and mounted on a donkey, even on a colt, the foal of a donkey.' This testimony underlies the whole story of the Entry, whoever tells it, just as Zechariah's thirty pieces of silver underlies the story of Judas the Betrayer. These storytellers, so extraordinarily gifted in the techniques of realism, are still engaged in the narrative expansion of an older poetic theme. The arrival from the Mount of Olives, the cries of Hosanna, are also messianic details, and it is worth noticing that here, as in the Temptation, Matthew and Luke make them known as such more than Mark does. Mark (though nowadays not everybody agrees) came first, and was subjected to narrative articulation and expansion.

Indeed, when we direct our attention to the techniques used in telling the varying story, we can't help noticing that once again it is Mark who is most enigmatic, much less concerned with what we still think of as the conventional amenities. For example, when he comes to the Cleansing he is far less direct and straightforward than the others (though in telling 'the story' we should almost certainly neglect him). In all accounts save his, Jesus enters the Temple and causes an immediate commotion. In Mark he simply looks around and then, because it is late, withdraws to Bethany. Next day, feeling hungry, he grows angry with a fig tree because it has no fruit (though, as the text informs us, 'it was not the season for figs'). Only then does he return to the Temple and cleanse it. The following day they find the fig tree withered.

Matthew, who deals separately with the fig tree, seems more workmanlike. In Luke the fig tree is quite distinct from this sequence and is treated as a parable. Only Mark entangles it with the Cleansing. His editor, Vincent Taylor, takes this to be a typical Markan muddle – such confusions, he argues, are indications of Mark's simplicity, and of the primitiveness of his version. He even adds that the story sounds truer because it is so obviously without art, 'not a product of imagination and invention.'

But all stories, however flat and awkward, are products of those forces; and it is, in any case, a good rule not to substitute premature evaluation for an effort at understanding. Mark goes about his business differently from the others. He favours one peculiar way of interrupting the normal process of serial narrative; he likes to nest one narrative element inside another, as for example when he places the story of the woman with an issue of blood as a parenthesis inside that of the raising of Jairus's daughter. It is a practice for which there are inexact precedents in the Old Testament, but no other book of the Bible shows Mark's attachment to the device. It makes the relation between the two elements quite other than it would be if they occurred in a simple serial sequence. As some modern analysts might say, the effect is to suspend metonymy in the interest of metaphor. There is a more substantial affinity between the elements than mere contiguity in the sequence could afford. Perhaps there is also a hint that one doesn't disturb the normal narrative order of things for nothing. But in the nature of the case the text does not explain why it uses this procedure. This nesting of senses must be interpreted by the reader.

Nineteen hundred years after Mark, disturbances of a similar kind became, in the hands of Conrad and Ford, means of forcing readers to contemplate differently the interrelations of the narrative elements of an 'affair' – of achieving effects beyond the power of simple chronological sequence and closure. More recently, such disturbances have grown more violent. In later fiction they are used to emphasise the lack of connection between narrative and some culturally agreed 'real' world outside it, to emphasise that all such reference is pseudo-reference. The intention is to force the reader to give up the comforts of traditional fiction, to accept the artifice of the artifact: the painting may be *of* something, but it is still a plane surface covered in oil paint. Mark presumably has no such ambitions; but his intercalations still belong to the continuing art of storytelling.

He isn't, that is to say, an avant-garde novelist; but unlike the other evangelists he saw value in this device. Here, at any rate, he is not inept. It is for us to ask why these narratives of the Cleansing and the Fig Tree are so interwoven. Does looking at a tree to see whether it has any fruit (when you know very well is hasn't: the season is wrong) resonate in any way with that first silent inspection of the Temple? Is the Temple something like a tree out of season, fruitless just when fruit is needed, when hunger, physical or spiritual, most requires to be satisfied? Does the withering of the tree have any relation of harmony with the foretold destruction of the Temple? Perhaps the collocation of Tree and Temple is another of Mark's mysteries or enigmatic parables.

My present interpretation, offered because such an offer seems obligatory, is neither here nor there; here is a space where something of the sort is called for, the sort of condensation that constitutes a point for interpretation in a dream narrative. Matthew and

Luke here, as in the Temptation, reduce that space by being relatively explicit, by complying more simply with normal narrative expectations, one thing at a time. Their Jesus enters the Temple, sees what is going on, and acts at once, just as he blasts the fig tree at once. They, like their hero, are anxious to get on with their business. Mark is much less interested in simply getting on, just as he is less interested in the full, decisive ending.

Of course I do not mean, by indicating this difference, to imply that the others did not know their business. Their stories are, at this point and at many others, well made. They ask the right sort of narrative questions, and provide satisfactory answers. What sort of Messiah is Jesus? How shall a visit that begins in a royal triumph end with the hero's death as a criminal? The possibilities of this turn are subtly realized. Since Jesus was the kind of Messiah who would triumph not as an earthly king (the Temptation story also told us that) but by suffering; his opponents, by denying his earthly glory and making him suffer, actually turn out to be his helpers. By their actions they do the opposite of what they intend. So, a little later, Judas, so much the Opponent that he is possessed by Satan (The Opponent himself), assists Jesus in the accomplishment of his quest, which must be achieved by his death. These writers understand irony, as when the true king is given a mock coronation. The label on the Cross, 'King of the Jews,' is meant as a gibe, but it is the truth. All this is very deft; the point of speaking about Mark's peculiarities is that there are more ways than one of making a story count; though it is not surprising that Matthew so soon ousted Mark from the position of First Gospel.

Stories, well enough told, are excellent mnemonics, and the success of more than one religion depends on them. I have been discussing parts of one such story. A father tries his son and sends him on a quest. He encounters opponents and helpers, who sometimes exchange roles (Judas, Pilate). The story presents enigmas which it later resolves, and others which it does not. It announces a king, makes it appear that the announcement was false, and then, by a remarkable turn, reaffirms its truth. Aristotle might have approved. Like all narrative, including historical discourse, this story obeys laws proper to narrative and not to event. There are certain metahistorical requirements, certain rhetorical necessities. There is a gap between the facts of the world referred to and the narration which seems to refer. It is a gap that changes shape with the passage of time, as we vary our prejudices, our notions of the truth.

And that is why the history of interpretation is continuous. We cannot restore in anything like its fullness the original sense and context of a particular telling or text, much less of the events to which it refers. And we should not treat the story as if it were a pane of glass only accidentally not transparent, which, given some hardly imaginable effort, we might clean or correct or dispose of, so revealing an undistorted truth. How much more sensible to study the mode of its partial opacity. How much better, in short, to interpret!

Let me, finally, try to sum up what the study of the two passages suggests to me. The three variant versions of the Temptation story usefully indicate the power of that threefold narrative to support interpretation. The insertion of that narrative, and of some of its surviving interpretations, into a new historical and generic context (such as Milton provided) is the method by which its potential to *mean* is preserved. Thus the story survives its immediate occasion and the loss of some of the senses it originally carried. It enters a future wherein it bears a burden of meanings not necessarily independent of the old, but more accessible and more necessary. Such, at any rate, is the history of interpretation not unduly constricted by an institutional scholarship so repressive as to propose for its sole hermeneutic aim the 'single correct interpretation.' Even those who profess to believe in that silencer of the imagination know it to be unobtainable. In secular criticism, at any rate, we have entered a period when simple historicism will no longer do, though defended by two groups, elegant but blinkered theorists on the one hand, and on the other the dull whom liberty alarms, and of whom we need take little account.

The second passage suggests something of the way in which, without much conscious effort, we preserve stories, and the sense of them, in our memories – by feats of forgetting, by reconstitution of the nuclear tale. But when we do make the necessary effort of attention we can see that each of our four versions makes its own 'synthesis of acts,' to use Aristotle's expression. It may be of a complex kind, like Mark's intertwined Fig Tree and Temple narratives; it will in any case have some measure of causal interrelation, and so some complexity. Telling it, we may reprimitivise it, so to speak – much as we do if asked to recount off the top of our heads the story of *The Good Soldier* or *The Sound and the Fury*. We create what some call the *fabula*, and at that low level the story survives; but the four varying versions remain to challenge us. And there interpretation grows more difficult. Performing it, we have the comfort, if we take it to be so, of working in a long tradition, stretching back to the evangelists themselves, interpreters all – and, indeed, far beyond them.

NOTE

In this essay I have drawn upon the following works: J. Dupont, 'L'arrière-fond biblique du récit des tentations de Jésus,' *New Testament Studies* 3 (1956–7), 287–304; B. Gerhardsson, *The Testing of God's Son*, Lund, 1966; J. Jeremias, *New Testament Theology I* (translated by J. Bowden), 1971; M. Steiner, *La tentation de Jésus dans l'interprétation patristique de Saint Justin à Origène*, 1962; S. Talmon, 'The Presentation of Synchroneity and Simultaneity in Biblical Narrative,' *Scripta Hierosolymitana*, xxvii (1978), 9–26; Vincent Taylor, *The Gospel According to St. Mark*, 2nd ed., 1966.

APPENDIX: THE SINGLE CORRECT INTERPRETATION

REVIEW PUBLISHED IN THE *LONDON REVIEW OF BOOKS*, 7–20 MAY 1981

Literary theory is somewhat bewilderingly in the news, and it is worth pausing over this well-written book, in which a young American Germanist develops his thoughts about the variety of it known as hermeneutics. One sometimes hears the word uttered in tones of deep distrust or derision, as if it were some foreign novelty recently imported into a soundly pragmatical Britain by trendy malcontents intent of disturbing the peace: in fact, it is very ancient, though it has, of course, widened its scope and altered its aims. In its earlier forms, it usually amounted to prescriptions and prohibitions relating to the interpretation of Scripture. Its promotion to the status of the science or art of interpreting texts generally was effected in the early nineteenth century by Schleiermacher; and it achieved with Heidegger a philosophical apotheosis. Modern hermeneutics is predominantly German in provenance. Central to it are Schleiermacher's principle of the hermeneutic circle, which will be mentioned below; and the distinctions developed by his successors between the natural sciences and humane studies (*Naturwissenschaften* and *Geisteswissenschaften*). Neither of these developments has attracted much comment in England.

So far as I know, there was not much American interest either, at any rate until 1967. This doesn't mean that problems classifiable as hermeneutic weren't discussed under other rubrics. One such problem is authorial intention, a favourite with critics on both sides of the ocean since the late 1940s. It is still in progress, but the terms of the discussion have altered a bit. Most forms of structuralist analysis exclude the author on principle, so intention simply isn't relevant. But although structuralism superseded pheno-menological criticism, which was of course intentionalist, the 'trad-itionalist' philology, equally opposed to both, was still intact. One result was the historically useful pitched battle between Barthes and Picard, a Sorbonne professor who reacted to Barthes's book on Racine with a pamphlet called *Nouvelle Critique ou Nouvelle Imposture* (1965), and so provoked from Barthes a reply entitled *Critique et Vérité* (1966). These books make the issues plainer, and Barthes's book is, if one may so put it, a classic defence of Modernist criticism, though a great deal has happened since 1966.

'Deconstructionist' criticism differs greatly from structuralism: one respect in which it does so is material to the present discussion. Since the deconstructionists mean to tell you what a text is saying in spite of itself, it has to keep something like the 'author's meaning' in place, so as to subvert it. But neither kind of criticism shows any concern for hermeneutics (though to some extent they have a common ancestry). The modern hermeneutist has an interest in intention quite different from that of the deconstructor. His need arises, historically, from the secularisation of his subject. Formerly it has been supposed that the text requiring interpretation – namely, the Bible – was omnisignificant, so that within certain constraints anything that could be said about it was likely to be true: there was no end to the task of explicating the intention of the divine author. Difficulties associated with changing interpret-ation therefore hardly arose. Moreover there was a powerful in-stitution that claimed the right to validate or suppress interpretations. The Reformation brought some changes in these arrangements: there was, as one might expect, some wild interpret-ation, but there was also a newly-orientated authority, more philo-logical and scholarly than before. It was this Protestant tradition that led eventually to Schleiermacher, whose object was entirely intentionalist in that he sought to restore the sense a text had had for its author and for the original audience.

As he saw it, the chief obstacle to bringing that off was what he called the 'hermeneutic circle'. In order to understand the part, you must understand the whole, which you can't do without understanding the parts. To break out of this bind you have to perform an act of divination: that is, you have to bring something to the text that was not already in it. This intuitive leap must be the historical warrant for all theories which allow the interpreter to make his own productive contribution to the text. Another way of saying roughly the same thing is to speak of a necessary prior understanding, *Vorverständnis*. This fore-understanding has a basis in common sense: the next sentence I speak is likely to be one that my interlocutor has never heard before, and it is probable that I myself do not know, when I embark upon it, precisely what its course and end will be. Yet neither of us will be hopelessly lost in mid-sentence. We know, if only intuitively, the grammar of the spoken language; we know the conversational context; and we know what is sometimes called the 'genre' of the sentence. But fore-understanding becomes a more complicated notion in the hands of such modern hermeneutists as Heidegger and Bultmann. My fore-understanding cannot be quite the same as that of St Thomas Aquinas or Spinoza or indeed of anybody whatsoever: which leads to relativism, and the opinion that because all fore-understandings are different there can be no one universally acceptable reading of a text.

There are, broadly speaking, two schools in modern hermeneutics. The one I've been speaking of so far has H. G. Gadamer as its best-known living representative. In his *Truth and Method* (1960, translated 1975) Gadamer speaks of a 'fusion of the horizons' in interpretation – the fusion of the horizon of the interpreter's historical present with that of the text in its historical past. The traditionalist idea that one ought to get out of one's own moment and place oneself in the historical context of the work under consideration is rejected as naive: *not* to transcend one's own moment is indeed held to be vital to interpretation. 'One understands differently when one understands at all,' says Gadamer. It obviously follows that there is no hope of a single interpretation held always and by everybody to be the correct one.

The rival school deplores this abandonment of the intentionalism of Schleiermacher and nineteenth century successors. The kind of hermeneutics it advocates is called 'recognitive' or 'reconstructive': in short, it takes the business of the interpreter to be the rediscovery of what the author meant by his text. Historical change can have no effect on that meaning. The most celebrated of the recognitive hermeneutists is E. D. Hirsch, whose *Validity in Interpretation* (1967) mounted a direct assault on Gadamer; his *The Aims of Interpretation* (1976) makes interesting but not, I think, substantive alterations to the arguments of the earlier book.

For Hirsch, there is a crucial distinction between 'meaning' and 'significance'. He sees that it would be absurd to deny that texts do get interpreted in different ways at different times and by different people: but those interpretations – or 'applications' – have to do, not with the meaning of the text, but with its significance. Since you can't have a meaning without a meaner, the meaning of a text can only be what the author meant by it. If you want to, you can relate this meaning to something else, and so attribute to it, or discover in it, a significance. Or, to quote Hirsch,

> Meaning is the determinate representation of a text for an interpreter. An interpreted text is always taken to represent something, but that something can always be related to something else. Significance is meaning-as-related-to-something-else. If an interpreter did not conceive a text's meaning to be *there* as an occasion for contemplation or application, he would have nothing to think or talk about. Its thereness, its self-identity from one moment to the next, allows it to be contemplated. Thus, while meaning is a principle of stability in an interpretation, significance embraces a principle of change.

There is of course a lot more to Hirsch, but here I need only add that his rigour does not prevent him from making some concessions to readers who are not disposed to follow him all the way. For instance, he allows that since hermeneutic theory 'has sanctioned just about every conceivable norm of legitimacy in interpretation . . . interpretive norms are not really derived from theory . . . theory codifies *ex post facto* the interpretive norms we already prefer.' And he goes on to say that in the last analysis the choice of such norms must be an ethical choice. What he really does is to make this a matter of correct professional conduct. 'Unless there is a powerful overriding value in disregarding an author's intention (i.e. original meaning) we who interpret as a vocation should not disregard it.' He concedes that 'anachronistic readings are not infrequently the best readings, but the original meaning has an ethical priority.' Of course it would be very convenient if everybody accepted this position. But some would think it wrong to do so, since the very concept of 'original meaning' seems to them questionable, to say nothing of their conviction that it would be inaccessible anyway.

Mr Juhl's book[1] begins with a critique of Hirsch, but it soon becomes evident that he is a disciple, and that his main object is to reduce his master's permissiveness. He will not have this choosing business. He disposes of the Gadamer party, a shade too briskly perhaps, and then settles down to turning the recognitive screws, taking the slack out of Hirsch, and presenting the intentionalist case in the most rigorous possible way. But, as will shortly appear, the intentionalist case looks rather drained and exhausted by the time he's done with it.

Although the theory is analytic, Juhl allows that it must be subject to empirical constraints: that is, he must pay attention to the ways in which persons interpreting texts actually behave. Otherwise he will find himself in Hirsch's position – merely making recommendations as to how they *ought* to behave. His strengthened form of the Hirsch doctrine goes like this: 'there is a logical connection between statements about the meaning of a literary work and statements about the author's intention such that a statement about the meaning of a work *is* a statement about the author's intention.' I suppose it follows that the most determinedly anti-intentionalist statement about the meaning of a work is necessarily a statement (normally false?) about the author's intention. This is more than Hirsch would want to say, and unless it is a mere tautology ('meaning' meaning 'author's intention') it leaves little room for 'significance'. And although Juhl endorses the meaning-significance distinction, he hasn't much time for significance. Intention is all. Devices for getting round it, such as arguments that literary texts do not make genuine assertions, are out of order. 'A fact will be evidence for the meaning of a literary work if and only if it is evidence of what the author intended to convey.' In short, a literary work has 'one and only one correct interpretation', and that would be a true statement of what the author intended.

It may be that Juhl's reader will at this point feel a certain exaltation at the prospect of an attainable happiness, a hermeneutic of perfect simplicity to be reached simply by marching through the rest of the book. But the going turns out to be rough. It is time to settle the question of what is here meant by 'intention', and first of all we are told to distinguish between what an author intends and what he *plans* to say, though if we are lucky enough to know the latter we may use it in evidence. This distinction extricates us from the old bind, familiar from ancient arguments about Blake's Satanic mills: as I understand it, the new position is that Blake *planned* to have them mean churches, but finally *intended* them to mean what they do mean, whatever that may be. Intention is what an author means by what he says. 'Any (and only) evidence of the author's intention is . . . evidence for the meaning of the work.' How do we come by such evidence except by divining the meaning of the text? How do we adjudicate between rival divinations?

As we have seen, Hirsch does not require the reader to use the author's intention as his norm of interpretation: within the limits of what is linguistically possible he can do as he pleases, though he *ought* as a professional to accept this norm, for if he does not the whole business turns into a mere game. This is far too feeble for Juhl, and part of his argument against it derives from an appeal to empirical evidence. But he seems to me to misread this evidence. He exaggerates the incompatibility of divergent interpretations, and neglects to point out that judgments almost never take the form of declaring one to be wholly correct and the rest wholly wrong. He has no interest in the notion, admittedly vague, of an institutional competence – of the manner in which people with a wide range of norms and prejudices achieve a measure of consensus, and actually do agree about the quality of individual interpretations, not only when they won't do but also when, possibly with some reservations, they are certified as acceptable. This messy but actual state of affairs is not something you can take into account if you believe that there is only one 'universally compelling norm' – the author's meaning.

What Juhl would probably say about the sort of agreement just mentioned is that it relates to significance and not to meaning. By way of enforcing this distinction, he considers Swift's 'Modest Proposal'. Somebody is quoted as having maintained that this work has 'something to say' about the Vietnam War, and his application is permitted as an instance of significance. The *meaning* of the pamphlet, however, is entirely a matter of Irish conditions in Swift's own time. But this is surely wrong: the most that could be claimed is that Swift so *planned* it. On Juhl's own argument, what Swift intended was what he wrote, and what he wrote is compact of ironies, opacities, interpretanda of many kinds, and the hermeneutic effort required to discover what they mean (and to so determine Swift's intention) is indistinguishable from that required for the elicitation of 'significance'. Swift's work reflects upon the desirability of massacring babies as a political expedient, and so what it says is not at all entirely a matter of Irish conditions in 1729, though it applies to those conditions, as no doubt it does to the Vietnam War; it would certainly be absurd to argue that Swift meant to discuss that war, and it would be absurd to say that he did not have Ireland in mind, but these considerations are insufficient to justify Juhl's retreat into an intentionalism far more primitive than the kind he is expounding.

The meaning-significance distinction gets him into more trouble when he looks at the common claim that certain literary works are 'inexhaustible'. To say this, he contends, 'does not imply that the meaning of a particular literary work is not what the author intended. It is perfectly plausible to suppose that what is inexhaustible about a particular literary work is not its meaning but its significance.' But this is Humpty-Dumpty stuff: if you reserve the expression 'meaning' for 'what the author intended' (however you explain that), it follows that nothing you will not allow into that category can be called meaning. Not for the first time one is reminded of the dangerous Damon Runyon character who forced people to gamble with him and threw the dice in his hat.

The remark about inexhaustibility seems, incidentally, to imply that meaning *is* exhaustible. But this is apparently not the author's intention (or plan), for he is committed to the view that meaning cannot change. He says that a literary work resembles a speech act, in which the very concept of meaning involves an author's intentional activity. The defence of this position is undertaken, in part, by the exploration of a very curious hypothesis. Supposing 'A slumber did my spirit seal' had been produced, not by Wordsworth, but by water erosion. Should we then be able to refer, in discussing the poem, to its 'speaker'? Juhl makes this a rhetorical question – no answer necessary but if one must be given it will be 'no'. But surely the answer is 'yes'. We could not suppose that 'my' and 'I' referred to a particular person with existence independent of the poem, but apart from that we could discuss it in quite the usual way. Juhl, however, is not even sure that we could call it a poem, or even that we could call the marks caused by the water erosion 'words'. But that he could recognise them as such is surely part of the hypothesis. Similarly he thinks that if *Coriolanus* (for instance) had been written over countless millennia by countless monkeys, we could not speak of its characters, for we can only make sense of statements about what a character does 'by construing them as statements about what an author has the narrator say'. But this, too, is wrong, unless we allow that such statements are always and only made by an author, whereas the hypothesis proposes that they have been made by water or monkeys: so that the test of the argument that a poem derives its meaning solely from its being an intentional act assumes what it sets out to prove. It is true that such a poem and such a play would not be speech acts, but for that to be telling it is necessary to agree with Juhl that to be a speech act is a necessary condition of a poem.

On the whole, Juhl is unlucky with his examples. He holds that to disambiguate a text by an appeal to its context constitutes an appeal to intention. For instance: if I make a phone call and next day, fearing that you might have misunderstood me, phone again in order to disambiguate my message, I am not altering the meaning of the first message but merely showing what I intended by it. This is so, but the application of it to literary contexts assumes, as recognitive hermeneutists always do, that there is no difference between a message and a text. The declaration that 'context will be able to disambiguate an utterance if and only if it constitutes evidence of a speaker's intention' has at best only a trivial relevance to literature. A phone call from Shakespeare might disambiguate a tricky line, but it could not disambiguate *Hamlet*, which it might be maintained, is undisambiguable. Juhl, however, wishes to apply his rule to all literary works, including *Finnegans Wake*. All are speech acts, and to be interpreted as speech acts are. He takes a look at Graham Hough's attractive proposal that we may detect an original 'illocutionary act' but must then go on to interpret an 'achieved meaning' that is typically *unintended*: but he rejects it in what one comes to think of as his usual way – that is, by broadening the sense of 'intention' to include what Hough means by 'typically unintended'. It seems to follow that all good statements of an intention should include what in more ordinary language is said not to have been intended.

Well on into the book Juhl has the thought that he could be accused of holding fast to a position that might be described as only 'trivially true': for example, the position mentioned above – that the meaning of a text is solely determined by the author's intention provided that we use the word to include what he did not intend. One agile and slippery paragraph seems insufficient to get him out of this fix. He has to claim that anti-intentionalists are really intentionalists without realising it, and has an odd skirmish with William Empson, whom he takes, mistakenly, as an exemplary anti-intentionalist, which could only be true if you were including his unintended intentions.

However, the climax of the argument comes, or ought to come, in the chapter headed 'Does a literary work have one and only one correct interpretation?' The answer is of course affirmative. If a work were to yield several correct interpretations, they would need to be logically compatible; and Juhl claims that empirically this is not the case. This is a mere assertion, and may be met with the counter-assertion that it very often *is* the case. But what we are waiting for now is an instance of a literary work with one and only one correct interpretation. Instead we are again told to think of literary works as utterances, and not to consider them *in abstracto*. We are further told that since critics actually do choose between possible readings it is 'intelligible to suppose' that there must be a right one. But it does not follow that because some are judged better than others, one and one only must be correct; and this chapter, which ought to be the strongest, is the weakest in the book. It makes what I take to be mistakes about literature so vast as to seem incorrigible, though of course one would have to change one's mind if the One Correct Interpretation were exemplified. It isn't: retreating from the empirical, Juhl argues only that there *must* be such an interpretation, even though it cannot be found; nor, if it were, could we expect agreement about its rightness. It exists only 'in principle'. We do as a matter of fact lack the necessary evidence.

Plain men may well decide that this refinement of recognitive hermeneutics is without much use. If the correct interpretation, though it exists in principle, is in practice (virtually indeed in principle) undiscoverable, why should they bother about it? There is even a danger that by one of those transvaluations favoured by Marxist critics Juhl's extreme hermeneutic rigour may be converted into a licence to say pretty well anything one likes about a text, since the one thing needful, on Hirsch's ethical or on Juhl's analytic view, is unsayable. Simple-minded stone-kicking intentionalists would, if they could bring themselves to read it, find this an unsettling book. And yet it is an interesting performance. Though it gives what I take to be a false report of what actually happens in interpretation, and though it is not always sufficiently considerate of rival approaches, it has the merit of not assuming a great deal that is often too crudely taken for granted.

REPLY BY MR JUHL

Professor Kermode's central objection to my book, *Interpretation*, is that I beg the crucial question as to whether the meaning of a text is indeed logically tied to the author's intention (*London Review of Books*, vol. 3, no. 8). I do so, according to Kermode, in three ways:

1 Kermode seems to assume that, on my view, only the meaning of the text constitutes evidence of the author's intention. 'How do we come by such evidence except by divining the meaning of the text?' I state in the Introduction very clearly how I am using the term 'intention', namely: what a man intended to convey is 'what he meant by the words he used' (or by his, or a speaker's, utterance). So Kermode's contention is that there cannot be anything which is evidence for what a man intended in this sense except the meaning of the text. But this is clearly not true. Surely an author's beliefs (expressed elsewhere), his other works, parallel passages, diary entries, or remarks by the author in other contexts about his work, and so on, are all evidence, though, of course, not *conclusive* evidence, for what the author meant by the words he used (or by a speaker's utterance or the whole work). Surely there is no merit in Kermode's suggestion that this sort of information does not constitute evidence of what the author meant.

2 Kermode endorses Graham Hough's view that what is not planned, premeditated or done with due forethought cannot

have been intended. But we do not always or even typically plan out in advance, 'with due forethought' or 'premeditation' what specifically we will say to someone else in a casual conversation, for example. Surely our intentions are typically formed in the process of formulating the sentences we use. Often there is no specific 'forethought' at all. Yet we do not, for that reason, say that most of what we say is said unintentionally, or that we did not mean what we said. If this is true, then Kermode is wrong in claiming that I stretch the term 'intention' so that it will 'include what in more ordinary language is said not to have been intended'.

3 Kermode claims that the distinction between meaning and significance, or my use of this distinction, begs the crucial question: 'if you reserve the expression "meaning" for "what the author intended" (however you explain that), it follows that nothing you will not allow into that category can be called meaning.' But I do not in fact regard the distinctions between meaning and significance as implying that the meaning of a work is what the author intended. Rather, I emphasise that 'this distinction does not, of course, show that the assumption (that the meaning of a literary work is logically tied to the author's intention) is correct. It may still very well be true that a literary work does not mean what its author intended and hence that "A Modest Proposal", for instance, is about *inter alia* the Vietnam War. What the distinction shows is that this does not follow from the fact that work survives its age.'

Kermode implies that I evade what is in fact one of the central tasks of the book: i.e. to show that anti-intentionalist critics, in speaking of the meaning of a work, are in fact speaking about the author's intention. He does not even mention that fact that I examine numerous and detailed examples of practical criticism by M. C. Beardsley, W. K. Wimsatt, J. Culler, M. Riffaterre, H. Bloom, C. Brooke-Rose, P. Szondi, H. R. Jauss, G. Hough, R. Jakobson and Lévi-Strauss, J. Wain, G. Dickie, J. Hospers, G. Hermeren, A. Isenberg, E. von Savigny, and others – all of whom reject the view that there is a logical connection between the meaning of a literary work and the author's intention. Kermode does not offer the slightest evidence that in any of these cases I beg the question. As for Empson: although I may be mistaken in taking him as an exemplary anti-intentionalist, certainly the major anti-intentionalist theorists of the past two or three decades have regarded his critical practice as among the best examples of the kind of criticism it was concerned to promote.

Kermode mistakenly attributes to me the view that the meaning of Swift's 'Modest Proposal' is 'entirely a matter of Irish conditions in Swift's own time'. Here is what I say:

> Let us suppose, for example, that Swift's 'A Modest
> Proposal' is merely about a certain unique historical
> situation [italics added] . . . This may not, of course, be true.
> I have made this assumption primarily to show that even an
> unduly restrictive view of what a literary work means is
> entirely consistent with the fact that a work may be of wider
> interest and of value to readers of later ages. . . . Swift no
> doubt intended to say something not *just* about a situation
> of his own time, but about certain general human
> tendencies.

Kermode appears to have misunderstood my discussion of the role of the context in disambiguating utterances in ordinary discourse and in literary works. According to Kermode, I assume that an author can disambiguate his text in exactly the same way as a speaker his utterance in ordinary discourse. I do not assume or claim this. What I do argue is, (a) that the meaning of an utterance in a literary work, just as in ordinary discourse, depends on the speaker's intention. I go on to argue, (b) that, though we cannot, of course, identify the speaker or a character in a literary work with the author, what the (or a) speaker means is what the author has him/her mean (intends him to mean). This may be wrong, of course, but it doesn't follow from it that 'a phone-call from Shakespeare . . . could . . . disambiguate *Hamlet*' – if for no other reason than that an author's statement about his intention is only *one* kind of evidence of intention and constitutes, as I emphasise, by no means incontrovertible evidence of his intention. But Kermode offers no argument or evidence for his claim. He simply asserts that *Hamlet*, 'it might be maintained, is undisambiguable'. Sure, it might be maintained. All sorts of things might be maintained.

But that does not give us a lot of reason to suppose that they are true.

Kermode contends that the last chapter is 'the weakest' because it doesn't actually produce 'the One Correct Interpretation' of a work. Since I do not claim that we can in fact find the correct interpretation of any given literary work, I do not see what could lead Kermode to expect that I would produce such an interpretation. In any case, he seems to think that 'this refinement of recognitive hermeneutics is without much use. If the correct interpretation, though it exists in principle, is in practice (virtually indeed in principle) undiscoverable, why should they [plain men] bother about it?' Who said they should bother about it? Kermode seems to be unclear about the issue. The issue, after all, is not: 'How can we help critics find the correct interpretation of a work?' On my view at least, they know that already. The issue is whether or not interpretations can properly be characterised as 'correct' or 'incorrect', or whether no sense can be attributed to these terms when applied to an interpretation. Kermode seems to be confusing Hirsch's position with mine. Hirsch is indeed concerned to change what he takes to be the state of interpretive practice. I have no such ambition. My aim is rather to analyse critical practice, to bring out our tacit assumptions, our logical commitments, in speaking about the meaning of a work, not to make recommendations as to what critics ought to do.

Kermode claims that I am 'a disciple' of Hirsch's. I find this somewhat strange, since I affirm, and try to establish, precisely what Hirsch denies: namely, that there is a logical connection between the meaning of a literary work and the author's intention. Hirsch holds that there is no such connection and that a critic can set up any normative conception he likes as his criterion of what a text means. Of course, Hirsch *recommends* that we *ought* to interpret texts in accord with the author's intention. But this is a position on a wholly different issue: i.e. what we *ought* to do, as opposed to what in fact (as a matter of logic) we do. Hence my view also cannot be characterised as 'a strengthened form of the Hirsch doctrine', since it is not 'a form' of Hirsch's doctrine at all. I must gratefully decline Kermode's compliment that my book 'has the merit of not assuming a great deal that is often too crudely taken for granted.' For if his main objection is valid, then I take at least as much for granted as those 'crude' chaps he has in mind.

213

REPLY TO MR JUHL

First, I confess that I did not fully and fairly state Juhl's opinion in my passage on 'A Modest Proposal'. Second, it seems clear that a man is entitled to say whether he is another man's disciple or not, and if Juhl says he isn't a disciple of Hirsch, then he isn't. But I do not think that I misrepresented the relation between their views, except in using that word. Juhl's starting point is the recognitive hermeneutic of which Hirsch is much the most influential American exponent; Juhl rejects his *ought* as inconsistent with the logic of the situation, but similar alterations of emphasis have been known to occur in followers, and this is all I meant. Juhl himself is clear that he has very little time for the rival party of Gadamer.

Juhl takes up some of my points, but not all. Here I mention first the ones he does discuss.

(a) It remains a question whether on Juhl's view a statement of intention made outside the text, or a probability inferred from other works, is reliable, let alone conclusive. For if I understand him he would reject such evidence as evidence merely of what the author planned to say rather than of what he intended to say; the evidence for that is the text. Critics used to be troubled by a passage in a letter of Jane Austen to Cassandra which appeared to state that the subject of *Mansfield Park* was 'ordination', for although Edmund's taking orders, and Mary Crawford's attitude to the clergy, are certainly relevant to the design of the book, it would not have occurred to most readers that ordination was what the book was *about*. Should they have said that Jane Austen's intention differed from her plan? It is only common sense to allow that intentions do not invariably achieve realisation. I suppose Juhl would maintain that in such cases one discounts the extratextual evidence; but it is hard to see why, on his view, he should ever want to use it, since it is valuable only if it tells what is already known; indeed if we know 'the correct interpretation already' we shall only confuse ourselves by attending to such evidence.

(b) It will not be denied that intended actions have unintended consequences, and it is no answer to say that in speech we may act without forethought, so that we are not acting unintentionally when we have no previously formulated intent. If I understand the position, the felicity of such statements is determined by their securing uptake which accords with the intention of the speaker, so that in so far as they have consequences unintended by the speaker they fail. No doubt he could have intended them to fail, and they apparently do so almost always; but this is to make of the identity of intention and meaning a vacuous dogma. It seems more sensible to agree that we say things unintentionally; to deny this is to make the proposition that the meaning of the text is what the author intended perfectly trivial.

(c) The allusion to Empson is not to be so easily dismissed by the remark that if he is not an anti-intentionalist more people than Juhl have misunderstood him. He has been saying clearly for at least thirty years that he regards anti-intentionalism as absurd. 'My intention,' he seems to say, 'is to be anti-intentionalist.' Juhl suggests that as he appears not to be anti-intentionalist he has misunderstood his intention. We may now see how subtle the concept of authorial intention has become; it is something that goes on in the heads of readers, not authors.

(d) On *Hamlet* I confess to some amazement that Juhl should suppose that it is up to me to provide evidence that the task of disambiguating it is impossible. What needs support is the view that it is possible. It is not enough to say that in principle it can be done; and I do not think that anybody who has applied himself seriously to the extraordinary complexities of this (or any comparable) work could think it anything but preposterous to say so. But I suppose Juhl's view amounts to saying that in so far as it has a meaning it is disambiguated already, so that we have done the job without knowing it, like Wordsworth crossing the Alps.

(e) I think I made it clear that I understood the differences between Hirsch, who is clear that he is talking about the ought, and Juhl, who prefers to talk about the is, as it seems to him. But I am still confused. A Single Correct Interpretation laid up as it were in heaven, or rather in the text, though we can never state it, is, as Juhl says, not a recommendation to interpreters. Nor do they need recommendations, for they 'know already'. Shakespeare would in any case be more likely to be wrong about *Hamlet* (that is, about his own intention) than they.

Holding these views, Juhl not surprisingly ignores my contention that there are, empirically, good and less good interpretations, not just one right one and lots of wrong ones. And he does not take up what I said about 'A slumber did my spirit seal'; rather surprisingly he could count on the support of Paul Ricoeur (*Interpret-*

ation Theory, Texas Christian University Press, 1976, p. 30); Ricoeur wants to reconcile the 'semantic autonomy' of the text with a conviction that it retains the characteristics of something said by somebody. But this is very partial support, and Juhl might not want it at the cost of having also to accommodate some version of 'semantic autonomy'. In any case I am still of the opinion that vulgar intentionalists would learn from a reading of his book that if they chose to defend their position instead of merely booing the opposition they might find themselves involved in an unwontedly strenuous intellectual exercise.

REPLY BY MR JUHL

(1) On the question of the relevance of an author's statement about his intention: I do not 'reject such evidence as evidence merely of what the author planned to say rather than of what he intended to say.' Nor do I believe or suggest anywhere in my book that the only evidence for what the author intended 'is the text.' I explicitly claim otherwise (see pp. 14, 88–9, 110–2, 146–8, 150).

Furthermore, while an author's statement about his intention may be a statement about what he plans to do, it need not be, e.g. in cases in which it is made after the work has been completed. And the difference between the two cases is a difference in the weight of the evidence: an author's statement about his intention shortly after the work has been completed carries, in general, greater weight than a statement as to what he plans to do. But that does not categorically disqualify the latter as evidence of what the author intended even though in some cases what an author says he plans to do may be unreliable independently of what he actually did (or meant), e.g. if he generally does not in fact do what he says he plans to do.

How we construe a literary work is, if I am right, logically tied to what we think the author intended and hence depends on a large number of (usually implicit) assumptions about the author's beliefs, attitudes, values, interests, his dialect or idiolect, and so on. Consequently, it is not surprising that no single piece of evidence as to the author's intention, including a statement by him (shortly after completion of the work) as to what he meant, is ever conclusive or incontrovertible evidence. It is always possible to construct a case in which the 'external' facts are such that we would discount an author's statement about his intention as incorrect. And occasionally we find such a case in practice.

As for the Austen example, I don't care much about what 'most readers . . . should have said.' I am more interested in what they did say. And I am quite sure that if they discounted Austen's statement about her intention, they will then have taken certain features of the text, in the light of numerous (implicit) assumptions about Austen, to be better evidence of her intention than her statement. In fact, if it could be shown that this is not the case, I would regard that as serious evidence against my thesis about the connection between the meaning of a literary work and the author's intention.

I certainly don't believe or claim that 'we know the correct interpretation already.' What we do know is how to go about finding, or rather looking for, the correct interpretation. (For although we may have the correct interpretation of a given work, we are not likely to know this, inasmuch as the existing evidence usually supports a number of different (incompatible) interpretations more or less equally well.)

(2) On saying something you didn't mean: I tried to show that intending to convey something (or meaning something) is not the same thing as planning to convey something. Hence I can certainly have intended to convey X, even though I didn't plan to convey X (e.g. say X with 'due forethought' or 'premeditation'). This clearly does not entail that I cannot say something which I didn't mean (or intend to say).

I also tried to show, however, that when the meaning of a literary work as a whole is at stake, there can be no discrepancy between what the author meant and what the work means. This might seem obviously counter-intuitive. The idea is this. When we are dealing with so complex an artefact as a literary work, we will rather say that the author was mistaken about his intention (I assume that we are interpreting a given work contrary to what the author said he intended) than say that so complex an effect could have come about by chance.

What I am claiming then is that a literary work cannot mean what its author didn't mean. Kermode is mistaken if he thinks that this makes the thesis 'perfectly trivial'. For it is not a stipulation but rather an hypothesis about the logic of interpretation. Hence any case in which a critic interpreted a literary work contrary to what he was convinced the author intended would constitute prima facie evidence against my view.

A case in point is Wimsatt's reading of Housman's '1887'. Here is what he says:

> Mr. Beardsley has cited the nearly parallel instance of A. E. Housman's angry attempt to deny the irony at expense of state and church manifest in his poem for Queen Victoria's fiftieth anniversary. 'Get you the sons your fathers got, And God will save the Queen.' Here a statement made in retrospect and under provocation, a kind of profession of loyalty to a sovereign, stands in sharp contradiction not only to the cunning details of the poem in question but to the well-known skeptical and cynical cast of poet's canon. (Wimsatt, 'Genesis: A Fallacy Revisted', section (4e))

Wimsatt is seemingly interpreting the poem contrary to what Housman meant. And yet consider what he does: he is casting doubt on the reliability of Housman's statement about his intention. Thus he speaks of 'Housman's *angry attempt* to deny the irony . . . a statement made *in retrospect* and *under provocation*, a kind of *profession of loyalty* to a sovereign. . . .'

In other words, contrary to appearances, Wimsatt is not interpreting the poem contrary to what (he thinks) Housman meant. Rather, he is arguing in effect that Housman didn't mean what he (Housman) said he meant.

And Wimsatt is not taking the meaning of the text as evidence for his reading, but rather certain features of the text ('the cunniɪg details of the poem') *in the light of* Housman's well-known views and attitudes ('the well-known skeptical and cynical cast of the poet's canon') as better evidence of Housman's intention than Housman's statement.

It is worth noting too that the example shows rather well the force of an author's statement about his intention. For unless it had considerable force indeed, it would be difficult to see why anyone, and especially Wimsatt, should feel any strong need – as he obviously does – to show that it is (in this case) unreliable. (For other examples, see pp. 124–47, esp. 140–7.)

(3) I am gratified to hear that Empson holds anti-intentionalism to be absurd. Kermode is mistaken, however, in saying that 'Juhl suggests that as he [Empson] appears not to be anti-intentionalist

he has misunderstood his intention.' I do not claim or suggest anything of the sort.

To reiterate: I may very well have been mistaken about Empson's metacritical views. The reason I chose to analyse his particular practice is that he was regarded by anti-intentionalists as one of the best examples of the sort of practical criticism they wished to recommend. Furthermore, since his criticism is certainly not obviously 'intentionalist' and since he is a figure whose work has had almost paradigmatic force for Anglo-American criticism of the last thirty years or so and especially for the New Critics, he is clearly a good example for the sort of confrontation (on the question of whether literary works can make truth-claims) I was interested in. After all, what I am interested in is analysing a *practice* and from the fact that someone holds certain metacritical views, it certainly doesn't follow that his or her practice will accord with those metacritical views (vide all those die-hard anti-intentionalists whose practice I examine in my book.)

(4) I take it that Kermode's point about *Hamlet* is that at least in this case there is no one correct interpretation. Since I devoted about 100 pages (Chapter VIII and the Appendix) to arguments for the claim that we can in principle determine the correct interpretation of a literary work, I did think that someone who claimed otherwise could be expected to produce some evidence or argument for that view. Or at least give some reasons why my arguments don't hold water. But simply to say that '*Hamlet* . . . it might be maintained, is undisambiguable' is to beg the question I tried to argue.

I don't understand why Kermode would suppose that 'It is not enough to say that in principle it can be done,' since I don't claim that it can (given the evidence we have) be done in practice. If it could, critics would have done it already. But it doesn't follow, nor is there any reason to believe, that it could not be done if we had the necessary facts.

(5) To say that there is such a thing as the correct interpretation of any given work doesn't preclude speaking of 'good and less good interpretations'. Since we usually don't know which is the right interpretation of a particular work, all we can say is that given the evidence we have, certain interpretations are somewhat more likely to be right, and hence in a sense 'better', others less likely.

(6) To return to 'A slumber did my spirit seal': Kermode badly distorts the arguments I give – based on this poem – about the appeal to the text (Chaper IV). Kermode is quite right in suggesting that I deny that we could, properly speaking, refer to 'the speaker' or 'a character' in a 'poem' produced by a monkey or water erosion. However, he is quite mistaken in supposing that my argument depends on this and hence 'assumes what it sets out to prove.'

What I do in fact argue in this chapter (and what Kermode completely ignores) is that under the assumption that a certain 'poem' has been produced by a monkey or by water erosion, we could not in principle explain the features of the 'text' in the way we typically do in interpreting a literary work and in the way we expect any interpretation to be able to explain those features. Furthermore, I argue that under the above assumption about the genesis of the 'poem', we could not *support* our interpretation by an appeal to textual features.

My argument may be wrong, of course. But Kermode does not even address himself to that argument. Instead he simply assumes that 'apart from [supposing] that "my" and "I" referred to a particular person with an existence independent of the poem, . . . we could discuss it in quite the usual way.' Who is begging the question?

(7) Finally, on the question of the relation between Hirsch's views and mine: my view is clearly not an 'alteration of emphasis', since Hirsch not only does not hold that there is a logical connection between the meaning of a literary work and the author's intention, but explicitly rejects this view. And the question whether there is a logical connection between the meaning of a literary work and the author's intention is after all the crucial issue in the controversy between intentionalism and anti-intentionalism. To say that we *ought* to construe a literary work in accord with the author's intention is to make a very different *kind* of claim.

NOTE

1 P. D. Juhl, *Interpretation: An Essay in the Philosophy of Literary Criticism* (Princeton University Press, 1981).

ACKNOWLEDGMENTS

Chapter 1 draws on material used in a Gauss Seminar at Princeton in 1970; it was originally published in *Harvard English Studies 2*, ed. Reuben A. Brower (1971). Chapter 2 was the Twenty-fourth W. P. Ker Memorial Lecture, delivered in the University of Glasgow in March, 1972 and published in that year by the University of Glasgow. Chapter 3 was a lecture delivered at the annual meeting of the English Institute at Harvard in 1972, and published in *Approaches to Poetics*, ed. Seymour Chatman, Columbia University Press, 1973. Chapter 4 was a lecture given at the University of Chicago in 1974, and published in the same year in *Critical Inquiry* 1 (University of Chicago Press). Chapter 5 was the Fourth Gwilym James Memorial Lecture delivered at the University of Southampton in March 1975 and published in the same year by the University of Southampton. Chapter 6 was a paper given at a symposium on 'Narrative: The Illusion of Sequence' at the University of Chicago in October 1979, and published in *Critical Inquiry* 7. Chapter 7 began as a brief paper delivered at the Modern Language Association of America conference in New York, December 1974 and revised for *Art, Politics and Will: Essays in Honor of Lionel Trilling*, ed. Quentin Anderson, Stephen Donadio and Steven Marcus, New York: Basic Books, 1977. Chapter 8 was a lecture given at Skidmore College in 1979, and published that year in *Salmagundi*, 43. Chapter 9, in various earlier forms, was a lecture given at

Deniston University, at the Divinity School, Cambridge, and at the Hebrew University, Jerusalem, in 1981. It was published in *Raritan Review* 1 (1982). The Appendix consists of a review published in the *London Review of Books*, 7–20 May, 1981, a response from the author of the book reviewed, Mr P. D. Juhl, *LRB* 6–19 August 1981, an unpublished comment on that response, and a further rejoinder by Mr Juhl. The Appendix apart, all these pieces have been revised for the present volume. I am grateful to all the publishers named above for permission to reprint my pieces, and to Mr Juhl for so kindly allowing me to print his work in my book. Many people have contributed to it by their comments after lectures and seminars, especially members of the University College Seminar mentioned in the Prologue; but Anita Kermode, whose eye for corrigenda is quite remarkable, has done most to make readable what she by no means always agrees with.

F.K.

INDEX